Concepts and Case Studies in

Threat
Management

Concepts and Case Studies in

Threat Management

Frederick S. Calhoun
Stephen W. Weston

CRC Press
Taylor & Francis Group
Boca Raton London New York

CRC Press is an imprint of the
Taylor & Francis Group, an **informa** business

CRC Press
Taylor & Francis Group
6000 Broken Sound Parkway NW, Suite 300
Boca Raton, FL 33487-2742

© 2013 by Taylor & Francis Group, LLC
CRC Press is an imprint of Taylor & Francis Group, an Informa business

No claim to original U.S. Government works

Printed in the United States of America on acid-free paper
Version Date: 20120507

International Standard Book Number: 978-1-4398-9217-6 (Paperback)

Library of Congress Cataloging-in-Publication Data

Calhoun, Frederick S.
 Concepts and case studies in threat management / Frederick S. Calhoun and Stephen W. Weston.
  p. cm.
 Includes bibliographical references and index.
 ISBN 978-1-4398-9217-6
 1. Violence--Prevention. 2. Criminal behavior, Prediction of. 3. Police training. 4. Threats. I. Weston, Stephen W. II. Title.

HM1116.C3523 2013
303.6--dc23   2012015286

Visit the Taylor & Francis Web site at
http://www.taylorandfrancis.com

and the CRC Press Web site at
http://www.crcpress.com

To our respective grandchildren
Silas Austin James Calhoun
and
Ariana Kaylene Sanchez,
Arrianna Nicole Salcido,
Mariah Anne Montero,
Gabriel Jose Salcido,
Samuel Stephen Salcido,
Angelo Vincent Saldana

Contents

Acknowledgments

A number of people offered insight and advice as we wrote this book. James Cawood, Gavin de Becker, and Mario Scalora served as peer reviewers and recommended publishing the book to Taylor & Francis Group. For that recommendation, we are sincerely grateful. Carolyn Spence, acquisitions editor, and Marsha Pronin, project coordinator, at Taylor & Francis Group, oversaw the publication of the book in a seemingly smooth and effortless process. It was a pleasure working with them both.

Later, James Cawood read the chapter on the need-to-knows and responded with well thought out advice on improving the discussion of those particular concepts. He greatly improved our discussion of those ideas. We thank him for taking the time to read and respond to us.

A number of folks worked very hard at putting together the "Glossary of Threat Management Terminology":

Denise Bulling, PhD, University of Nebraska Public Policy Center
Frederick Calhoun, author and threat management consultant
James Cawood, MA, president, Factor One
Larry Golba, MA, University of Nebraska Public Policy Center
Brandon Hollister, University of Nebraska Public Policy Center
J. Reid Meloy, PhD, Forensis, Inc.
Mario J. Scalora, PhD, University of Nebraska–Lincoln
Rachel Solov, president, Association of Threat Assessment Professionals
Stephen Weston, JD, author, University of Nebraska Public Policy Center
William Zimmerman, United States Capitol Police

Although this is a first attempt at cataloging the emerging vocabulary of threat management, it is a noble effort—and a very worthwhile one. We hope that it will serve as a building block for future growth of the profession.

Finally, we want to thank the board of directors of the Association of Threat Assessment Professionals (ATAP) for allowing us to print ATAP's Code of Conduct and for working with us on the glossary.

New Concepts Emerging From the Professionalization of Threat Management

1

Professionalization has come to the field of threat management. It has developed a systematic theory unique to the field. Recognized authorities have emerged. The community has sanctioned its legitimacy as a profession and it is finding its own ethical code of conduct. Threat management is beginning to grow its own culture, complete with a vocabulary of its own. As is common to all other professions, threat management now offers training for the uninitiated.[1] Although the field yet has a way to go, it is well along the path to becoming a profession.

One product of this ongoing professionalization is the discovery of certain key concepts that, until now, have not been identified or defined. In the following pages, we identify several of those concepts, define them, and then illustrate them with real-life case studies. For example, one concept that has emerged is the recognition that assessing a potential threat situation requires knowing certain information inherent in the situation. This information, which we call the *need-to-knows*, gives a measure for each assessment and informs future fact finding. Identifying what is known leads to the threat assessment, while recognizing what is unknown guides the fact finding. Internalizing the need-to-knows allows the threat management team to make sound threat assessments and to gauge how informed each threat assessment is by comparing what is known about a particular situation against the complete set of need-to-knows.

The concept of case dynamics posits that the interaction between the subject, the target, and the threat manager is constantly changing. Actions the subject takes cause reactions by the target and the threat manager. The reverse also holds. Actions the threat manager takes—or does not take—cause a reaction by the subject. Applying a threat management strategy changes the chemistry of the relationships. Proper threat management requires understanding the dynamics and the synergism and using that understanding to inform how the situation is handled.

Understanding the power of inhibitors, including the influence of missing inhibitors or recently lost inhibitors, must inform the choice of the most appropriate threat management strategies. Assessing what the subject has to lose by using violence can give great insight into the subject's intent, motive, and ability. Conversely, discovering which inhibitors are lacking or, worse

yet, which inhibitors the subject may have recently lost can signal how imminent the violence may be. Individuals who believe that they have nothing
left to lose are more likely to resort to violence compared to individuals who
perceive that they have value in their lives.

Recognizing the differences among the different venues of violence helps
pinpoint the subject's possible motive, evaluate the innate security of that
venue, and assess the nature of the relationships within that particular venue.
Those factors help determine the potential for violence targeting that venue.
While the subject *always* has to traverse the path to intended violence, regardless of venue, the differences inherent in the various venues profoundly affect
the subject's motives. Domestic violence differs from public figure violence—
not in the process of violence, but rather in the subject's motive and goal.
Workplace violence has its own unique attributes, as does violence toward
gathering places and violence toward representative targets. Exploring those
differences gives a whole new perspective to the nature of violence.

Certain of these concepts have a negative effect. Threat managers must
avoid building information silos caused by not sharing information with other
agencies, organizations, and involved individuals. Similarly, threat managers
must also refrain from bunkering down in their own organization or agency,
seeing only their problems rather than understanding that potentially violent
subjects may target other agencies, organizations, involved individuals, or
society at large. Solving the threat manager's organization's problem with the
individual may risk transferring the problem somewhere else.

Instead, the threat manager should see beyond his or her own organization and work with other involved entities to ensure that the problem is
resolved all around. Finally, falling into the temptation of holding fast to
myopic management strategies is shortsighted. Applying threat management
strategies has to be seen within the overall context of the situation and the
changes and synergy that inevitably occur. Applying a strategy and failing
to assess its effectiveness continuously risks making the situation worse. The
only way to avoid silos, bunkers, and myopic management strategies is to be
aware of their existence and their dangers.

Concepts and Case Studies in Contemporary Threat Management ana-
lyzes these concepts in detail. It also illustrates each point with realistic
case studies and real-life examples. The book explores in depth the current
state of the threat management process. It aims to enhance the profession's
understanding of that process. Readers of this book will come away from
it with a fuller understanding of the concepts undergirding the profession.
Enhancing that understanding will improve our approach to the challenge of
identifying, assessing, and managing individuals who pose a risk of violence.

Finally, we append a first attempt at compiling a glossary of terms used
in the emerging profession of threat management. The glossary is a joint
effort between us and researchers at the University of Nebraska's Public

Policy Center. We do not claim this glossary to be exhaustive or definitive. It is, instead, a first stab at identifying and defining a set of terms common to the profession. By compiling this new vocabulary, we hope to move the professionalization of threat management a bit farther down the road. It is a start, at least.

Presenting a Practical Approach to Threat Management

Our previous books on contemporary threat management addressed different aspects of the threat management process. In those books, we detailed our view of the most appropriate methods for identifying, assessing, and managing potentially violent situations; defined the paths to impromptu and intended violence; and drew a sharp distinction between hunters, who intend to commit violence, and howlers, who seek only to frighten or connect emotionally with their target. The books first hypothesized about the *intimacy effect* and then confirmed its validity. We looked at the findings of the research and explored how that research could be applied in practical ways to real-life situations. With each book, we strove hard to provide very practical strategies and tactics for implementing our approach. We tried to present these strategies and tactics in such a way that they could be readily understood, easily remembered, and immediately implemented.

We also illustrated each point and concept with actual, realistic case studies. Some were drawn from today's headlines, some were based on our own case experiences in running threat management programs, and some were derived from the experiences of other threat assessment professionals. These carefully chosen examples helped substantiate the point under consideration by showing how that point actually applied in real-life situations. The illustrations also animated the concept. They took the point beyond dry definitions to vibrant example. If nothing else, the case studies helped prove that what we offered was not some pie-in-the-sky intellectualizations, but, rather, a pragmatic, workable approach.

Our aim has always been to arm threat managers with realistic ideas and approaches that they could keep fresh in their minds and immediately implement in their day-to-day work. We also framed our discussions in such a way that they did not require an advanced degree in psychology or criminology to understand or put into practice. Indeed, we went to great lengths to provide sensible, straightforward advice. We shunned jargon and obtuse language in favor of simplification—a kind of blue-collar approach to the challenge of identifying, assessing, and managing potentially violent individuals.

Fortunately, each of the books was well received. That positive reception, we believe, resulted directly from the practical approaches we took and the myriad case study illustrations we presented. The approaches provided reality; the case studies brought our points to life. *Concepts and Case Studies in Threat Management* plays, again, to those strengths. We offer here a set of useful concepts, each illustrated with case studies to show how the concept applies within the reality of the contemporary threat management process. Each is framed and exemplified as practically and realistically as possible.

Scope of the Book

This book goes beyond our previous works by introducing various concepts that directly impinge—for well or ill—on the threat management process. Some of these concepts, such as the effects of *case dynamics* and the impact of *intervention synergy,* are as often detrimental to the process as they are beneficial. Yet, the threat manager or, better yet, the threat management team, needs to be aware of the existence of these effects and impacts. Such awareness offers the only viable way of channeling the effect or impact toward an enhanced response. Ignoring them is always at the threat manager's peril.

Other concepts come more under the control of the threat manager or management team. Keeping in mind that the importance of *proportionate responses* and *flexible strategies* resides well within the control of the threat manager. They represent crucial concepts in controlling the only thing the threat manager absolutely controls: his or her response to the developing situation. As Gavin de Becker wisely pointed out some years ago, anything the threat manager does or does not do might

- make the situation better
- make the situation worse
- have no effect on the situation

Keeping the response proportionate to the subject's behavior and being ever mindful of the need for flexibility in applying any of the threat management strategies help the threat manager gauge whether or not the situation is better, worse, or unchanged. Obviously, if things grow worse or remain unimproved, the threat manager needs to consider applying a different strategy or combination of strategies. Threat management is a dynamic process of assessing, responding, reassessing, and revising the response.

Not only is the protective response necessary for ensuring target security, but it is also a crucial step in managing the target's response to what often is a frightening or disturbing situation. One of the certainties of contemporary threat management is that if a target is not offered a protective response, he or she will surely develop one. Doing so can put the target at odds with the threat management response. It also takes control of the response away from the threat manager or threat management team.

The protective response, then, becomes personal rather than objective and, possibly, inflated rather than proportionate to the actual situation Protective responses can also be minimized by the target or ignored altogether due to fiscal, organizational, political, media image, convenience, or personal issues. These considerations have little chance of improving the situation. Therefore, taking the response away from the target helps advance the overall response.

Some of the concepts, such as the effect of inhibitors on the subject's personal life and the impact of the *intimacy effect,* are profound influences, again for well or ill, on the outcome of the situation. Every individual has in his or her life certain influences that hold the balance between taking violent action or not resorting to violence. We call these influences *inhibitors.* They are such things as family ties, financial resources, holding down a good job, religious beliefs, mental and physical health, comfortable living arrangements, self-worth, and dignity. When inhibitors are strongly in place, most people are inclined not to do anything that would put them at risk. But when inhibitors start to fall—and when they do, it is usually like dominoes toppling—then individuals become at greater risk of turning to violence as a way to solve their problems.

Consequently, threat managers need to find out what inhibitors are in the subject's life and how those or other inhibitors can be put in place and strengthened. Thus, knowing about inhibitors is crucial to any threat assessment, while manipulating or taking care not to disrupt the subject's inhibitors is an effective tactic for defusing the risk of violence.

Inhibitors can be overruled by the *intimacy effect.* In our previous book, *Threat Assessment and Management Strategies: Identifying Howlers and Hunters,* we appended a research paper written by Debra M. Jenkins that validated our hypothesis that the more interpersonal or intimate the relationship between subject and target is, the greater is the value of threats as preincident indicators of future violence. Here, we take that effect and show how the threat manager must always address it when conducting a threat assessment and evaluating the strength of a subject's inhibitors. It is a practical, easy test to incorporate in each assessment. Further, it helps remind us that every potential target, no matter how prestigious or powerful the target's position in society, has a personal life involving interpersonal and intimate relationships.

Case Illustration: Anatomy of a Suicide

Sometime in 2010, John Jack's life started spiraling downward with such force that it toppled his inhibitors. The fall culminated in Jack's death by suicide. He suffered mental health problems and then began drinking heavily. The drinking caused him to miss work and created disputes with his landlord. In the fall of 2010, the landlord called

Melbourne, Florida, police to complain that Jack was drunk, driving a motorcycle, and "distraught." Palm Bay Hospital, where Jack worked, fired him in October for poor work attendance. In early November, Jack texted his friends with the simple message, "Goodbye." Clearly, Jack's inhibitors were toppling.

On November 4, Jack returned to the hospital to say good-bye to his former colleagues. He went to the cafeteria kitchen, but something went wrong. Instead of farewells, Jack began threatening the employees and brandishing a pistol. He then barricaded himself in a room, where he shot himself with the firearm. (*Source:* Associated Press, "Gunman Commits Suicide After Fla. Hospital Ordeal," November 4, 2010)

For the first time, we examine here the differences among the different venues for violence. In our previous books, we have always insisted that, regardless of the venue, every subject has to engage in behaviors associated with one of the paths to violence. Those behaviors are recognizable and, therefore, assessable and manageable. In this book, we take a look in the opposite direction. That is, we ask about the unique aspects of the various venues for violence and how those attributes affect the potential for violence. What is it about public figure violence that separates it from other targets? How does workplace violence differ from intimate partner violence? Do attacks on gathering places have distinguishing attributes? How do assaults on representative targets stand out? Analyzing these differences helps put the situation in its proper context.

Finally, we discuss the practices that threat managers should always avoid. Creating information silos not only keeps what the threat manager knows from other professionals, but also isolates the threat manager from information that those other professionals may have. Similarly, adopting a bunker mentality for one's own organization may let the problem subject loose on other entities or individuals. Individuals advancing along the path to intended violence are everyone's problem. Diverting them from one target may, in effect, direct them to another target. Instead, the subject should be managed away from violence altogether.

Threat managers should also avoid focusing on myopic management strategies. Losing sight of when a strategy is failing or becoming so wedded to a particular strategy creates inflexibility within very dynamic situations. Flexibility and a willingness to change as situations change are key to effective threat management.

Organization of the Book

Unlike our previous books on contemporary threat management, this book does not try to be a primer on the threat management process. Instead, we take a different approach. In this chapter, we introduce that approach and identify a set of what we consider to be fundamental elements undergirding contemporary threat management. These elements also spawn many of the threat management concepts identified and exemplified in the subsequent chapters. Our purpose is to highlight basic issues inherent in the threat management process. By bringing them to light, we hope to refine and improve that process.

Each of the following chapters focuses on individual concepts that we believe are vital to the contemporary threat management process. In each chapter, we first define and discuss the specific concepts and any auxiliary elements, and then we illustrate the concepts with one or more case studies. Throughout, we strive for simple explanations that avoid jargon. To each concept, we apply a simple test: Does it make sense in a straightforward, commonly understood manner? It passes that test if we can discuss it in plain, unvarnished English.

Between the discussions of these fundamental concepts, we insert a case study that we describe and analyze in depth. Each case study illustrates the concepts identified in the book. The case study opens with background information and then an analysis of the events; it ends with an outline of multiple lessons learned from the case. The critiques are intended to draw useful, practical lessons from real events and, sometimes, real tragedies. The profession of threat management deals in life and death situations. As professionals in that profession, we must be prepared to learn from the tragedies as well as the successes.

The cases flesh out the concepts that affect the contemporary threat management process. We draw them from real-life situations precisely because threat managers operate in the real world, where their decisions and approaches frequently tread the very thin line between controlling problematic behavior or devolving into chaos, between making the situation better or making it worse. Our attention cannot afford to drift away from that fundamental reality.

At the end of each case study, we list a number of issues of interest from that particular case. These lessons help identify some of the *do's* and *don'ts* of contemporary threat management. Studying previous cases best illuminates the strengths and weaknesses of making threat assessments and applying threat management strategies. The critique is not criticism, but an honest effort to learn and, by learning, to improve our approach.

Finally, we conclude the book with an initial glossary of threat management terms prepared in association with the University of Nebraska's Public Policy Center. This glossary represents an initial stab at standardizing the terminology that is beginning to come into play in the emerging professionalization of the field of threat management. Every profession ultimately develops a specialized vocabulary unique to the demands generated by that profession. Contemporary threat management has developed enough specialized terms that an initial glossary seems entirely appropriate and timely. Having a glossary should also fuel the continued professionalization of the field.

A Brief Review of the Fundamental Elements of Threat Management

In our previous books, we identified at various times and places what we now consider to be fundamental elements of contemporary threat management. Since we have described each element in considerable detail previously, we will not belabor or repeat those descriptions. Yet, precisely because these elements are fundamental, it behooves us to provide a brief summary of each one here because we derived the concepts described in this book from these fundamental elements. Contemporary threat management essentially organizes itself around these core ideas. Understanding them is essential to any understanding of the threat management process. They provide, in effect, the best way to think about and understand threat management. They are the pillars upon which that process stands.

Two Forms of Violence

Violence comes in one of two forms: impromptu or intended. Impromptu violence is an unplanned, spontaneous outburst resulting in physical violence. The subject did not come to the encounter planning to commit violence, but the chemistry of the moment—the emotional interaction between the subject and the target—generated the resulting violence. Since impromptu violence is emotionally driven, it attempts to achieve an immediate goal. Even if targeted at a particular person, the violence is spontaneous.

Case Illustration: The Angry Spitter

Daniel Malone ran a stop sign on Christmas Eve, 2008, in Bonner County, Idaho. Four days later, First District Court Judge Justin Julian rejected Malone's plea of innocence and refused Malone's request for leniency because the violation occurred on Christmas Eve. Instead, the judge fined him $75. Furious, Malone glared at the judge before "maliciously expelling a large amount of saliva" onto the carpet in the hallway of the courthouse. For that impetuous act of anger, the judge found Malone in contempt of court and sentenced him to 2 days in jail. (*Source:* "Man Spits on Court Floor After Traffic Conviction," Associated Press, December 29, 2008)

Conversely, intended violence is a planned, premeditated physical assault conducted by the subject against one or more targets. The subject approaches the encounter fully intending to commit violence. Intended violence tends to be very focused, even if the targets are selected randomly. Although emotions affect the motive, the violence itself is quite controlled and purposeful. The subject has thought out how the violence will occur and acts according to the plan.

Case Illustration: Practicing for the Fort Hood Shooting

Major Nidal M. Hasan, a U.S. Army psychiatrist, killed 13 and wounded 32 fellow soldiers at Fort Hood, Texas, on November 5, 2009. On August 1 of that year, over 3 months before he opened fire, Major Hasan purchased a laser-equipped semiautomatic pistol. In the intervening months, Hasan completed a course on concealed handguns and practiced shooting at a shooting range once or twice a week. He used silhouette targets of human forms, rather than the traditional bull's-eye. He also seemed to prefer shooting at the head and chest rather than center mass. Hasan also bought up to eight boxes of ammunition a week and added extensions to the pistol's ammunition clips.

Hasan intended to shoot as many people as he could. He chose his weapon, purchased it, and took the time to practice shooting it. (*Source:* "Hasan Repeatedly Visited Firing Range Before Fort Hood Rampage," *Washington Post,* October 22, 2010)

Impromptu violence tends to be less fatal because any weapons used are usually weapons of opportunity—fists and feet, spittle, loose objects, or equipment that happens to be within the subject's reach at the time of the encounter. Intended violence, because it is planned, usually results in more lethality. The subject has plenty of time to decide on a weapon, obtain it, and even practice with it prior to the encounter.

Although threat managers must contend with both forms of violence, impromptu violence usually erupts and dissipates before the threat manager can apply any preventive strategies or interventions. Most of the responses to impromptu violence are punitive and after the fact. Consequently, most threat managers focus their attention and energy on preventing acts of intended violence.

The Paths to Violence

Violence, whether impromptu or intended, is a process of incremental behaviors culminating in an attack. That process is best conceptualized as paths to violence along which the behaviors are acted out. The paths are illustrated in the following figure.

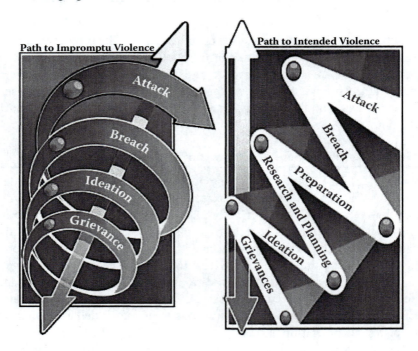

As the two paths illustrate, both impromptu and intended violence include behaviors associated with developing a grievance, settling on the idea of committing violence, breaching the target's security, and launching the attack. Intended violence also involves behaviors associated with researching and planning the attack and then making preparations required by the plan.

Impromptu violence usually takes place very fast; hence, it is displayed as a spiral winding quickly from grievance to attack. Intended violence is a more deliberative process. It can take mere moments to occur or days, weeks, months, or even years, to be consummated. Thus, time presses on impromptu violence, but has little impact on intended violence.

The most important lesson derived from the paths to violence is to focus on the behaviors associated with each path. Because violence is a process of incremental behaviors, those behaviors are recognizable. Recognizing that a subject has stepped out on the path to violence is the first step in preventing that individual from completing the path. What makes the violence preventable is diverting the behaviors—that is, essentially getting the subject off the path.

Elements of the Contemporary Threat Management Process

Threat management consists of three distinct elements:

1. Identifying the potentially violent subject
2. Assessing the subject's actual risk of violence
3. Managing the subject away from the potential violence

Identifying potentially violent subjects is best done by focusing on any behaviors associated with either of the two paths to violence. Once those behaviors are identified, then impromptu violence can be interrupted or punished. Identifying behaviors associated with the path to intended violence allows for gathering information and making a thoughtful threat assessment. Assessing the subject's actual risk of violence can be accomplished by asking about the subject's intent, motive, and ability to commit a violent act. Managing the subject away from potential intended violence requires the threat manager to apply one or more intervention strategies based on the subject's behaviors and his or her intent, motive, and ability.

Hunters and Howlers

Contemporary threat management involves dealing with two very different types of problem individuals. Hunters truly intend to commit a violent act. Consequently, they engage in the behaviors associated with intended violence. That is, hunters develop a grievance, resolve themselves to violence, research and plan their assault, make preparations for it, breach the subject's security, and attack.

Case Illustration: The Poisonous Hunter

In the spring of 2003, parishioners at the Gustaf Adolph Lutheran Church in New Sweden, Maine, took ill after drinking coffee at the church after Sunday services. One man died; 15 others were injured. The coffee, police investigators later found, was laced with arsenic.

Several days later, Daniel Bondeson, a 53-year-old potato farmer and a member of the church, shot himself in the chest. His suicide note took responsibility for the poisoning. Bondeson claimed that he was upset that people in the church did not like him and that someone had spiked his coffee with something that gave him a stomachache. He confessed to his lawyer that he did not intend for anyone to die, just to suffer like he did. Unfortunately, the chemical he used contained arsenic.

Bondeson was a hunter whose planning and preparation got away from him. He had a grievance, got the idea of taking revenge, planned the act, made his preparations, and then spiked the coffee and watched the parishioners drink it. Whether he planned to kill them or give them a stomachache mattered little once he stepped out on the path to intended violence. Not all plans and preparations go the way the hunter wants. (*Source:* Pam Belluck, "Poisonings at Church Are Termed Retaliation," *New York Times,* April 19, 2006)

Howlers lack the resolve to commit violence. Instead, they seek to frighten their target or establish some kind of relationship with the target. Howlers make threats, draw attention to themselves, and cause fear in their targets, but they do not get past the ideation stage on the path to intended violence. For howlers, the simple act of communicating with the target suffices, regardless of how disturbing or frightening that communication may be.

Case Illustration: The E-Mail Prankster

Eight days before President Barack Obama's inauguration as president, the FBI's Washington office received an e-mail stating, "I'm going to assassinate the new president of the United States of America. P.S., you have 48 hours to stop it from happening." A second e-mail threatened to blow up the Mall of America outside Minneapolis, Minnesota, with 40 pounds of C4 explosive and TNT planted on seven cars in the parking lot.

Shortly thereafter, FBI agents arrested Timothy Gutierrez, aged 20. Gutierrez claimed that he had hacked into the FBI's computer website. "I wanted to see what was really going on," Gutierrez said. "There are 500 acres of encryption data, but I found a slip through it. There's always a hole." According to Gutierrez, he left the two e-mails on the FBI's computer as a prank and "didn't think they would actually find" the messages.

Gutierrez surrendered to the FBI on January 29, 2009. Seven months later, he pled guilty and received 4 years' probation, the first year under house arrest, complete with an electronic bracelet. The e-mails proved to be an expensive prank.

Gutierrez was a classic howler. (*Sources:* "Colo. Man Accused of Threatening Obama Surrenders," Associated Press, January 30, 2009; "Obama Threat-Maker Gets Probation," Lubbock Online, Lubbock *Avalanche-Journal,* August 1, 2009)

Although hunters are far more dangerous than howlers, both types of problem individuals have to be managed. Howlers cause fear; they cannot be ignored. Indeed, ignoring them tends to embolden them to make more frequent and more strident communications. There is even the risk that a howler may transform into a hunter. Thus, it becomes just as important to deal with a howler as it is to deal with a hunter.

"At This Time"

The three most important words in the threat manager's lexicon are the prepositional phrase "at this time." First employed by the United States Secret Service, the phrase freezes each threat assessment in time. It serves as a pointed reminder that the assessment is founded on the known facts under consideration. New facts or previously unknown information may compel a change in the assessment in the future. As a result, threat assessments have very short shelf lives. They are current only at the moment at which they are completed; they do not extend beyond the information known at this moment, this time.

Case Illustration: The Changing Former Employee

In the spring of 2011, the Acme Corporation fired one of its line supervisors for negligence and failure to come to work. During the termination meeting, the employee threatened his supervisor and a coworker. The supervisor reported the threat to the company's threat management unit. Based on the threat, the former employee's motivation, and his personal knowledge of the targets and the layout of the factory, the threat management unit initially rated the potential risk as high at this time.

Two days later, however, the unit determined that the former employee had gotten another job at a nearby factory. A check of the former employee's personnel file showed that he had been married nearly 20 years, owned his own home, and had a son in college. Based on the presence of these strong inhibitors, the unit assessed the potential risk as low at this time.

A month later, the former employee left several messages on his former supervisor's voice mail claiming that he had been fired from his new job and blaming the supervisor for causing his problems. The voice on the messages was slurred, suggesting that the former employee had been intoxicated when he made the calls. Based on the loss of the new job, the new threats, and the possible alcohol abuse, the threat management unit assessed the potential for violence as high at this time.

Two weeks later, another employee, who knew the former employee socially, reported to the threat management unit that the former employee's wife had left and had filed with the court a request for a restraining order against the former employee, claiming domestic abuse. Based on the loss of an important inhibitor and the use of violence, the threat management unit again assessed the potential for violence as high at this time.

The next day, police arrested the former employee for violating the restraining order and for physically assaulting the estranged wife. The threat management unit monitored the judicial proceedings against the former employee. At the end of the trial, the judge found the former employee guilty and sentenced him to 3 years in the penitentiary. Once the threat management unit confirmed that the former employee had been admitted into the prison, they assessed the potential risk as low at this time. (*Source:* Hypothetical situation based on authors' experience)

Consequently, every threat assessment, to maintain its internal honesty, must include—indeed, must conclude—with the acknowledgment that the assessment is frozen *at this time.*

Empathy

Assessing problem individuals, whether hunter or howler, requires understanding the world as the subject sees or perceives it. Empathizing with the subject does not mean sympathizing or agreeing with him or her. It means, instead, seeing the situation from the subject's point of view in order to determine the subject's emotional investment in the issue, the subject's grasp of reality, and the subject's intent and motive. Empathizing also helps measure the subject's ability to cause harm. At times, this requires the threat manager to be out of his or her comfort zone and really put himself or herself in the other guy's shoes. Not all the subjects who come to a threat manager's attention have good jobs, live in comfortable homes with their families, or even have a firm grip on reality. Some subjects have lives with difficulties and challenges that we can hardly imagine.

Case Illustration: The Folks at the Buckhorn Lodge

The Buckhorn Lodge is a roadside tavern in the Sierra Nevada mountain range in California. It is an old place that has hosted gold miners, loggers, hunters, bikers, and dam construction workers over its 150-year existence. Like many of these mountain taverns, its only neighbors are the gas station, a small country store, and the 50-space mobile home park spread out behind the lodge. This is a stereotypical "rough place" with more than its share of parolees, drug addicts, and people on the edges of society. The nearest deputy sheriff has to respond from the county seat 45 minutes away on mountain roads. Due to past problems, the volunteer fire department and the ambulance service wait for the sheriff's deputy to arrive before going to the tavern or mobile home park during emergencies.

Recently, the Buckhorn Lodge hosted a pool tournament. The wrong guy won: He was not a local resident. Therefore, the folks at the bar beat him unconscious and threw him out in the dirt parking lot. A traveler on the road saw him lying there and called 911. When the sheriff's deputy arrived, he could find no one who had witnessed the attack and, according to one patron (a 30-year-old pregnant woman drinking a beer and smoking a cigarette on the tavern's front porch), most residents doubted that he had ever been in the bar at all.

One Leg Tom is a very frequent patron at the Buckhorn. Two years ago, he passed out drunk and fell into a bonfire that had been built at the mobile home park. A subsequent infection resulted in loss of a leg and an addiction to pain medication. When Tom is drunk, which is fairly often, he is known to launch himself from his wheelchair and attack other bar patrons. Tom is feuding with the chain store pharmacy in town where he gets his medication. He gets other bar patrons to drive him to the county seat once a month to get his medication and his angry, crazed behavior has become a problem. He always wants more medication and he is accusing the pharmacy workers of conspiring against him.

He has been arrested for disturbances at the pharmacy and has had several stays in the county jail. When he is released, the jail staff is always happy to get him off their hands.

The pharmacy employees are fearful of Tom and they reported the problems to the corporate headquarters in Sacramento. The corporate attorney looked at the information provided and determined that they could not deny service because they are the only provider in town and they have an obligation to serve indigent patients through a contract with the state. She looked at the legal options and, working with other attorneys, she crafted a strongly worded cease-and-desist letter. She sent the letter to Tom by registered mail. After 2 weeks, the letter was returned unclaimed. She contacted the postal carrier to find out why the letter was unclaimed. The postman informed her that Tom could not read and never accepted any mail.

If Tom could read, how effective would this type of intervention have been? How impressed would the folks at the Buckhorn Lodge have been if they had read the letter? The attorney selected a course of action that would be effective with other attorneys and people in her world—not the world of the Buckhorn Lodge. (*Source:* Authors' personal knowledge)

Empathizing with the subject requires suspending belief and accepting what the subject does or communicates as—for the moment—a true description of the situation. It requires stepping into the subject's mind and seeing things through his or her eyes. That is best accomplished by analyzing the subject's behavior, communications, past history, and any other information pertinent to the assessment. The threat manager should always ask: "What does the subject want? What may be at risk from the subject's point of view? Is the subject behaving in such a way to indicate that he or she is trying to accomplish something or to protect something dear to him or her?"

Empathy is also crucial in measuring the impact of the *intimacy effect*. That effect must always be assessed from the point of view of the subject, regardless of the reality of any relationship or lack of relationship between the subject and the target. If the subject has a delusional belief that he or she has an interpersonal or intimate relationship with the target, then the *intimacy effect* is in play.

New assessments require new exercises in empathy, regardless of how problematic the subject's behavior may become.

The Spectrum of Threat Management
Strategies for Defusing the Risk

In our previous books, we identified and described in detail the nine threat management strategies that threat managers can draw upon to defuse the risk posed by the subject. We believe the range to be definitive; that is, these strategies are the complete range of options from which the threat manager chooses the best and most suitable for the case at hand. The spectrum along which these strategies are arrayed from least confrontational to most confrontational is illustrated in the following figure.

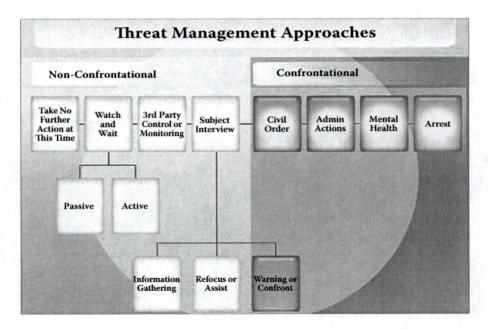

Briefly, the strategies are defined as the following:

- *Take no further action at this time* is the conscious decision, based on a low-risk assessment, that no further action beyond the assessment is needed.
- *Watch and wait* is the conscious decision, based on a low- to moderate-risk assessment, that the best strategy is to wait for the subject's next move. This can be done passively, meaning that no more information is gathered, or actively, meaning that information continues to be collected on the subject and the situation.
- *Third-party control or monitoring* relies on a third party who has some influence or relation with the subject to control the subject's problematic behavior or to monitor the subject and report the subject's activities to the threat manager.
- *Subject interview* involves actually interviewing the subject to gain information from the subject's point of view, to exploit opportunities to resolve the subject's issue, or to confront the subject with the warning that further problematic behaviors will be punished.
- *Civil order* entails involving the judicial system through the issuing of a restraining or stay-away order or some other judicial precept directed at halting the subject's problematic behavior.
- *Administrative order* relies on using an organization's disciplinary process to address the subject.
- *Mental health* means involving the mental health community in addressing the subject's behavior through an involuntary or voluntary commitment.
- *Arrest* involves charging the subject with criminal behavior in support of having the subject arrested.

How these strategies are used in practice will be illustrated in the case studies and case illustrations throughout the book.

Format for Threat Assessments

In compiling a written or oral threat assessment, we strongly recommend following the format we first outlined in *Threat Assessment and Management Strategies*. This format is the best way for any threat manager or threat management team to present a written or oral threat assessment. Used consistently, the format allows the assessor to think through the situation logically and comprehensively and to communicate effectively. It also explicitly draws attention to what is currently known about the situation, which helps highlight the blank spaces of the unknowns. It helps give a sense of urgency and seriousness to what are always urgent and serious situations.

The format consists of the following four basic questions.

1. What Do We Know About the Situation at This Time?

Provide a summary of the facts known and verified *at this time* without embellishment or descriptive phrasing. In other words, the answer to the first question is a straightforward synopsis of what is known at the time at which the assessment is prepared, without unnecessary adjectives or adverbs, and told in an objective, unembellished, straightforward way. The synopsis should include a plain statement of what exactly prompted the assessment in the first place. Was there a threat, a suspicious activity, an inappropriate communication or contact? What happened to prompt this assessment at this time?

The statement of facts also explicitly acknowledges what critical facts are unknown at the time of the assessment. Expressly identifying the knowns and the unknowns helps measure the validity of the assessment. It also points the way for finding out what needs to be known and where the gaps are in the current assessment. This exercise contributes directly to guiding the protective investigation. Subsequent assessments can then be compared to this one to ensure that the new knowns are factored into the reassessment.

2. What Is the Assessment of the Known Facts at This Time?

Assess and analyze all of the facts known *at this time.* The assessment should weigh the method of delivery of the inappropriate communication or contact, address the potential impact of the *intimacy effect,* determine what inhibitors are in place in the subject's current life situation, and provide a detailed rationale in support of the assessment. Of absolute importance, the assessment needs to be tied directly to the facts known at the time of the assessment. It should avoid at all costs any conjectures or speculations.

At the same time, the assessment should weigh the unknowns against the knowns. In any situation, certain factors carry more weight in the assessment than other factors. Knowing about a recent purchase of a weapon, loss of essential inhibitors, or escalating activity along the path to intended violence obviously carries tremendous weight in any realistic threat assessment. Conversely, positively knowing that none has occurred would lower the assessment. Obversely, not knowing one way or the other that any of these events has occurred would not weigh as heavily, if at all, in lowering the assessment.

The context in which the inappropriate communication or contact occurred is equally as important as the circumstances prompting the assessment. Is there evidence of significant changes in the subject's life or situation? Are those changes positive or negative? Has his or her attitude or demeanor undergone any changes, including any changes in communications or contacts with the target? Did the subject understand the impact of his or her words, actions, or activities? Seeing the situation within its larger context gives form and fiber to the assessment.

3. What Is the Recommended Protective Response?

Based on the assessment and the situation, develop a recommended protective response at this time. The response should be directly proportionate to the level of risk identified in the threat assessment for a defined period of time. Most importantly, a response is crucial, even if it is merely a personal security briefing for the target. Conducting such a briefing reassures the target that the situation is being taken seriously and that actions will be taken to alleviate or mitigate any risks. Threat management requires managing both the subject and the target. It is especially important to ensure that the target does nothing to aggravate the situation.

4. What Are the Recommended Threat Management Strategies?

Based, again, strictly on the threat assessment and the level of risk, recommend the most appropriate threat management strategy or strategies (if any) for now, based on what is known and unknown. The strategies should be proportionate to the assessment and applied flexibly. A reassessment should be conducted as soon as the strategy or strategies come into play or more information is discovered.

The threat manager needs to keep in mind that once a strategy or strategies have been applied, the very nature of the situation has radically changed. For every action taken by the threat management team, the subject will have a reaction. The threat management team needs to be able to react appropriately to that reaction. This requires a reassessment of the situation and, possibly, seeking more information or the adoption of different threat management strategies. These, in turn, will prompt new reactions from the subject, necessitating new assessments, more information, and new strategies from the team.

Summary

We propose addressing the concepts and case studies described in this book in a practical, straightforward manner. The concepts will be presented in realistic, easy to understand descriptions, and the case studies will help bring the points to life. The concepts derive from seven overarching elements of the threat management process: the two forms of violence; the two paths to those forms of violence; the process of identifying, assessing, and managing individuals of violent intent; dealing with hunters and howlers; the concept of "at this time"; the need for empathy; and the spectrum of threat management strategies.

From these elements, we have derived the concepts of threat management "need-to-knows," case dynamics and intervention synergy, the impact of inhibitors, and the differences in the different venues for violence. These concepts and the case studies illustrating them will be explored in the next chapters.

Notes

1. Parsons, T. (1968). Professions. In D. L. Sills (Ed.), *International encyclopedia of the social sciences* (p. 536). New York, NY: Macmillan; Carr-Saunders, A. M. (1966). The concept of professionalism. In H. M. Vollmer & D. L. Mills (Eds.), *Professionalization* (p. 4). Englewood Cliffs, NJ: Prentice Hall; Calhoun, F. S. (1996). *The trainers: The federal law enforcement center and the professionalization of federal law enforcement* (p. 3). Glynco, GA: The Federal Law Enforcement Training Center.

Case Study
Piecing Together the Puzzle

2

In April 2009, the Kansas office of the Federal Bureau of Investigation received a letter from Scott Roeder's ex-wife's current husband.[1] The letter alleged that Roeder had threatened to physically harm Dr. George Tiller of Wichita, Kansas. Dr. Tiller was a controversial abortion provider, one of only three or four doctors in the United States specializing in late-term procedures. Roeder, also a Kansas resident, was a known opponent of abortions who embraced the so-called "justifiable homicide" doctrine.[2] That view postulated that saving the lives of unborn fetuses justified killing abortion providers. According to FBI spokesperson Bridget Patton, the agency "found no specific, credible threat in the letter."[3] Based on that threat assessment, the Bureau took no action.

During April and May, Roeder began attending Sunday services at the Wichita Reformation Lutheran Church—the same church that Dr. Tiller and his family attended. In the past, the church had been occasionally picketed by antiabortion protesters. Members of the congregation knew about the controversy surrounding Dr. Tiller and were sensitive to protesters at the church, but there is no evidence that anyone raised an alarm about Roeder's new church attendance.[4] Later, several members of the church would state that his presence during services seemed suspicious.[5]

On May 1, someone vandalized Dr. Tiller's clinic. The vandal severed the wires to the closed-circuit television (CCTV) cameras and poked a hole in the roof, which led to extensive water damage. Three days later, an anonymous caller telephoned the clinic and threatened Dr. Tiller's life. On May 5, Dr. Tiller's attorney, a former Kansas U.S. attorney, wrote the FBI informing them of the vandalism and the threat and requesting an investigation into Freedom of Access to Clinic Entrances (FACE) Act violations at the clinic.[1] No one appears to have made any link between the new husband's letter and the subsequent vandalism and telephone threat.

On May 23, someone glued the door locks at a clinic in Kansas City. A week later, the clinic director identified Scott Roeder gluing the locks to the same clinic doors on the CCTV surveillance tapes. The director recognized Roeder because he regularly picketed the clinic. The director reported the incident to the FBI and gave the Bureau the license plate number of the car Roeder drove. Because May 30 was a Saturday, the report was probably handled by an FBI watch officer who—again, probably—may not have had any knowledge of the reported vandalism and threats to Dr. Tiller's clinic.

No evidence exists to suggest that anyone tied the events at the two clinics together. There is not any evidence indicating that Dr. Tiller knew about the vandalism at the Kansas City clinic or that that clinic's director knew about the vandalism and threats to Dr. Tiller's clinic. Although we have a clear view now of Roeder's antiabortion activities in the spring of 2009, at the time, the picture was disassembled, like pieces of a puzzle scattered about.

The next day, May 31, 2009, Roeder shot Dr. Tiller once in the head while the doctor was standing in the vestibule of his church handing out bulletins.[5] A few hours later, police pulled Roeder over on the highway and arrested him for murder. He was driving the car with the same license plates that the Kansas City clinic director had reported to the FBI a day earlier.[1]

In hindsight, the events leading up to the May 31 shooting appear to give positive indicators that Roeder had stepped onto the path to intended violence toward Dr. Tiller. Unfortunately, at the time, no one with the FBI or within the prochoice community or at Dr. Tiller's clinic had the vantage point to see the whole picture. The clarity of hindsight merely underscores the murkiness that clouds the process of conducting accurate threat assessments. The practice of threat management requires peering into the mists obscuring the future. The view improves with the addition of new information, but gaining that information at the right time is itself a challenge. It requires relying on preexisting channels of communication and acting on new information as it comes through those various channels.

The information about Scott Roeder in the spring of 2009 clearly shows him moving from civil protests to unlawful actions that continued to escalate until he pulled the trigger of his newly bought pistol. The lessons we derive from Dr. Tiller's assassination include the importance of good communications and information sharing, especially among communities as close-knit as the prochoice movement and its relations to law enforcement.

Background

George Tiller was no stranger to death threats. Over the course of his 30-year career providing abortions, Dr. Tiller became a lightning rod to the antiabortion movement. Protestors stood outside his clinic daily trying to dissuade patients from entering. Larger, well-organized protests led by Operation Rescue and other national antiabortion groups periodically targeted the clinic. As recently as the spring of 2007, Operation Rescue had organized one large demonstration at the clinic from May 17 to May 20.

Others went beyond protest demonstrations. In August 1993, Rachelle Shannon, an antiabortionist who had previously specialized in clinic arsons, shot Dr. Tiller as he left his clinic at the end of the day. The bullet hit him in the left elbow and ricocheted into the right elbow. Over the course of the next

16 years until his assassination, Dr. Tiller's clinic was bombed and vandalized. He was targeted with death threats, as well as investigated by state prosecutors and law enforcement. In 2009, the state attorney filed charges against Dr. Tiller for violating Kansas abortion laws. The court acquitted Dr. Tiller shortly before his assassination.

As a result of the protests, threats, and attempted assassinations, Dr. Tiller drove an armored car, frequently wore a bulletproof vest, and often carried a pistol, though he had neither with him at the church. He and his family lived in a gated community. Clearly, Dr. Tiller was sensitive to the risks posed against him. Various prochoice organizations also recognized the nearly constant threat facing the doctor. Law enforcement, both at the local and federal level, also understood the high-risk nature of Dr. Tiller's practice. On several occasions, deputy U.S. marshals provided physical security to Dr. Tiller and his clinic. Over the years, the local FBI office received numerous reports of vandalism to the clinic and threats to Dr. Tiller. Wichita police routinely kept order among the protestors who daily demonstrated outside the clinic. Tragically, what was lacking was good communications between the various groups—law enforcement and prochoice—concerned with Dr. Tiller's security.

Scott Roeder was no stranger to law enforcement. In the mid-90s, according to his ex-wife, he underwent a "drastic personality shift" to become a radicalized antigovernment, antiabortion fanatic. He quit his factory job and became an itinerant, moving nearly constantly around Kansas. "He wanted a scapegoat," the ex-wife explained. "First it was taxes—he stopped paying. Then he turned to the church and got involved in antiabortion."[4] In April 1996, police in Topeka, Kansas, pulled Roeder over because his car had improper license plates. Roeder's homemade plates read, "Sovereign private property. Immunity declared by law. Non-commercial American."[4] When officers searched the car, they found ammunition, a blasting cap, a cord fuse, a one-pound can of gunpowder, and two 9-volt batteries, one of which was connected to a switch for triggering a bomb.[4] Roeder was sentenced to 24 months' probation with intense supervision, but his conviction was overturned on appeal 18 months later. The search of the car, the court ruled, was improper.[2]

Suzanne James, who at the time was director of victim's services for Shawnee County, remembered seeing Roeder during one of his court appearances. "He was part of the One Supreme Court, a Freeman group based out of Shawnee County," James told a reporter for the Kansas City Star. "He was fanatic about a lot of things. I went to one of his court appearances and thought, 'This guy is dangerous.' There were a lot of red flags that came up about him."[2]

Increasingly in the late 90s, Roeder's focus shifted from antigovernment extremism to antiabortion extremism. In 1996, Regina Dinwiddie, a prominent Kansas City antiabortionist, met Roeder while picketing outside the Kansas City Planned Parenthood clinic. Roeder, she remembered, walked into the clinic and asked to see the doctor. The doctor came out and Roeder stared at him for nearly a minute. Finally, he said to the doctor, "I've seen you now." Roeder then turned on his heel and walked away, leaving the doctor and his colleagues unnerved.[2]

From there, it would have been easy to zero in on his fellow Kansan, Dr. Tiller, who was one of the antiabortion movement's most hated providers. Roeder participated in the May 2007 protest at Dr. Tiller's clinic organized by Operation Rescue. Someone using the name Scott Roeder posted a comment on Operation Rescue's blog commending the protestors, adding,

> Sometime soon, would it be feasible to organize as many people as possible to attend Tillers [sic] church (inside, not just outside) to have much more of a presence and possibly ask questions of the Pastor, Deacons, Elders and members while there? Doesn't seem like it would hurt anything but bring more attention to Tiller.[2]

In the spring of 2009, Roeder told a fellow demonstrator that he had attended Dr. Tiller's trial every day. He called the proceedings a "sham." According to the other demonstrator, Roeder "felt the system had bitterly let down justice and let Tiller go free."[4] Apparently, the idea of somehow confronting Dr. Tiller at his church resurfaced in Roeder's mind. Around this time, April and May 2009, he began showing up at the Wichita Reformation Lutheran Church on Sunday mornings, usually sitting quietly in a pew. Several congregants reported seeing Roeder in church repeatedly in the weeks leading up to the shooting. "He didn't seem in place," one congregant told an Associated Press reporter. "I was suspicious of him." Roeder also drew the attention of church members because of an overwhelming odor around him. He smelled like ammonia.[5] These suspicions do not appear to have been reported to law enforcement or to the doctor himself.

It was also around this time—March or April 2009—that Roeder indicated to his ex-wife his intention of physically harming Dr. Tiller. That prompted her current husband to write to the FBI. Someone vandalized the clinic in early May and someone threatened Dr. Tiller over the telephone. Both the vandalism and the threat indicated an escalation in the protest activity going beyond demonstrations to actual acts of violence.

On May 18, Roeder purchased a Taurus .22 caliber pistol. He picked the weapon up 5 days later—the same day on which someone glued the door locks on the clinic in Kansas City, a 3½ hour drive from Wichita. The next day, May 24, Roeder again attended services at the Wichita Reformation Lutheran Church. Dr. Tiller was absent that Sunday. The next weekend, on Saturday, May 30, the Kansas City clinic director identified Roeder on the surveillance tapes and reported Roeder to the FBI.

Then, on Sunday morning, May 31, Roeder and Dr. Tiller went to church.

Analysis

In hindsight, Scott Roeder's May 31, 2009, rendezvous with Dr. Tiller at the Wichita Reformation Lutheran Church appears as a fairly straightforward, albeit lengthy, progression from family man to antigovernment, antiabortion radical and then to assassin. During this time, he shed many of his inhibitors, including his marriage, family, employment, and steady domicile. By the mid-90s, Roeder had bought into the justifiable homicide doctrine, but held back on taking such action, probably hoping someone else would. His wait proved in vain. In late May 2009, Roeder escalated his protest activities by gluing the locks at the Kansas City clinic.

But when the state failed to prove that Dr. Tiller had violated Kansas abortion laws, Roeder made the decision to step out on the path to intended violence. He researched the doctor's church and its Sunday morning rituals, made his plans, prepared himself by purchasing a weapon, drove himself to the church in time for Sunday services, and then approached Dr. Tiller and, without hesitation, put the gun to the doctor's head and pulled the trigger. Brandishing the weapon to hold the other two ushers at bay, Roeder escaped in his car. Police arrested him several hours later.

The FBI received a warning in April specifying that Scott Roeder intended to harm Dr. Tiller. Despite the vandalism to the clinic in early May and the subsequent telephonic death threat directed at Dr. Tiller, the FBI held to its "no specific, credible threat" assessment. Even after, although at the 11th hour and on a Saturday, the FBI received notice that Roeder was acting out by gluing the Kansas City clinic's doors, the assessment held. The vandalism at Dr. Tiller's clinic and the Kansas City clinic evidenced a sharp escalation in Kansas antiabortion activity in the spring of 2009, but no one appears to have seen the larger picture until after the assassination.

As Attorney General Eric Holder said to a meeting of prochoice groups in his office a few weeks after the assassination, "We blew it."[1]

A Brief Note on the Silo Effect and Its Impact on This Case

The so-called "silo effect" undoubtedly had a profound impact on the FBI's response to Dr. Tiller's situation in the spring of 2009. The term *silo effect*, popular in business and organizational communities, refers to a lack of communication and sharing information between individuals, departments, field offices, and headquarters in a single organization. The silo effect is the opposite of systems thinking in an organization. The silo effect takes its name from the farm storage silo: Each silo is designated for one specific grain. Each silo ensures no mixing of different grains or, in organizations, no sharing of information. Any large organization risks this problem to some degree.

In this case, Roeder was acting out in several Kansas cities. According to the clinic personnel, they reported each incident to the FBI. But questions remain: Did the information on the threat reported by the new husband ever end up at the same FBI desk as the subsequent vandalism, the phone threat, and Dr. Tiller's attorney's request for an investigation into FACE violations? Did the identification of Roeder as the person vandalizing the locks ever reach the proper FBI desk on a Saturday? Were the various incidents seen as a broad investigation or were they each considered isolated incidents? Did local law enforcement know of the threats and the acts of vandalism? Probably not.

Threat managers need to combat the silo effect continuously. The larger and more geographically spread out the organization is, the larger the potential problems are.

The silo effect undoubtedly also affected the Kansas prochoice community. Did the information from Kansas City ever reach Dr. Tiller or other clinics in Wichita? Were they all informed of the threats made by Roeder? Did Dr. Tiller and the other clinics in Kansas routinely share information concerning security events at their individual clinics? Did the Kansas City clinic manager view the vandalism at his clinic as potentially part of a larger series of attacks toward other clinics in Kansas?

Another factor in this case is the expectations of the clinic management versus the reality of FBI operations. Did the clinic believe that calling the FBI was the magic formula that would solve all security problems? Did the FBI share that belief?

From any target's point of view, a number of issues need to be considered in order to offset the silo effect and any unrealistic expectations when reporting threat information. These include the following:

- Does the organization to which the reports go have a legal or contractual authority to manage the case?
- Does it have the resources and expertise to handle a threat assessment?
- Are the reports going to one person or different people at different locations?
- Is there a 24/7 operation to receive and assess reported problems?
- What type of information should be reported?
- Are resources committed to the case?
- Is the law enforcement agency responsive to the situation or does it only record and file the report?
- Does the agency have boots on the ground or is it an office operation only?
- Does the agency handle assessments only or will it manage security also?

- Is it responsible for keeping others informed, including other potential targets and local law enforcement?
- Is the agency going to handle only this situation or will it also manage all future problems with the subject and, if so, for how long?

Lessons Learned

1. Threats should never be ignored or dismissed out of hand. Given how controversial Dr. Tiller was, he was always at a high risk of violence precisely because of the controversy. As a result, any threat toward him should always have been treated as credible. Instead, what appears to have happened is that Dr. Tiller's constant state of high risk inured both him and law enforcement. Living for nearly 30 years at high risk caused a kind of complacency, an acceptance that being at high risk was the norm, not the aberration. In that context, threats and vandalism were commonplace and not seen as indicators of escalating activity. If one is always at high risk, how can indicators of increasing risk be seen, much less assessed, accurately?

2. Threats need to be assessed within the context in which they occur. Even a cursory inquiry into Scott Roeder, based on the new husband's letter, would have uncovered the fanatical nature of his beliefs, his commitment to the justifiable homicide doctrine, and his increasing fixation on Dr. Tiller. After all, news reporters uncovered as much within days of the shooting.

3. Time is of little consequence when someone embarks on the path to intended violence. Roeder maintained a grievance against abortion providers in general and, increasingly, Dr. Tiller in particular, for years before he began acting on the idea of actually taking action himself. What seems to have prompted him toward the assassination was the state's failure to convict Dr. Tiller of violating Kansas abortion laws. The failure of lawful measures to stop Dr. Tiller's practice may have convinced him of the necessity to take unlawful means. Once Roeder accepted the idea of taking action himself, he moved quickly through research and planning (attending the church services), preparation (buying the pistol), breach (approaching the doctor in the church vestibule), and attack (shooting Dr. Tiller). The church location seemed to have a significant hold on Roeder's imagination, as though he had decided it was the most appropriate place to stop Dr. Tiller.

4. Situations containing the risk of potential violence are dynamic, not static. Consequently, the threat manager needs to reassess the situation whenever changes occur or new events happen, including

simply the passing of time. That is the only way to identify patterns of behavior, escalations toward violence, or de-escalations. Once the letter from the current husband was assessed in April, Dr. Tiller's situation should have been reassessed in May—immediately after the vandalism to the clinic and again after the telephonic death threat. Information about Scott Roeder should have been continuously assessed and reassessed as well. The appropriate protective response should have been continuously reevaluated as new information, such as the vandalism to the Kansas City clinic, was reported.

5. Threat managers must avoid focusing too tightly on a specific bit of information and thus missing the larger picture, like the blind men, each of whom touched a different part of the elephant and concluded that each had a different animal.

6. The vandalism to Dr. Tiller's clinic and, later, to the Kansas City clinic indicated an escalation in antiabortion activities in that area, but it is not clear that anyone put the disparate events together. Stronger communication channels within the prochoice community in Kansas and beyond may have picked up the increase in illegal protest activity. Had they done so, they may have been able to present a stronger case to the FBI that the risk to Dr. Tiller had increased.

7. Law enforcement also failed to note the escalation in protest activities. In April, the FBI discounted the information from Roeder's ex-wife, perhaps considering the letter a "poison pen" letter. A month later, the escalation in protest activities occurred. Although Roeder may or may not have vandalized Dr. Tiller's clinic or did the first gluing of the locks at the Kansas City clinic, an eyewitness did identify him gluing the locks on May 30. That incident could have given more credence to the April letter, had anyone had time to put the two together.

8. Most importantly, the events leading up to the assassination underscore the need for multiple communication channels. The various entities within the prochoice community, including clinic personnel and the several national prochoice groups, need better ways for collecting information on antiabortionist activities and to share that information immediately with all the law enforcement agencies with jurisdiction over the different areas. As the Southern Law Poverty Center has repeatedly demonstrated in dealing with individuals associated with various hate groups, private sector organizations have a lot more freedom in collecting information on private citizens than law enforcement does. By analyzing the information it collects, the center is able to alert appropriate law enforcement organizations to new trends, disturbing patterns, and suspicious individuals.

9. Entities and individuals sharing a common commitment to a particular cause, whether it is prochoice or antiabortion, religious beliefs, gay rights, or any of thousands of other causes, have the opportunity and, hence, the advantage of fostering close-knit communities. Such communities facilitate sharing information, especially any news adversely affecting the cause and its components. Common causes can result in common risks. It is very much in the cause's best interest to establish that communication and to be constantly alert for improving the ways in which information is shared.

10. Finally, Dr. Tiller's unusual situation raised its own unique challenges to assessing threats against him. Dr. Tiller lived in a near constant state of high risk. National antiabortion groups targeted him as the worst of the worst. Elements of the extremist fringe focused on him. So how can one assess a threat against someone who is already at high risk, but who cannot afford any more security than that already in place? If someone is at high risk, is there such a thing as a higher risk, or even the highest risk? Tragically, Dr. Tiller's assassination answers that question affirmatively. The lesson for assessing someone already at high risk is to avoid the complacency that inevitably comes from living day to day at a high state of alert. If high risk is the constant state, then any assessment of new threats begins with the constant state as the baseline. That allows for recognizing higher risks, even the highest risk.

Notes

1. Presentation prepared by the Feminist Majority Foundation.
2. Thomas, J. L. (2009, May 31). Suspect in Tiller's death supported killing abortion providers, friends say. *Kansas City Star.*
3. Associated Press. (2009, November 14). National briefing, Plains, KS: FBI was warned before doctor's killing.
4. Saulny, S., & Davey, M. (2009, June 2). Seeking clues on suspect in shooting of doctor. *New York Times.*
5. Davey, M. (2009, July 29). Witness tells of doctor's last seconds. Associated Press.

Case Dynamics and Intervention Synergy 3

In threat management cases, the only constant is that the cases are constantly in flux. Subjects continue to act and react, their life situations change, targets respond, and the actions of the threat management team enter the chemistry of the situation. Even if the target is an inanimate building or place, changes in its security or even a news report about the facility can cause new reactions from the subject. New developments, often unrelated to the relationship between subject and target, continue to occur. These prompt different actions from the subject. Those reactions generate their own dynamics—and so it goes, on and on.

This process contrasts to a traditional criminal, civil, or administrative investigation. Typically, an event or crime occurs, facts are gathered, a report is written, a decision is made and implemented to resolve the situation, and the paperwork is filed. Threat management cases do not follow this pattern, primarily because all the action is done prior to the crime or critical event. The threat manager attempts to evaluate, channel, or control behavior in real time while the events occur. In a traditional case, the story has been written. In a threat management case, the story is ongoing and the threat manager is both a participant and one of the authors.

Threat management teams that ignore these case dynamics do so at the peril of the target. The threat manager needs to incorporate the concept of dynamic situations into the handling and management of the case. Indeed, once a threat management strategy or strategies are applied, that intervention creates its own synergy that dramatically changes the chemistry of the situation. Accounting for the subject's response, as well as the target's response, to that synergy provides a fuller assessment of the changing situation. The threat manager should never assume that any situation stays static. It is simply not the nature of the field.

This chapter explores and illustrates the twin concepts of case dynamics and intervention synergy. We discuss, too, ways in which the threat manager can use each concept to better enhance the security of the target and the management of the subject. Although both are simple concepts—indeed, even self-evident—they are often overlooked or ignored in handling threat management situations. For this reason, we emphasize the vital importance of incorporating each concept into the threat manager's handling of any situation.

Finally, we address the issue of threat management ethics. As the field professionalizes, ethical considerations emerge. For example, consciously redirecting a subject toward another target should be avoided. Terminating an employee because she is the victim of domestic abuse in order to decrease the risk of the domestic violence spilling into the workplace should also be considered unethical. The Association of Threat Assessment Professionals has developed a code of ethics for anyone working in this field. We append it to this book. More than that, we encourage professionals to abide by it.

Case Illustration: The Truth Will Out

Charles Lee "Cookie" Thornton, an independent contractor, owned an asphalt company in Kirkwood, Missouri. He also had a long-running dispute with the town government. Going back to the 1990s, Thornton believed that city officials had promised him lots of work on a new development near his home, but, according to Thornton's brother, all he got were "scraps." He also received approximately 150 code violations, tickets, and citations amounting to thousands of dollars in fines. Thornton began airing his protests at town council meetings.

According to press reports, "the asphalt company owner raged at council meetings that he was being persecuted, mocking city officials as 'jackasses' and accusing them of having a racist 'plantation mentality.'" He often carried placards to the council meetings to enhance his protests. Police arrested him twice on disorderly conduct charges and the council considered banning him from the meetings altogether, but ultimately decided against such a move.

In 2007, Thornton filed a lawsuit in federal court claiming that his arrests for disorderly conduct violated his First Amendment rights of free speech. A judge in St. Louis dismissed the lawsuit on January 28, 2008, determining that "any restrictions on Thornton's speech were reasonable, viewpoint neutral, and served important governmental interests."

Ten days later, Thornton again went to the town council meeting—this time armed with a handgun. He killed three council members and two police officers and critically wounded the town mayor. Throughout the rampage, Thornton kept repeating the phrase, "Shoot the mayor." Police charged into the room and killed Thornton.

According to press reports,

Gerald Thornton, Mr. Thornton's brother, told CNN on Friday that his brother felt that his 'constitutional protections' had been violated and no other options were available to him. 'My brother went to war tonight with the government,' Gerald Thornton said in an interview with a local television station after the incident. 'He decided that he could no longer verbally work it out.'

In another interview, the brother said, "This was not a random rampage."

Thornton's dynamic relationship with the city government continued for years until he reached a point at which he believed that he had run out of legal options. Before going to the council meeting, he left a note on his bed stating, "The truth will come out in the end." (Sources: Mike Nizza and Carla Baranauckas, "Mourning in Missouri as Shooter's Motives Emerge," Associated Press, February 8, 2008; "Town Struggles After City Hall Shooting," Associated Press, February 9, 2008)

The Dynamics of Threat Management

The reason that threat management cases remain constantly in flux is simple and straightforward. These cases involve willful, thinking beings who respond and react to changing stimuli in an unpredictable world. The subject acts toward the target; the target reacts to the subject, which prompts a response from the subject. The spiral continues in an unending series of actions and reactions. Cookie Thornton protested at town council meetings; the council responded by having him arrested. The protests continued, as did the arrests. Thornton took legal action, apparently pinning his last hope on the federal courts. Ultimately disappointed, Thornton ratcheted up his protests with gunfire. With each protest, each arrest, and every stage of the lawsuit, the situation between Thornton and the town council changed, sometimes escalating, sometimes de-escalating, until Thornton made the final escalation. As much as the town council undoubtedly wished Thornton would just go away, so, too, he wished for the justice he perceived had been denied him a dozen years earlier and continued to be denied with each code violation, ticket, and citation. That give and take, spiraling up and down movement, typifies most threat management cases.

In the past, we presented the threat management process as phases or a series of steps as follows:

- Gather initial facts
- Make initial assessment
- Develop protective response
- Conduct fact finding
- Reassess continuously
- Select and implement management strategy
- Schedule follow-ups

We have always indicated that some steps could be done simultaneously. While this is a valid method for teaching a process to apply consistently, some threat managers may be tempted to implement it at times in a static or rigid way, as though each step must go in order and only after the preceding one. We now present companion concepts to the threat management process that counter such rigidity. We call these concepts *case dynamics* and *intervention synergy*.

When a threat manager is in the middle of an active threat situation, he or she gains information from a variety of sources concerning what the subject has done or is doing. New information also comes in about the subject and the situation itself, including how the target is reacting and how well the initial protective response is working. This information is the first element of the threat management dynamic: the knowns. Typically, a known is like opening a new door for the fact finding: It raises more questions. These unanswered questions, along with any other missing information, are the second element of the dynamic: the unknowns. The threat evaluation of the knowns and unknowns at any given time is the third element of the dynamic: the assessment. The fourth and final element of the dynamic are the security decisions made and countermeasures taken based on the assessment or reassessments: the protective response.

As Figure 3.1 illustrates, many factors impinge on the threat management dynamic. The figure also emphasizes that the threat management team may not have all the information needed to complete a full assessment. What is known can be quite disturbing; what is unknown is harrowing. The dynamic also requires reassessments of the situation whenever new information is uncovered or there has been new activity by the subject, target, or outside influences, such as the judge's dismissal of Thornton's lawsuit. The threat manager should also reassess the situation whenever the protective response is initiated or changed because that also fuels the dynamic.

As new information is reported or discovered, unknowns remain or become known, assessments evolve and mature, and protective responses are

Figure 3.1 Case dynamics.

constantly being reevaluated based on the impact of the other three elements. This is a fluid, ever changing process we call the case dynamic. We defined the case dynamic as

> *the evolving interaction between the knowns, the unknowns, and the need to continuously assess each in determining the appropriate protective response at any given point in time*

Far from remaining static, threat management cases constantly change, sometimes amazingly quickly and at other times agonizingly slowly. But change is always there and the astute threat manager recognizes that dynamic and accounts for it in managing each case.

The subject may even react to a lack of response by the target. If the subject expected a response to his or her action in contacting the target and none occurs, the subject may feel it necessary to escalate his or her next action to ensure getting the target's attention. This dynamic introduces considerable uncertainty into the progress of threat management cases. That uncertainty is what makes accurate predictions difficult.

Since subjects are willful, they act in willful ways that may follow irrational patterns. Delusional subjects follow their own reality. Other mental illnesses also distort how the subject perceives and behaves. The subject's motive may or may not make sense to reasonable people; it matters only that the motive makes sense to the subject. It does not take a degree in psychology to understand that individuals tend to behave in ways that make sense to them (even if not to anyone else) or that meets their needs. That simple insight should also be factored into any threat assessment.

In a further complication of the dynamic, subjects can change. They adopt new opinions, find new grievances, switch targets, or otherwise sow confusion over the situation. Inhibitors—or the lack of inhibitors— may prompt a subject to change behaviors. As long as Thornton believed that he had a chance in federal court, that belief inhibited him from taking more drastic action. Once he lost faith, he had nothing to lose. Subjects evolve, their evolution frequently guided by external events and the dynamics of the situation. Threat managers need to remain cognizant that people change day to day, moment to moment. Never assume that the subject's current behavior will be the same today as it was last week or will be next week.

Case Illustration: The Change of Heart

Naser Jason Abdo enlisted in the United States Army in April 2009. Private Abdo was stationed at Fort Campbell, Kentucky, when his unit, the 101st Airborne Division, received orders to deploy to Afghanistan.

Abdo changed his mind about serving the United States. A devout Muslim, Abdo decided that Muslims should not be deployed to fight in a war zone against other Muslims. "I was under the impression that I could serve both the U.S. Army and my God simultaneously," Abdo told a CNN reporter in the summer of 2010:

> As the time had come near to deployment, I started really asking myself and taking the question more seriously whether God would accept what I was doing and whether I was really meant to go to war as opposed to the peace that Islam preaches.

In late 2010, Private Abdo contacted the Military Religious Freedom Foundation seeking support for his discharge as a conscientious objector. Zachari Klawonn talked with Private Abdo over the telephone for a half-hour. Klawonn came away from the conversation determined to keep clear of Private Abdo. "He was very anti-American, anti-Western, anti-Army," Klawonn said in an interview with a *Washington Post* reporter. "There was something off about his demeanor. I said it would not be wise to take this guy on as a client."

Private Abdo continued his campaign alone. The Army granted him conscientious objector status in May 2011. His discharge, however, was put on hold when Army officials discovered child pornography photographs on his computer. Shortly after, Private Abdo went absent without leave.

Private Abdo traveled from Fort Campbell to Fort Hood, Texas, in late July 2011. He took a taxi to a gun store where he purchased weapons and smokeless gunpowder. His behavior, however, aroused the suspicions of the store clerk, who contacted police. After tracing the taxi route, police went to Private Abdo's motel. Among the items they found in his room were a military uniform with Fort Hood patches, a pistol, shotgun shells, and an article on "how to make a bomb in your kitchen" from the English-language Al Qaeda magazine *Inspire*. Police also found bomb-making materials. Private Abdo admitted to police that he specifically planned to attack Fort Hood, the scene of the November 5, 2009, shooting rampage by Major Nidal Malik Hasan.

At his arraignment hearing, Private Abdo refused to stand when the judge entered the courtroom. When the proceedings ended, Private Abdo shouted, "Nidal Hasan, Fort Hood 2009!" as officers escorted him out of the courtroom. He also called out the name of an Iraqi girl whom U.S. soldiers had raped and murdered in 2006. (Sources: J. David Goodman, "Soldier Held Amid Claim of Terror Plot at Fort Hood," *New York Times*, July 28, 2011; Peter Finn and Jason Ukman, "Naser Abdo, an AWOL Soldier, Accused of Plotting Fort Hood Attack," *Washington Post*, July 28, 2011; Peter Finn and Alice Fordham, "Naser Abdo, AWOL Soldier, Charged in Fort Hood Bomb Plot," *Washington Post*, July 29, 2011)

The Role of Time

Time also plays a role in the threat management dynamic, but not in ways that are self-evident. Cookie Thornton continued collecting code violations, tickets, and citations even as he continued protesting those fines for a dozen or more years. He became an expected, routine appearance at the town council meetings. No one assessed him as a threat—only as a pest. But then the dynamic turned when the federal court dismissed his lawsuit. Denied what he no doubt thought his day of justice in court, Thornton decided to escalate the situation with gunfire. Time neither slowed him down nor turned his attention elsewhere until he became convinced that his options were now limited only to violence.

Time can also be an accelerant. In March 2006, at the Fulton County, Georgia, courthouse, a judge presiding over a rape case ordered District Attorney Paul Howard to keep out of a debriefing of the jurors who had acquitted the defendant. When Howard attempted to attend the debriefing, the judge told the attending deputy sheriffs to take Howard to a detention cell. Howard resisted. He waved his arms to keep the deputies at bay, but managed to hit a female deputy in the shoulder. He also pushed her against the wall as he tried to get back into the courtroom.[1]

Unlike Thornton, whose grievance was long running, Howard's grievance was immediate and pressing. He waited barely seconds before turning to violence. Comparing these two cases or any of the thousands like them forces the conclusion that time always plays a part in the threat management dynamic—but not a static or consistent part. The importance of time changes depending on the circumstances and the subject's perceived needs. Time became pressing to Howard because what he wanted—to attend the jury's debriefing—was going on right then. Time became pressing for Thornton only after years of protesting when he became convinced that his legal remedies had run out. At that point, the timing of his attack depended on the next scheduled session of the town council.

The Role of the Uncontrollables

Case dynamics are not restricted to the interplay between subject and target. Other events, even events unrelated to that interplay or dispute, occur that affect the subject's life, emotions, behaviors, or attitudes. Threat management cases do not play out in an insulated bubble, isolated from the world. Quite the contrary, the cases take place very much in the world and are easily influenced by life events. The subject's lifestyle and life situation can change, often dramatically. These changes can serve as trigger events pushing the subject into some new course of action.

Changes may have positive or negative impacts. A disgruntled former employee may find new employment in another state, thus taking the subject's attention away from the former employer. Someone in the subject's life may die, thus pushing the subject into despair and desperate action. The subject meets a new woman and falls in love, thus distracting his attention from the original target. Another subject wrecks his car and breaks his leg, thus incapacitating him for a period of time.

We call these outside events the "uncontrollables." The threat manager may not even know that they have occurred, much less be able to manage them. Subjects have lives and lives constantly change with each passing day. The world happens.

Case Illustration: Changing Information, Changing Assessments, Changing Strategies

Paul V. volunteered. He volunteered for the reelection campaign of a state senator and he voluntarily protected the women volunteers, particularly the candidate's daughter. Paul informed the campaign manager that another volunteer was harassing the daughter. The campaign manager turned the report over to the threat manager. He also advised that Paul seemed to be infatuated with the daughter. Paul had repeatedly asked her out on a date and remained undaunted by her refusals. He also became jealous whenever he saw any other man talking to her. Recently, he had begun leaving small presents for her on her desk.

The threat manager ran a criminal history check, but found nothing of concern. Paul had no registered firearms. After a few discreet inquiries, the threat manager learned that several of Paul's colleagues considered him strange because he frequently spoke of how he protected other people. At this point, the threat manager assessed Paul as low risk.

Nonetheless, the threat manager felt that the situation warranted a subject interview. Using Paul's expressed concern about the other volunteer harassing the daughter, the threat manager and her partner interviewed Paul and encouraged him to describe in detail his voluntary role of protector. Paul confided that he had volunteered on other political campaigns in Nevada and Arizona and always found some female in need of his special protection. He bragged to the two threat managers about his skill in martial arts and his expertise with knives and firearms. He also volunteered that he owned several unregistered firearms.

The threat manager checked records in Nevada and Arizona and reached out to law enforcement officials in each of those states. She learned that Paul had been committed to a mental hospital in Minnesota after attempting to board an airplane with a firearm. The U.S. Secret Service reported that their agents had arrested Paul for approaching a foreign dignitary under Secret Service protection with a knife. The Secret Service committed Paul based on a diagnosis of paranoid delusions. Nevada records uncovered an incident in which Paul had led police on a high-speed car chase that ended in an accident that left Paul partially disabled.

The threat manager reassessed Paul as high risk. She arranged for the reelection campaign to notify Paul that his volunteer work was no longer needed. In addition, the threat manager arranged for local police to confiscate Paul's firearms based on his mental health history. The threat manager also arranged to monitor Paul closely and keep in frequent contact with him. The close monitoring continues. (*Source:* Authors' personal knowledge)

Accepting Good News

Not every change in the threat management case dynamic has a deleterious effect on the situation. As surprising as it may seem, good things sometimes do happen. The threat manager needs to be aware of that fact and watch for it. Too often, threat managers fall into a jaded, pessimistic worldview that distorts their perceptions and blinds them to the occurrence of positive events in a subject's life that also have a positive effect on the situation. It is a little like looking only at the dark side of the moon and missing the harvest full moon.

That being said, it is still best to hope for the best, prepare for the worst, and recognize the difference.

Case Illustration: The Hoax

Boone, North Carolina, police and the faculty and staff at Appalachian State University responded with alacrity to a report that a masked gunman had been seen on the university campus. The university initiated a campus-wide lockdown while police officers conducted a thorough search of the 1,300-acre campus containing 19 academic buildings, 20 residence halls, 4 dining halls, 11 athletic facilities, and a large library. The sprawling campus represented a significant challenge to the small police force, but the report with its implied threat could not be ignored.

Then police officers interrogating the individual who made the report got him to admit that he had made the whole story up. Acting on the good news, police immediately announced that there was no armed or masked person on the campus. The lockdown and search were ended. The fabricator faced a misdemeanor charge of filing a false police report. (*Source:* Associated Press, "Cops: N.C. Campus Gunman Report Was Hoax," March 4, 2008; http://www.appstate.edu/about/)

Intervention Synergy

The concept that we call *intervention synergy* describes an additional complication and intensification of case dynamics. When an action is taken toward the subject in a threat situation or the target reacts in some way detectable to the subject, a fifth element enters the case dynamic: the intervention. This action creates what we call intervention synergy, which is defined as

> *the case dynamic intensified by the stimulus of what the threat manager or target does or does not do in response to the threat situations.*

The concept involves the complex interaction that occurs whenever one or more of the threat management strategies are applied. This differs from the normal case dynamics because applying an intervention strategy is wholly under the control of the threat manager (hopefully). It is a conscious choice to do something, even if the something is to take no further action at this time. The willful act of applying an intervention strategy unavoidably creates its own synergy between the subject, the target, and the threat management team.

As Figure 3.2 illustrates, intervention synergy derives from the complex interplay between the knowns, the unknowns, the intervention strategy or strategies applied by the threat manager, and the need for constant threat reassessment and reevaluation of the protective response. All of these factors play off each other constantly. The result is a complex smorgasbord of activity—of action, reaction, knowns versus unknowns, uncontrollable events, reassessment, and reevaluation. Throughout the interaction of those rapidly evolving factors, the threat manager must constantly determine the effectiveness of the current intervention strategy and the accuracy of the overall assessment.

Figure 3.2 Intervention synergy.

Three controlling principles heavily influence how the intervention synergy plays out. The first characteristic consists of the short shelf life of any threat assessment. A threat assessment is nothing more than a quick snapshot in time. The assessment includes all the known information that has gone on before and recognition of the unknowns, but nothing of what is to come. As a result, assessments rapidly deteriorate from the moment they are completed. New information and changes in the situation promote that aging process and require continuous reassessments of the new information or the changed situation. Even applying a new threat management strategy ages the current assessment because now the situation has been altered, for good or ill, by the willful action of the threat management team.

Understanding this principle aids the threat manager in constantly accepting new information and recognizing changes in the situation. This introduces flexibility in managing the situation. It also allows for the recognition of good news when it occurs. In short, by accepting the fact that, by their nature, assessments are short lived, the threat manager can better deal with the effects of both the case dynamics and the intervention synergy.

Case Illustration: The Angry Employee

Austin C.'s supervisor reported that Austin had been acting erratically the past few weeks and was beginning to frighten his colleagues. Specifically, on several occasions he had lost his temper and yelled at other employees. Last week, he had kicked a chair in the break room so hard that the back of the chair put a hole in the plaster wall.

The threat manager began an initial fact-finding inquiry and learned from a concerned friend of Austin's that Austin's wife had recently left him for another man and that Austin's son urgently needed surgery on a life-threatening tumor. The wife had also filed a lawsuit seeking possession of the couple's house. From Austin's personnel file, the threat manager learned that Austin had been with the company for 27 years and had received numerous bonuses, commendations, and promotions for exemplary performance. Austin also volunteered on the company marksman team and had served 2 years as the team's captain.

Based on the poor status of Austin's inhibitors, his acting out his anger, and his familiarity with and ownership of firearms, the threat manager assessed Austin as a high risk for workplace violence. The manager recommended compelling Austin to get a fitness-for-duty evaluation and to seek assistance from the company's employee assistance program (EAP).

Austin did not respond well to the required fitness-for-duty evaluation and refused to seek help from EAP, saying that counseling was for the weak willed. Although clearly angered by the direction to get a fitness for duty, he did go to the psychologist on the company's retainer. The psychologist recommended giving Austin a week off and paying for him to go to anger management classes.

Again, Austin angrily complained about the time off and the anger management classes. The threat manager reassessed the situation and determined that the intervention strategy had increased Austin's anger toward the company and his supervisor, thus increasing the potential risk. The manager agreed with the psychologist's recommendation, but added that company security should be made aware of the situation and be prepared to confront Austin if he showed up at work during his time off.

A week later, Austin's friend reported that Austin and his wife had reconciled and that Austin's son had survived the surgery with a positive prognosis. The threat manager agreed to let Austin return to work. Although Austin exhibited hard feelings toward his supervisor for the fitness-for-duty evaluation and time off, he did not show any signs of anger toward his colleagues, and his supervisor commended his work performance. (*Source:* Hypothetical illustration based on authors' experiences)

The second principle admonishes the threat manager to avoid allowing previous assessments to cast a shadow on new assessments. At most, previous assessments should be used solely as a yardstick for determining if the situation is improving or getting worse. An initial assessment of high risk does not mean that the situation will always be high risk. Conversely, an initial assessment of low risk does not mean that the situation will always be low risk. Each assessment has to stand on its own; it has to assess all the knowns that the threat manager has identified and recognize the unknowns. As new information comes in or as the subject engages in new behaviors, that new information and those new behaviors need to be assessed independently of the previous assessment. Each assessment should account for all the information available at that particular moment in the life of the case.

Case Illustration

Emily U. wrote graphic stories for her AP English class describing situations involving school shootings and killing other students. She used the names of other students in the class and portrayed herself as the shooter. Disturbed at the gruesome nature of the short stories, Emily's teacher contacted the school district's threat management team. The teacher also supplied the team copies of four of the short stories that Emily had thus far written for the creative writing class.

The threat manager read the stories and reviewed Emily's official student file. She learned that Emily was a junior, had a straight-A grade point average, was a member of the school's film club, and had won an award for creative writing her sophomore year. The threat manager also knew that recent school shootings in neighboring states had everyone involved in education very concerned and focused on potential future shootings. The threat manager determined that Emily's writings were of enough concern to warrant an interview with Emily.

Emily's father accompanied her to the interview and refused to let the threat manager speak directly to Emily. He threatened to sue the school district for harassing his daughter. The father pointed out that the creative writing class teacher had, at the beginning of the year, sent the students home with a letter from the teacher to the parents encouraging the parents to let their children's imaginations have complete free rein, even if that resulted in their imaginations going to "extreme places." The father felt that this was where Emily's imagination had gone.

The threat manager elected to implement a third-party monitoring of Emily through all her teachers, rather than just the creative-writing teacher. As the school year progressed, Emily's interest in school violence waned. Her short stories focused more on romantic themes. By the end of the year, the threat manager assessed Emily as low risk. When she returned the next year, she never wrote about violence again. (*Source:* Hypothetical illustration based on authors' experiences)

The third principle recognizes that, once the threat manager responds to a situation, the manager has altered the chemistry of the situation simply because the subject knows that the threat manager or someone is now actively involved. How the subject responds to that involvement creates the synergistic relationship between subject, target, and the threat manager. Any action by the threat manager will have one of three outcomes:

- The action will make the situation better.
- The action will make the situation worse.
- The action will leave the situation unchanged.

Consequently, the threat manager should assess each intervention strategy by its immediate and long-term outcomes. Strategies that make the situation better should be continued, strategies that make the situation worse should be discontinued, and strategies that leave the situation unchanged should be refined or abandoned in favor of a strategy aimed at improving the situation.

Case Illustration: Chemistry for Life

Amy C. approached the threat manager to confide that she was in an abusive relationship with her husband. She asked about the support that she could expect from the company if she left the relationship. The threat manager advised her that the company would do everything it could to protect her at work, but the company could not extend that protection after hours. The threat manager advised her to get a restraining order from the court requiring her husband to stay away from her. He also recommended that she get counseling and other support from the company's employee assistance program. He provided her with a list of nearby women's shelters.

Three days later, Amy's husband called the threat manager and threatened to kill him and blow up the company because the threat manager had encouraged Amy to leave the marriage. The threat manager tried to calm the husband down, but to no avail. He ended the call by warning the husband that if he tried to get on company property, he would be arrested for trespassing.

After the call, the threat manager alerted company security to be on the lookout for the husband. He also warned Amy that her husband had reacted badly to her leaving. The threat manager then conferred with company attorneys to see what action could be taken based on the husband's threat to kill him and blow up the company. The attorneys advised that, at this point, the husband could deny making the threat and there were no other witnesses. The threat manager arranged to tape future phone calls.

Once a threat manager applies a threat management strategy, he or she becomes part of the chemistry of the case. (*Source:* Hypothetical illustration based on authors' experiences)

In threat management, not only does every action foster a reaction, but the lack of action may also cause new actions by the subject. Making the conscious decision to take no further action at this time or adopting a watch-and-wait approach may frustrate a subject who expected a reaction from the target. That frustration may prompt the subject to escalate his or her behaviors in order to get the reaction that he or she expected. Intervention synergy thus posits that the decisions of the threat manager will become part of the situation regardless of any action or inaction the threat manager adopts in reaction to the subject's behavior.

Ethics of Threat Management

When the threat manager is involved in an active case and the dynamics and intervention synergy of the situation are in play, he or she can be presented with dilemmas or challenges involving the ethics of threat management. These ethical challenges involve taking steps that put others at risk, not thoroughly doing everything to lessen the overall risk (not just the risk to the threat manager's organization), conflicts of interest, allowing undue influence to pervert the threat assessment, applying inappropriate intervention methods, and abandoning the weak to protect the powerful. We have set out the most common ethical dilemmas so that the informed threat manager can possibly avoid them or at least be aware of their existence prior to being confronted with these challenges in the middle of a critical case.

Sending the Problem to Someone Else

This involves inappropriately routing a threatening or inappropriate subject to another government agency or an individual so that the subject will stop contacting the protectee or client. The usual form is telling the subject something like, "The councilman can't resolve your [delusional] problem; the rays harming your body are a federal problem. Why don't you go to the federal building and see if they will help you?" Although such threat managers are trying to divert the subject away from their protectee, their approach is done in a cynical, frat-boy prank approach that does nothing but increase the subject's frustration and possibly cause potential harm to another location or person. Professional threat managers should strive to be better than that.

Solving the Problem but Leaving Others or the Public at Risk

This is the situation where intervention methods are implemented that may keep one target safe, but ignore risk to other targets or leave the public at large at risk. A typical situation is when, in reaction to a significantly dangerous subject, the potential target is moved away from harm and significant security is set up for the target's benefit. However, in an effort to be discreet or even secretive, other potential targets are not protected or notified.

What can be even more damaging is when a threat manager has information about a threatening subject with lethal means available and the threat manager does not inform law enforcement of a potential risk to public safety. At times, this challenge involves one law enforcement or security organization not informing other agencies of a potential risk. Sometimes confidentiality or privacy concerns are the excuse. Threat managers must always keep in mind the risk to the public—not just the target—and find ways to share information properly.

Assessment to Enhance Security Profits

Assessments made to enhance security profits involve a potential conflict of interest when assessment and security are provided by the same person or organization. Organizations that sell security, including protective details and security hardware, are venturing into the field of threat assessment as part of a sales component. The opportunity exists to increase profit for the security side of the house by inflating the level or severity of the threat assessment potential. Professional threat assessment should be based only on appropriate criteria and not motivated by profit.

Inappropriate Influence

Inappropriate influence results from undue influence on the level of threat or the confrontation level of the intervention due to the stature or influence of the target. There are times when, in an effort to please a powerful official or client, pressure may be applied to the assessment team by administrators to make the problem go away or make the target happy with the service provided. At times, the targets themselves make it clear that they want the person punished even though no crime has occurred. This type of attempted influence is a fact of life in large organizations that have powerful protectees who can make or break careers.

Pressure can also come from within an organization to assess a subject as a threat to gain an advantage in an unrelated dispute or justify a past decision. For example, being assessed as a threat would be an advantage if the organization is involved in a whistleblower or wrongful termination lawsuit with the subject. Professional threat assessment and management should be based only on appropriate criteria—not on political favoritism or gaining some advantage.

Case Illustration: Impeaching the Judge

Some years ago, a private citizen became irate at a U.S. district judge because of the judge's ruling in the individual's lawsuit. Shortly after the judge handed the decision down, the individual approached the judge at a local restaurant and told the judge that he, the loser in the lawsuit, fully intended to do everything in his power to have the judge impeached—the only legal method for removing a federal judge from the bench.

Panicked, the judge reported the incident to the U.S. marshal for his district, describing it as a threat to his life, rather than his livelihood, and demanding protection. This placed the marshal in the uncomfortable position of having to tell the judge that the private citizen was well within his rights to try to convince Congress to impeach the judge. The judge was not happy with that response. (*Source:* Authors' personal knowledge)

Intervention Proportionate to the Threat

The interventions applied should be only as confrontational as the level of the threat. For example, a subject assessed as low risk should not receive an intervention as if he or she were a high-level threat because he or she is bothersome, annoying, or consuming too much time. Professional threat assessment and management sometimes require patience and restraint.

Abandoning the Weak to Protect the Powerful

Abandoning the weak to protect the powerful involves taking inappropriate actions against the target of a potential threat in an effort to protect the more important individual or organization. One form that this takes is to recommend termination of a victim of domestic violence to ensure that the offender does not bring violence into a workplace. Victims do not usually choose to be the target of potential violence and interventions should not place targets at a greater risk to protect other potential targets.

Summary

In this chapter, we reviewed the concepts of case dynamics and intervention synergy. Case dynamics refers to the ever changing nature of threat management cases. This involves the action–reaction syndrome. The subject acts toward the target, the target reacts or does not react in the way that the subject wanted or expected, and the situation changes. Intervention synergy results from the subject's response to any threat management intervention. Together, case dynamics and intervention synergy describe the changing chemistry of any threat management case. Threat managers need to be mindful of how these concepts influence the course of events in any situation involving a subject intending to act out violently toward a target.

The chapter also addressed the emerging need for an ethical code of conduct among active threat managers. The Association of Threat Assessment Professionals has crafted a code of conduct and everyone in the field should familiarize himself or herself with its content. We addressed such ethical issues as sending problem individuals to someone else, solving one's own problem while leaving the public or others at risk, enhancing security profits at the risk of the target, and other ethical issues. These, too, affect the case dynamics of any threatening situation.

Notes

1. Associated Press. (2006, April 28). Special prosecutor tosses warrant for DA.

Case Study
The Dynamo

4

A supervisor at a large federal security agency received a telephone call from the local police department. The officer informed the supervisor that the day before an employee of the agency had been involved in a road rage incident. A woman had cut the employee off. In response, the employee followed the woman to her house, where he drove onto her front lawn, got out of his car, and shouted obscenities and threats at the woman. The woman copied down the employee's license plate number as he drove off. The officer also informed the supervisor that, 6 months earlier, the employee had been arrested by the police after he had picked a fight with his ex-wife's new boyfriend at the employee's daughter's school play. The ensuing fight was so disruptive that the school had canceled the play.

The supervisor checked the employee's personnel file and determined that, contrary to agency policy, the employee had not reported the arrest 6 months earlier. The employee had had performance issues in the past—primarily issues about not getting along with colleagues. After consulting with the Employee Relations Department and the field attorney, the supervisor proposed suspending the employee for 6 days for failure to report the arrest. The supervisor prepared a letter to the employee notifying him of the proposed disciplinary action. Once the employee received the letter, he had 7 days to appeal. Once handed the letter, the employee reacted angrily and threatened to file a grievance for hostile work environment.

On the third day of that interim, the employee got into a shouting argument with his team leader over what the proper standard operating procedure was for a particular security action. During the heated argument, the employee stated to the lead, "Let's take this outside and finish it." Witnesses to the argument stated that they understood the statement to be a threat to go outside and fight.

Based on the latest incident, the supervisor, again in consultation with Employee Relations and the field attorney, determined to withdraw the proposed 6-day suspension and to propose, instead, terminating the employee from the agency. The supervisor prepared a letter to the employee proposing the termination. Again, the employee had a week to respond to the proposal before the termination went into effect. At this point, given the volatile nature of the employee's recent behavior, the supervisor contacted the agency's threat manager who oversaw the agency's Workplace Violence Prevention Program.[1]

The threat manager considered the dynamics of the recent events in assessing the situation. Clearly, the problem employee had suffered a loss of inhibitors that contributed to his violent outbreaks. His marriage had broken up and he was apparently concerned with his ex-wife bringing a new boyfriend into his daughter's life. The employee evinced continued signs of stress with the road rage incident and with the threat to the team lead. The police charges against him for the fight at the school play still hovered over him. Although the employee evinced no signs of substance abuse, that could not be ruled out. Those dynamics were about to be exacerbated further by the federal security agency through the proposed termination. The combination of the case dynamics and the intervention synergy greatly increased the risk that the employee would respond negatively, possibly even violently, to the proposed termination.

The threat manager did not oppose the proposed termination. Rather, he recognized that *how* the supervisor handled the termination would go a long way toward managing the employee's response. He counseled the supervisor on how to handle the termination meeting. The supervisor should keep the meeting focused on the future and not let the employee engage in a debate about the incident or his past behavior. The supervisor should keep the meeting brief, pointed, and matter of fact. If possible, the supervisor should arrange for law enforcement to be nearby, just in case the employee's behavior escalated.

The supervisor followed the threat manager's advice and the termination meeting went smoothly. The employee turned in his identification badges and access controls and left the building without incident.

Analysis

At first, the supervisor focused only on the administrative violation of failing to notify the agency of the arrest instead of the bigger, more volatile situation of a troubled employee who had been involved in at least two violent incidents and was going through a serious, life-altering dispute. Not recognizing the precarious dynamic of the situation, the supervisor initiated an intervention by the disciplinary action without recognizing the synergy that it produced.

The threat manager was not involved until the employee threatened the supervisor in reaction to this intervention.

The employee showed a typical pattern in that after losing one inhibitor (his divorce), other inhibitors also started to fall. The resulting pressure on him increased the risk of losing his temper. Once his temper took hold, he became increasingly prone to violence and threats. That dynamic, coupled with the effect of intervention synergy, made managing him out of the workplace a delicate, high-risk task. But, with reason and careful preparation, doing just that can be accomplished.

Lessons Learned

1. Threat managers should never assume that they know everything going on in the life of a subject under assessment. Indeed, the best assumption is just the opposite—that is, that many other events are taking place and putting pressure on the subject, some of which are caused by the potential target.
2. Inhibitors act like dominoes: When one falls, it frequently topples other inhibitors. The employer was about to topple another significant inhibitor by terminating the employee.
3. When bad things start to happen, it becomes increasingly difficult to change directions, so a subject's downward fall tends to be like a snowball rolling downhill: The problems get bigger and bigger.
4. The increased risk of terminating a problem employee who has demonstrated a capacity for violence is not reason enough to cancel the termination. However, that increased risk does mean taking extra precautions and being more sophisticated in how the termination is handled.
5. Policies should be in place in the organization requiring early involvement of a threat manager when situations such as this are reported. Training should also be provided to all supervisors in threat indicators and the process to follow when they are confronted with a threatening situation.
6. If the threat manager was involved after the first report, more information could have been gathered and a more comprehensive intervention could have been employed that was designed to channel potential synergy and prevent the threatening outburst in the workplace. For example, after the initial report and fact finding, an interview could have been conducted with the employee to get his side of the situation. If the suspension was warranted, it would also have been packaged with EAP counseling, supervisor participation, and follow-up progress meetings. The threatening outburst and subsequent termination could have been avoided.
7. In many workplace environments, this employee's misconduct would not have resulted in a termination, which would have necessitated the more creative intervention strategies discussed. You would not want a termination to be overturned or drag on with appeal after appeal.

Notes

1. These facts are based on the authors' personal knowledge.

The Need-to-Knows

5

Threat assessments, at their most basic level, consist of evaluating whatever information the threat assessor has at the time of the assessment. Something has to have happened or some situation must exist to prompt conducting the assessment. Otherwise, the assessor has nothing to assess.

Perhaps the target received a threatening or ominous letter or telephone call. The target may have reported some specific suspicions or a feeling of unease due to particular events or activities. The subject may have approached the target. On occasion, the target may have done something that provokes opposition or creates controversy. Whatever happened, *something* happened or is happening that the assessor needs to assess. Thus, the assessor always has a specific situation or incident to evaluate.

In certain circumstances, the assessor may need to assess an overall situation, rather than a specific incident or event. Has the target taken a prominent or controversial stand on an issue or ideological position? Does that stand or position generate opposition? Does that opposition risk violent responses? These situations tend to be long term and controversial. In effect, the target focuses enmity on himself or herself.

Case Illustration: Assessing a Situation

On August 24, 2004, two Chechen women, hiding explosives in their bras, brought down two Russian airliners when they detonated the bombs midflight. All on board both flights were killed.

In response to the two bombings, the administrator of the Transportation Security Administration (TSA) ordered a new procedure for searching airplane travelers in the United States. Called the "upper torso pat-down," the procedure involved physically frisking selected passengers going through the security checkpoints.

The upper torso pat-down generated fierce opposition among many individuals. The TSA Contact Center was soon inundated with e-mails and telephone messages protesting the new security measure. A large number of the communications threatened harm to any screener who conducted the pat down, especially on females. The threats also targeted the administrator as the person who implemented the new security.

Each threat had to be assessed on its own merits, but the overall situation also had to be assessed. The procedure generated such a public outcry, as well as a high number of explicitly threatening contacts, that the situation itself posed a risk. As long as screeners continued to conduct upper torso pat-downs, a high risk of both impromptu and intended violence existed toward the screeners. An equally high risk of intended violence toward the administrator also existed because the public clearly identified him as personally responsible for the offending procedure. (*Source:* Authors' personal knowledge)

In addition to knowing that something happened to prompt the assessment, the assessor also knows that the target, at this moment, exists. If the target is taken out—either killed (a person) or destroyed (property)—the assessor obviously has no need to make an assessment. The time for assessing the threat directed at Dr. Tiller was when the FBI received the second husband's letter, or after the vandalism to the clinic, or after the telephone threat, or after parishioners noticed Roeder at the church. No one needed a trained threat assessor when Roeder made his lethal approach toward the vestibule; the threat then was immediate and obvious.[1] Once Roeder shot the doctor, no one needed to make a threat assessment. The threat had been carried out.

Knowing that something happened that needs to be assessed means that threat assessments focus on the past or the present. For this reason, we emphasize that assessments are not predictions of future behavior; they are focused analyses of what has already happened—what the subject and target have already done or not done. By analyzing past and present events, the assessor looks for clues or indicators to project the likelihood of potential future events. But no assessment can predict with any certainty what will happen next or what the subject will do next. Predictions are the province of angels and fools; they have no place in assessing potential threats.

Not everyone in the field of threat assessment agrees with our position on predictions. Gavin de Becker, for one, writes about making "high stakes predictions."[2] The term, however, strikes us as too precise and too clear, something altogether too certain in an uncertain world. We challenge anyone to support a real-life assessment that a particular subject *will*, without doubt, commit a violent act in the very near future.

Consider the comparison to weather prediction. With all the years of study and modeling in the field of meteorology, meteorologists hesitate to say 100% chance of rain; they always qualify their so-called prediction by saying 60% or 70% chance. We know of a number of situations in which the subject, fully intending and desirous of attacking his or her target, crossed the breach stage along the path to intended violence, but then found himself or herself incapable of actually committing the violent act.[3] Any assessor assessing their behaviors as they traversed the path to intended violence would have identified them as at a very high risk of violence, even though ultimately they simply did not have the ability to commit the violence—thus do predictions fall before the unpredictable events in the unseeable future.

The best that can be said for any assessment is that the subject is or is not engaging in behaviors that, in the past with other subjects, have resulted in those subjects committing violence. Those behaviors increase the probability that the current subject poses a risk of violence. Probabilities or projections, of course, are not certainties; hence, we shy away from any predictive claims.

There is no standard model for conducting threat assessments or even agreement on what to call the process of analyzing the potential for violence. Two professional organizations, The American Society for Industrial Security (ASIS) and the Society for Human Resource Management (SHRM), recently released a set of professional standards that opted for the term "violence risk assessment" in lieu of threat assessment. The groups argued that the term "threat assessment" is too closely associated with the same term used by the insurance industry to mean something other than determining the potential for violence.[4]

Some groups in the behavioral health field use the term behavioral threat assessment to differentiate their assessments from threat assessments of situations or geographic locations. Other experts have developed their own approach to assessing the risk of violence. J. Reid Meloy developed a "biopsychosocial model for violence risk assessment."[5] The United States Capitol Police developed a distinctive approach for assessing the risk to members of Congress.[6] J. Chris Hatcher developed a threat assessment model consisting of five distinct categories. The model was described in detail by James Turner and Michael Gelles after Hatcher's untimely death.[7] James Cawood and Michael Corcoran, who also prefer the term violence risk assessment, developed an assessment grid methodology for making an assessment.[8]

This lack of consensus on both what to call the process and how to conduct it reflects different approaches or formats derived from different professional fields and different experiences. The purpose of a threat assessment may also be different based on the varied needs of the user. Is the assessment for litigation purposes to defend a client's actions? Is the assessment designed to assist an executive in making a policy decision? Is it for the purpose of justifying the allocation of resources or for fiscal disbursement? Is it for the purpose of protecting an individual or asset?

In truth, it hardly matters. What does matter is addressing the incident or situation in the most organized, thoughtful, and pragmatic way possible. All the rest is just quibbling over semantics. We, for example, stick to the term "threat assessment" regardless of its association with the insurance industry. Our preference for it stems from its commonsense understandability. It makes sense to us in a way that "violence risk assessment" does not. We note that the premier professional association in the field is the Association of Threat

Assessment Professionals (ATAP). In our previous books, we described in detail our approach to conducting practical threat assessments.[9] We stick by those approaches precisely because we find them pragmatic and useful.

We use the term "threat assessment" to mean the analysis of an incident or situation after a determination has been made that the incident or situation under assessment has crossed a threshold for becoming inappropriate or disconcerting. For this reason, we have always recommended that the threat manager, regardless of venue, develop a clear, precise definition of what behaviors represent the threshold for determining when to conduct an assessment. A clearly defined set of inappropriate behaviors will help the threat manager separate the wheat from the chaff, thus sparing the threat manager from wasting significant amounts of time assessing incidents or situations that did not, in fact, need to be assessed because nothing objectively inappropriate or disconcerting actually happened.

We begin the threat assessment process only after the defined threshold has been crossed. Further, our approach relies on analyzing only the facts known at the time of the assessment. We do not allow for educated guesses, hunches, speculations, suspected psychological diagnoses, or any other information that is not based on actual facts known at the time. We realize, of course, that this approach is frequently only a partial assessment because much that is not known is excluded from the assessment. For that reason, we understand threat assessments to be an ongoing process of continuously reassessing the situation or incident as new information becomes available or new incidents occur.

That process also takes into account the effects of case dynamics and intervention synergy. We build into the process the recognition that any threat assessment is only a snapshot frozen in time with a very short shelf life. Any assessment at any point in the continuum of constant reassessments must always end with "at this time," thereby freezing the assessment in time and space.

In addition to freezing the assessment in time and space, we introduce in this chapter the practice of recognizing how informed any assessment is at the time at which the assessment was conducted. The threat assessment process consists not only of assessing the situation or incident based on the facts currently available, but also of assessing how much information—and the relative importance or significance of the information available—went into the assessment.

By necessity, assessments made early on tend to be poorly informed because of the lack of information on which the assessment was based. Nonetheless, regardless of the lack of information, an assessment has to be conducted in order to determine the appropriate protective response or make operational decisions. Lives hang in the balance, thereby denying the threat manager the luxury of waiting for more information.

This is a crucial concept. In reality, threat managers frequently have to assess an incident or situation based on very little information. But the paucity of information is no bar to assessing what information is available. It simply means that the assessment is a minimally informed one, but based on the best information available. The necessity of this reality derives from the very nature of threat management: *Lives hang in the balance and decisions need to be made, thereby denying the threat manager the luxury of waiting for more information before rendering an opinion.*

As more information becomes available, subsequent assessments become better informed. We discuss in this chapter a set of 20 variables that we call the threat assessment "need-to-knows." The need-to-knows consist of individual areas of inquiry that, summed together, provide a comprehensive array of factors and behaviors contributing to the potential for violence. A fully informed assessment takes into account information about the incident or situation for all 20 of these variables. That, of course, is an ideal rarely achieved in reality.

As a further complication, as we discuss later, the value of any single one of the need-to-knows varies according to the circumstances and context of the incident or situation under assessment. Although using the need-to-knows sounds complicated, working with them greatly assists the threat manager in making informed assessments. They also allow the threat manager to recognize just how well informed each assessment is at this time.

Understanding the Need-to-Knows

For every assessment, we have identified information that the assessor needs to know in order to make a fully informed threat assessment. These *need-to-knows* cover a wide spectrum of information and information sources. Explicitly identifying them during each assessment helps the assessor identify what is known and not known at the time of that assessment. The unknowns can then be used to guide additional fact finding, the results of which will be factored into new assessments. The balance between the knowns and the unknowns also determines how informed the assessment is at this time.

We do not claim that our list of *need-to-knows* is comprehensive or definitive across all fields and specialties engaged in conducting threat assessments. Psychologists and mental health professionals undoubtedly look in other areas related to their fields. They have their own need-to-knows.[10] Rather, we developed our list as a practical, commonsense list of information that, if known, can be analyzed to form a solid threat assessment in which the threat manager can have a high degree of confidence.

Certain information inheres in every situation under assessment. These *always knowns* provide enough information to support an assessment, just a minimally informed one. Nevertheless, necessity frequently requires the assessor to rely solely on the always knowns simply because that is all the information that the assessor has initially. Lack of information about every single need-to-know is not a bar to conducting a threat assessment. Rather, lack of information is a guide to further fact finding. The assessor does not have the luxury of not making a threat assessment simply because one or more of the need-to-knows remain unknown. The initial assessment has to be made on what is initially known. In doing so, the assessor realizes that much information remains to be collected and factored into new assessments.

Consider this scenario. The assessor receives a report that a certain target received a voice mail stating, "I'm going to kill you." The message was left on the target's office voice mail. The call was made at 2:00 a.m. The target claims that he does not know why anyone would make such a threat. Based on that simple sentence in that circumstance, the assessor can make an initial threat assessment to determine the degree of risk to the target at this time. That determination will guide the protective response and the need for future fact finding, if any. The always knowns provide the foundation for the initial assessment when little is known about the threat. The unknown need-to-knows guide the future fact finding. How much is unknown determines how well informed the assessment is at this time.

In this situation, the assessor knows several facts that give insight into the threat:

- The subject chose to telephone the target rather than write or make an approach.
- The subject also chose to make the call at a time when the target was likely not to be in his office.
- The subject also chose to remain anonymous.
- The threat was clearly intended to arouse fear in the target.
- The target does not know anyone who had reason to make the threat.

Based on these limited facts, the assessor can make an initial assessment that the threat poses little risk to the target at this time, based on the subject's choices to avoid personal contact (by telephoning at 2:00 a.m. and remaining anonymous, each the mark of a howler). As more information is uncovered or if the subject does something else, future assessments may change, but for now the assessor has enough information for an initial, minimally informed assessment.

By comparison, two Tampa, Florida, television stations each received a telephone call by someone who identified himself as "Scorpio." He told the operator at each station that "there is a contract out on" a specific assistant U.S. attorney (AUSA). Scorpio concluded each call with the statement, "He will be eliminated. I rode alone with [the AUSA] yesterday at 10:00 a.m." The

AUSA confirmed that a lone man had been on the elevator with him at about that time the day before.[11]

In this case, the assessor knows several facts supporting an assessment of high risk:

- The subject approached the target, thus exposing himself to being confronted or identified should the AUSA remember what he looked like.
- The subject chose to reveal that approach by making the telephone call.
- The subject clearly intended the threat to frighten the target.
- The subject is seeking public attention by contacting the media.
- The subject is identifying with a famous murderer from the past.

Unlike the anonymous, early morning telephone call, the subject's choice of getting physically close to the target indicated his ability and intent to do so, thus escalating the risk to the AUSA. As more information is uncovered or if the subject does something else, future assessments may change, but for now the assessor has enough information for an initial, minimally informed assessment.

Often, beginning threat assessors ask, "When does the assessor have enough information to make a competent assessment?" The question is misleading because it assumes that an assessor has the prerogative of deciding not to make an assessment based on too limited an amount of information. Yet, that is never an indulgence any assessor can afford. The target who received the voice mail stating, "I'm going to kill you," needs—indeed, demands—to know: "What is the risk to me, right now?" The assessor has to answer that basic question even though all the assessor knows is that he or she is assessing a telephone message expressing a direct threat to that particular target at this point in time. The assessor can qualify the assessment by saying that it is poorly informed and much more needs to be known, but even so, the assessment must stand by itself, if only temporarily.

Not all of the *need-to-knows* can be pulled together for every assessment, but the assessor always needs to ask about them or attempt to find the information. Thus, it becomes just as important to recognize what is not known at the time at which the assessment is made. This allows the assessor to rate how informed the assessment is at this time. If a lot of questions go unanswered, the assessment is minimally informed. If most or all of the questions are answered, the assessment is well or optimally informed.

Consequently, the *need-to-knows* serve as a checklist of what questions the assessor should always ask in every assessment. They also act as a guide to future fact finding and as a rating of how informed that particular assessment is at this time. The assessor should also keep in mind that the need-to-knows are not simple questions designed for a yes or no answer. Rather, they are best considered as areas of inquiry, with the answers to the questions dictating the urgency and relevance of the information.

We do not intend for this chapter to offer a comprehensive discussion of information gathering or investigative methods. Instead, we identify what types of information or areas of inquiry should be a priority during threat assessment fact finding and how that information relates to a competent assessment. We assume that the general investigative rules of determining who, what, when, where, why, and how of any situation are strictly followed and that information from a direct source is always preferred over second-hand or unverified content. We also assume that when a question is answered, all appropriate follow-up questions are asked to complete a line of inquiry.

In this chapter, we identify for the first time the type of information and the several areas of inquiry that make up the best informed assessments. Pulled together, the assessor can use this information index as a yardstick to measure exactly how much information is factored into the assessment and how much information needs still to be gathered. We offer here a way to gauge the context surrounding every threat assessment.

In any protective or security environment, assessments often have to be made on the run, based on very thin information. In any venue, situations may occur in which little information beyond the always knowns is available. The threatening voice mail can conceivably be left on anyone's answering machine, whether a public figure, coworker, classmate, ideological opponent, or former intimate. Regardless, threatening situations require threat assessments, no matter how much is known and, just as importantly, how much is not known.

Beyond the always knowns, the setting itself may contain additional information to feed the assessment. In certain environments, such as judicial, mental health, workplaces, and corrections facilities, volumes of historical and expert evaluation information can be gathered quickly before making the initial assessment. Case files and personnel records may contain a treasure trove of information on the subject. In other environments, ready access to previous encounters with the subject and previous assessments may be drawn upon when making new assessments. The setting and context determine what information is readily available to feed into the threat assessment. The need-to-knows consistently guide the information collection.

Time, too, impinges on every threat assessment, sometimes as an advantage and other times as a profound disadvantage. Consider two different situations: (1) A deputy sheriff at a courthouse assesses a failed bombing of a judge's car by a prior litigant who left angry graffiti at the scene, and (2) a mental health professional prepares an assessment on the risk of releasing a violent offender from prison to a halfway house. The courthouse threat manager operates in a different universe from that of the mental health professional in terms of case urgency, target fear, organizational pressure, information needs, access to resources, and the necessity of making an immediate assessment that determines the course of action by others. In those two vastly different situations, the mental health professional has one thing that the deputy sheriff does not have: *time.*

Consider, too, that the type and priority of the information to be gathered will significantly differ for each scenario. The deputy will be less concerned with the subject's family history of neglect and abuse than the mental health professional will be. The mental health professional will be less worried about the subject's current whereabouts and access to the target than the deputy will be. The nature and circumstances of the situation under assessment determine which of the individual need-to-knows are the most important for that situation at this time.

The urgency, circumstances, and environment surrounding the situation under assessment determines when and how often the threat manager will have to make assessments. The need to assess the threatening voice mail may not be as pressing if it targets a public figure compared to an ex-wife by the former husband—or Scott Roeder calling Dr. Tiller. In some cases, the threat assessment will have to be made before all the optimum information is available. In pressing situations, assessments will be necessary for making basic operational decisions, such as "Does this situation need to be followed up? Who will do it? How soon? How fast?" Threat assessments done on an active case are part of a continuous process that starts with the first information reported; it is not a theoretical exercise or a long-term research project.

Case Illustration: Threats to Goldman Sachs

In late June 2007, as many as 20 newspaper companies across the country received a letter threatening the investment firm Goldman Sachs. Each letter was handwritten in red ink on loose-leaf paper. Each was signed "A.Q.U.S.A." The letters contained the warning, "Hundreds will die. We are inside. You cannot stop us." The letters bore postmarks dated in late June from the New York boroughs of Queens and the Bronx. Newspapers in Seattle, Washington; Boise, Idaho; Corpus Christi, Texas; Fort Wayne, Indiana; Bayonne and Newark, New Jersey; and cities in Vermont, Ohio, and North Dakota each received the same letter.

That was the only information available to law enforcement and security officials at the investment firm. Yet, an assessment still had to be made. While taking the threats seriously, both law enforcement and Goldman Sachs security officers deemed the threats not to be "highly credible." (*Source:* Associated Press, "FBI Probe Threat to Goldman Sachs," July 6, 2007)

Regarding access to information, that depends on the environment and the authority of the threat manager. A few basic concepts include the following:

- It is better to develop information resources prior to when the assessor may urgently need them.
- Information will not flow to you unless you take steps to have it sent your way. Developing rapport with relatives, neighbors, landlords, or supervisors so that they will report the subject's behavior can be the difference between a successful or thwarted attack.
- If the assessor cannot get confidential records (e.g., mental health records), then witness observations (a neighbor saw the subject naked in the snow holding a toy rifle) may have to suffice.
- Information received from the subject should also be used in the assessment. The assessor does not need to have a psychology degree to conclude that a subject who claims to be acting out the violent commands coming from the voices in his head is not mentally stable.
- Understand that the always knowns are sufficient for making the initial assessment, however poorly informed it may be, while the remaining need-to-knows will guide future fact finding.
- The most basic and important concept is to recognize the information needed to make better informed assessments and to use that recognition to GO ASK QUESTIONS!

Using these concepts effectively will enhance any threat management program.

The Need-to-Knows

We have developed a list of the need-to-knows for any situation under assessment. We formatted the list as questions that the threat manager should ask whenever making an assessment. In so doing, we are not attempting to provide a comprehensive list of all information needed in every situation. Rather, we identify here what we consider to be the high-priority information areas critical to forming an informed threat assessment. The need-to-knows are an extraordinarily useful compendium of the type of information that makes a fully informed assessment. Using them as an index:

- Segregates the knowns from the unknowns in any assessment, thus rating the assessment
- Helps determine the protective response
- Guides future fact finding

In effect, asking the need-to-know questions at any point in the threat management process provides a ready measure of what information is

Table 5.1   The Need-to-Know Questions

1. How did the subject choose to approach the target?
2. What about the situation indicates the subject's identity and physical proximity to the target? In other words, who and where is the subject?
3. What about the situation indicates whom or what the subject is targeting? In other words, who or what is the target?
4. What about the situation indicates the type of venue being targeted and what about the venue gives insight into the subject's intent, motive, and ability?
5. What about the situation indicates whether or not the intimacy effect is in play? In other words, what is the nature of the relationship between the subject and the target?
6. What about the situation relates to the subject's choice of context, content, and circumstances?
7. Is the target currently accessible to the subject?
8. Does the subject have the ability and motivation to take advantage of any current accessibility to the target?
9. Is there a known history of previous contacts with the target or other targets by this subject?
10. Does the subject have a history of violent or threatening behaviors, including any criminal behavior?
11. What is the subject's knowledge about the target's current situation?
12. Is the subject seeking knowledge about the target and the target's current situation?
13. Does the subject's behavior indicate mental health issues, including suicidality?
14. Does the subject possess, have access to, or give evidence of a fascination with weapons?
15. Is the subject currently seeking to obtain a weapon?
16. What is the status of the subject's inhibitors, including any recent losses?
17. Has the subject exhibited controlling, isolating, or jealous behaviors toward the target?
18. Does the subject have a history of abuse of alcohol, drugs, or prescription medicines?
19. Does the subject have any relevant medical issues?
20. Has the subject engaged in any final-act behaviors?

known at that time against what information is not known at that time. Consequently, the concept of the need-to-knows is fundamental to effective threat management (Table 5.1).

How Did the Subject Choose to Approach the Target?

For any conceivable situation under assessment, the subject who created the situation makes certain choices that give the assessor insight into the subject's intent, motive, and ability—the trifecta of informed assessments. These choices form the always knowns of any threat assessment. For example, in most cases, the subject consciously chooses how to approach or bring himself or herself to the attention of the target. The subject has a choice of five different methods of approaching:

1. Approach the target through writing, including letters, e-mails, text messages, graffiti, Internet blogs, social network postings, or any other written or electronic format that the subject knows or has confidence that the target will read.
2. Approach the target through the telephone, including pagers and voice mails.
3. Allow, whether intentionally or not, information about the subject's violent intent to leak out to third parties, including through Internet postings, diaries, comments, or suspicious behaviors that other individuals can pass on to the target or to authorities.
4. Approach the target verbally, such as making a threat or other ominous spoken statements to the target in person and face to face.
5. Approach the target through some suspicious activity, such as stalking, conducting target research near the target, or prowling around areas where the target happens to be.

An exception to these five approach methods is information about a situation gleaned from an informant—especially if the subject is unaware that he or she is being informed upon. What the informant reports that the subject is doing or saying, provided the informant is credible, gives the assessor insight into the subject's plans and activities. Consequently, in informant situations, the assessor must always first assess the informant's credibility, including possible motivation, before assessing what the informant claims.

In situations when the subject chooses the approach, that choice gives a strong indication both of the subject's intent at the time of the approach and the subject's current ability to harm the target. Subjects who choose to approach through writing or the telephone keep a safe distance from the target. That physical separation strongly suggests that the subject's intent at this time is to frighten or disturb, rather than to cause actual physical harm.

Subjects who leak their violent intentions put themselves at risk of exposure, but not necessarily at risk of immediate physical harm. Leakage tells the assessor little about the subject's true intent, but it does give considerable insight into the subject's motive and ability. Electronic media make information eminently shareable. However, that "shareability" comes at the cost of losing control over the information.

The Internet offers a tempting way to justify one's actions, to show to the world the slings and arrows of one's own outrageous fortune. Blogs, social media, and other ways to post comments and observations have proved very attractive to many individuals of violent intent.[12] Yet, in choosing to post these ruminations on the Web, the subject risks exposing to the world—and the threat manager—his or her motives, plans, and current place along the path to intended violence. As with written and telephonic approaches, electronic postings are done from a physical distance between subject and target.

Conversely, subjects who choose to approach the target verbally in person put themselves in physical proximity to the target, thus putting themselves at risk of physical harm. Similarly, subjects who approach the target in some suspicious way are also putting themselves in physical proximity to the target. This behavior strongly suggests that the subject is prepared to harm the target now or in the near future.

The concept of determining the physical proximity between the subject and target, bolstered by the understanding that the subject controls that proximity, provides a crucial insight into determining whether the subject is a hunter or a howler.[13] Subjects who choose to maintain a physical distance between themselves and the target are acting, at this time, like howlers. Subjects who choose to put themselves in close physical proximity to the target are acting, at this time, like hunters. That choice provides a significant insight into the mind of the subject to the threat manager.

The choice, too, is one of the always known variables. It is present in every situation under assessment. Without it, the threat manager has nothing to assess. Even when assessing controversial situations, such as the TSA administrator's decision to conduct upper torso pat-downs, the public's response involved various methods of communicating, including e-mails and telephone calls to the TSA Contact Center, Internet blogs, and physical approaches to airport security screeners.

Consequently, the importance of this need-to-know derives from the insight it gives the threat assessor into the subject's intent, motive, and ability. How the subject chooses to approach the target reveals much about the subject's current intent because the choice itself is under the subject's control. That choice, then, becomes a significant indicator of the subject's current motive.

Thus, for purposes of the threat assessment, the assessor should always ask what about the situation indicates how the subject chose to approach the target.

What About the Situation Indicates the Subject's Identity and Physical Proximity to the Target? In Other Words, Who and Where Is the Subject?

The subject, again with the exception of informant reports, also chooses whether or not to reveal his or her identity. In the case of the threatening voice mail, the subject chose to remain anonymous. Combined with the choice of approach, the assessor can have confidence that—at this time—the subject intends to frighten or disturb the target rather than cause physical harm.

Compare the telephone call with Scott Roeder's lethal approach to Dr. Tiller. Although Roeder never revealed his name, he revealed himself and his car to witnesses who were subsequently able to report his physical description and license plate to the police. By being in the church in person, Roeder exposed his identity. As he moved toward the vestibule of the church where Dr. Tiller stood chatting with another usher, Roeder revealed his intention to approach his target physically.

As with method of approach, the subject's choice of whether or not to reveal his or her identity and physical proximity to the target is also one of the always knowns of any threat assessment. Essentially, it is a simple question. Either the subject chose to provide enough information to reveal his or her identity or the subject chose to hide his or her identity by not providing sufficient information or by maintaining a safe distance from the target. Consequently, for any situation under assessment, the assessor must determine who and where the subject is at this time.

This is a basic issue. Assessors usually cannot assess access, relationship, violent history, or many of the other need-to-knows without knowing the identity of the subject. Some of the challenges that may occur are the subject's use of pseudonyms, symbolic names such as "the Watcher," or someone else's name as a dirty trick. Maintaining a database of past contacts will help in identifying subjects who choose to remain anonymous.

One of the common data points collected by threat managers is unique characteristics or wording of any inappropriate communication or contact. Comparing the unique characteristics of the current situation to previous incidents or situations may help identify the subject. Networking with other organizations that have threat management programs and asking the threat managers to compare unique characteristics of the situation under assessment with previous incidents in their databases may also have positive results.

Even if the assessor cannot identify the source of an inappropriate or threatening contact, a thoughtful analysis of the content can provide significant information for feeding the assessment. For example, the mayor of a city receives an angry text message on his city phone accusing him of molesting a minor female several years ago. The message ends with a promise to make him pay for this crime with his life. A few days prior to the text, the local press reported the accusation. The police determined that the allegation had no merit. A trace of the phone text revealed that it was a cloned phone that was now deactivated.

What useful information can be assessed from this incident, especially as it relates to assessing the subject? The writer keeps track of local issues in the press. The press attention was a few days old, so probably the text was not an impulsive act. The writer is sufficiently organized to use texting and purposely keep his identity concealed. He or she was motivated enough to send a death threat message. He or she did sufficient research or had access to the mayor's cell phone number and was sophisticated enough to utilize a cloned phone. Most importantly, by sending a text message, the writer chose to maintain a physical distance between him or her and the mayor. That choice allowed the writer to express his or her murderous outrage from a safe distance.

There are also unique characteristics of this communication that may be useful when compared to other communications, such as press motivated, cloned phone, use of texting, access to private phone numbers, and any specific threat wording. A check of the city's threat management records may find similar factors in previous situations. If not, putting what happened into the files or database will ensure its recovery in the event that the mayor receives other texts from the subject in the future.

Consequently, the importance of this need-to-know is that it provides the threat manager information on the current and immediate relationship and physical proximity between the subject and the target.

Thus, for purposes of the threat assessment, the assessor should ask what about the situation indicates the subject's identity and physical proximity to the target.

What About the Situation Indicates Whom or What the Subject Is Targeting? In Other Words, Who Is the Target?

The subject also chooses to specify or not specify exactly what his or her target is and what his or her physical proximity to the target is at the time when the situation under assessment occurred. To go back to the "I'll kill you" voice mail message, the assessor needs to determine who the phone number belonged to in order to gain insight into who is the target. The fact that the subject did not specify a target, again coupled with the choice of approach, strongly suggests a general desire to cause fear or unease rather than physical harm. Roeder, by comparison, intended to harm Dr. Tiller specifically.

Threats may be vague or confusing as to whom the actual target might be. This is particularly true in threats toward government, large institutions, or iconic locations, such as the Golden Gate Bridge. Is the threat toward an individual? The building itself? The entire government? Sometimes, the threat manager will have to assess the situation by considering the target to be more than one person or location. That involves considering different factors. This is also a basic issue that must be determined to assess the nature of the relationship, target knowledge, and, most importantly, whom or what to protect.

Sometimes the potential target is a location either specific or symbolic to the subject's grievance. This has been the case in attacks on courthouses and churches. At other times, it is a type of location where people who meet certain characteristics congregate. This has been the case in targeted violence incidents against minorities, gays, and Jews.

When the subject's underlying grievance is a desire for recognition or to "be somebody," the venue or person targeted is designed for maximum attention. Often, attacks on public figures or famous locations fall into this category.

This need-to-know is crucial because it focuses the threat assessor on determining who or what is the potential target. Identifying the target through the subject's choice of being specific or general provides the threat manager another insight into the subject's intent, motive, and ability. As with the first two need-to-knows, target identification or lack of identification is another always known. Without some kind of target, no matter how general, there is nothing to assess.

As defined by victim selection, intended violence falls into one of three categories. Targeted violence is very specific in choice of victim; that is, targeted violence is aimed at specific, clearly identified individuals. Conversely, opportunistic violence is very general in its choice of victims; that is, opportunistic violence targets victims in general because they happen to be at a certain place at a certain time or because they are members of a group, such as a particular religion, sexual orientation, political affiliation, or other identifying unit. The third category of intended violence, generally the most lethal, is a combination of targeted and opportunistic violence. That is, the subject targets specific individuals, but uses that opportunity to use violence against anyone else who happens to be near or around the targeted individuals.

Case Illustration: Targets and Opportunities

Early in the morning of August 1, 1966, Charles Whitman went to his mother's apartment in Austin, Texas, and killed her in her sleep. He returned to his own home, where he killed his wife while she slept. He took the time to explain in his journal that he killed the two women to spare them the embarrassment and humiliation for what he intended to do later that day.

Later that morning, Whitman hauled a footlocker loaded with weapons, ammunition, and other supplies to the top of the University of Texas clock tower. He killed the receptionist on the 28th floor. He then went out on the observation deck and began shooting anyone who came into his rifle sights. He continued firing for over an hour and a half, killing 15 (including his wife and mother and another victim who survived for 2 weeks after the shooting spree), and wounding 31. Three policemen stormed the observation deck and killed him.

Whitman first engaged in targeted violence against his mother and his wife and then switched to opportunistic violence against random individuals who happened to be within range of the clock tower observation deck. It proved a lethal combination of intended violence. (*Source:* Calhoun and Weston, *Contemporary Threat Management*, pp. 11–12)

Consequently, the importance of this need-to-know is that it focuses the threat assessor's attention on determining exactly and precisely whom or what the subject is targeting. That determination will help the assessor formulate the best protective response. It will also help guide future fact finding.

Thus, for purposes of the threat assessment, the assessor should ask what about the situation indicates whom or what the subject is targeting.

What About the Situation Indicates the Type of Venue Being Targeted and What About the Venue Gives Insight Into the Subject's Intent, Motive, and Ability?

The subject chooses the venue in which the situation occurs. That choice gives the assessor insight into the subject's knowledge about the target and its current level of security, as well as the subject's intent, motive, and ability. Subjects targeting a current or former spouse know a great deal about their target's routines, job location, ability to protect himself or herself, and other intimate details. These subjects do not need to engage in much target research because they already know so much about the target.

Subjects pursuing a public figure are less likely to know the target's routines or ability to protect himself or herself. Those subjects have to engage in considerable target research in order to find out where the target lives or where the target will be at any given moment. That research exposes the subject to detection because target research requires engaging in noticeable behaviors, such as stalking, target research, and other information-gathering behaviors.

Other venues tell as much. Subjects planning an act of workplace violence against a current or former workplace know a great deal about the target because the subject currently or previously worked at that workplace. Subjects who attack places where people gather know where those places are, but they know little about the individuals they target. Similarly, subjects who attack representative targets know what the target represents—a gay bar or Jewish community center—but they may know little about the level of security at the site. Identifying the venue for the potential violence enables the threat assessor to put the assessment and the situation in context. We discuss in a later chapter the similarities and differences among the various venues for intended violence. That comparison sheds considerable insight into the situation under assessment.

Unfortunately, venue is not one of the always knowns for any given situation or assessment. The subject may choose to disguise his or her affiliation to the target so that the threat assessor may not know or be able to identify what it is about this subject and that target that is driving the subject toward an act of violence. Because venue sheds so much light on the subject's motive, it behooves the threat manager to move quickly to determine the exact relationship between subject and potential target.

Consequently, the importance of this need-to-know comes from allowing the threat assessor to determine some sort of context for assessing the situation. It also gives clues as to the subject's motive and ability.

Thus, for purposes of the threat assessment, the assessor should ask what about the situation indicates the type of venue being targeted and what about the subject's connection to that venue gives insight into the subject's intent, motive, and ability.

What About the Situation Indicates Whether or Not the Intimacy Effect Is in Play? In Other Words, What Is the Nature of the Relationship Between the Subject and the Target?

What the subject chooses to convey gives the assessor insight into the nature of the relationship between the subject and the target. Leaving a threatening telephone message, for example, clearly shows that the subject feels animosity toward the target or targets. Roeder's choice of behavior also showed considerable animosity toward his target. By comparison, subjects who engage in unwanted pursuit of a love interest are not showing an adverse relationship, but, rather, an unrequited love relationship.

The latter two need-to-knows also shed light on the presence or absence of the intimacy effect. How the subject expresses or perceives his or her relationship with the target, combined with the choice of venue, provides the assessor with considerable evidence regarding the impact of the intimacy effect. Was the target who received the threatening telephone call recently divorced or otherwise had recent contact with the former spouse? Did the telephone belong to a supervisor who recently dismissed a disgruntled employee? Those situations would strongly suggest that the intimacy effect is in play. Whoever called Dr. Tiller's clinic and left the threatening message was likely not on interpersonal terms with the doctor or his staff.

We consider it essential to know the nature of the relationship between the subject and the target because it strongly affects the value of threatening words as a predictor of potentially violent approach. Is the relationship intensely interpersonal, such as marriage, or far distant, such as a private citizen targeting the U.S. president? Is the relationship somewhere in between, such as a coworker, neighbor, judicial official, or business acquaintance? The relationship is assessed from the point of view of the subject based on his or her beliefs and version of reality. Also, threats toward public figures are not necessarily based on a distant relationship, but may be related to a contact in their interpersonal or private lives.

The subject's relationship to the target may not always be readily apparent. Public figures have private lives; strangers whom they may have unwittingly offended sometimes target ordinary individuals. Incidents of road rage are good examples of the latter. Still, the importance of asking the question arises from focusing the threat assessor on gauging the nature of the relationship between subject and potential target. Recognizing that the threat manager does not yet know the answer can be just as important as knowing it.

Consequently, the importance of this need-to-know derives from its insight into the chemistry between the subject and the target. It also helps in assessing threats, as well as the subject's intent and motive.

Thus, for purposes of the threat assessment, the assessor should ask what about the situation indicates whether or not the intimacy effect is in play.

What About the Situation Relates to the Subject's Choice of Context, Content, and Circumstances?

The subject controls the context of the situation under assessment, at least initially. What was it about this moment in time that prompted the subject to initiate the situation? Why did the subject make the threatening phone call when he or she made it? Why did he or she choose the words used in the context presented? Was the call likely to go to voice mail, as opposed to someone likely being around to answer the telephone? Why did Roeder suddenly start attending services at Dr. Tiller's church, thereby arousing suspicion among some of the other parishioners? The threat manager should always ask the questions: Why this target? Why here? Why now? Why this method of approach? Ask what else is going on that may be related, such as controversial disputes or unresolved conflicts.

Circumstances and context are one of the always knowns, if only in part. Every situation has some context. The threat manager, though, has always to remember that he or she may be seeing only part of the context, only some of the circumstances. At first, the threat manager will see a conflict only from the point of view of the target. The subject may have an entirely different point of view. This means that the threat assessor needs to avoid becoming too wedded to previous threat assessments. As more of the context and circumstances become clear, the threat assessment will change.

Consequently, the importance of determining circumstances and context of the situation results from allowing the threat assessor to root the situation in time and place.

Thus, for purposes of the threat assessment, the assessor should ask what about the situation indicates the subject's choice of circumstances and content.

Is the Target Currently Accessible to the Subject?

The first step in the threat management process is to locate the target and make sure that he, she, or it is safe at this time. At the same time, the assessor can make an initial determination of the target's current accessibility to the subject. This is not the time to be overconfident in any established security. If there is an access opportunity, a determined hunter will find the opening. Tiller had security at home and work. He carried a weapon. But he had neither while at church, where Roeder killed him. The assessor must keep in mind that accessibility changes as the situation evolves.

For example, in a domestic violence scenario, the battered wife has no protection while at home, except if the husband is in custody. When the husband bails out of jail, the wife is accessible again; however, the wife can move to a confidential battered women's shelter, making herself inaccessible to him.

In a threat toward a government agency, the agency has significant security and is forewarned. The assessment of that inaccessibility improves when the assessor determines that the subject lives 10 hours away, has no vehicle or money, and only leaves his house to buy beer.

Pay close attention to travel issues. Does the subject have an unusual pattern of travel? Is it toward or away from the target? Does the subject disappear for periods of time? Does he or she live 2 hours away, but visit a location near the target? Does he or she travel near the target for no discernable reason? Does the subject have resources near the target?

Case Illustration: The Traveling Threatener

An assistant DA started receiving disturbing letters from a prison inmate whom she had prosecuted for stalking and rape. It was clear from the letters that he was now fixated on her. When he was paroled, a stay-away provision was added to his conditions of parole. After he violated parole and was listed "at large," she received a sexually explicit letter from him postmarked from Mexico. The situation rapidly escalated when it was discovered that a former cellmate had rented a house on the same block on which the DA lived. The subject was apprehended attempting to cross back over the border after an alert was arranged with the border patrol. (*Source:* Authors' personal knowledge)

When a specific target is known, target accessibility is another of the always knowns. When the subject simply seeks targets of opportunity, his or her accessibility can also be deduced based on what opportunities the subject is looking for. Subjects intent on wreaking violence against members of a particular group, such as religious affiliation, sexual orientation, ideological affiliation, or simply shoppers at a shopping mall, will go to places where the group members congregate.

Consequently, the importance of this need-to-know comes from allowing the threat assessor to see the situation in its current state and to formulate countermeasures to the subject's next steps.

Thus, in determining target accessibility, the assessor balances between subject capabilities and intentions, including ability to travel, access to resources, motivation, and intent on targeted or opportunistic violence, or both, versus target accessibility and level of security. Consequently, one of the first questions the assessor needs to ask is, "Where is the target at this moment and how accessible is the target to potential danger?"

Does the Subject Have the Ability and Motivation to Take Advantage of Any Current Accessibility to the Target?

Simply because the target is accessible to the subject does not mean, *ipso facto*, that the subject will take advantage of that vulnerability. Howlers, for example, may have easy access to their targets, but they only use that access to frighten or disturb the target. Because that is their only intent, they have no purpose in getting closer to the target.

The steps along the path to intended violence can help the assessor determine if the subject wants to exploit any current accessibility to the target. Does the subject exhibit any research and planning behaviors? Is the subject actively preparing for an assault? Has the subject breached the target's security? These types of behaviors give the assessor insight into the subject's intentions regarding gaining access to the target.

The subject's willingness to exploit a target's accessibility may not always be readily apparent. Howlers, who make up the vast majority of problem individuals, do not actually intend to access the target beyond their threatening or inappropriate behaviors; yet, the stakes are altogether too high for the threat manager to play the odds that the current situation under assessment involves a howler. Prudence demands that, barring positive evidence that the subject is a howler, the threat manager has to act as if every situation involves a hunter.

Consequently, the importance of this need-to-know derives from providing the threat assessor a current snapshot of where the subject currently is and what the subject is currently doing.

Thus, the assessor should look beyond the target's potential vulnerabilities to determine if the subject is exhibiting any behaviors indicating that he or she intends to exploit those vulnerabilities and is acting to further that intention.

Is There a Known History of Previous Contacts With the Target or Other Targets by This Subject?

Subjects who behave inappropriately toward the current target frequently have histories of similar behaviors toward the same target or similar targets. It is important to ask about previous contacts and suspicious incidents that may be related. Maintaining a threat management database or even basic recordkeeping and networking with other threat managers is a good way to learn about previous subject behaviors.

How a subject behaved in the past in the same or similar circumstances gives the best insight into assessing how the subject will behave in the future. Howlers frequently engage in the same annoying, but ultimately nonviolent, behaviors toward a series of targets or multiple targets. Seeing that behavior in previous situations gives the assessor insight that the behavior may be repeated in the current situation.

Conversely, in assessing a subject who has acted out violently in previous situations, the assessor has to recognize a high risk that the subject will act out violently in the current situation. In a workplace violence venue, an assessor may be asked to assess the degree of risk during an upcoming termination meeting. Knowing that the employee is being terminated because he acted out in anger with violence toward another employee is a strong indicator that the risk of violence during the termination meeting is high. When assessing past problematic behavior, seek out detailed information. How similar is the past situation to the problem today? How did the subject react to interventions? If the behavior stopped, why did it stop? Is the status of inhibitors the same in both situations?

Unfortunately, the threat assessor may not be privy to a subject's past behaviors in similar situations. The current situation may be unique, the subject may have recently moved to the area, or the subject's life condition may have changed so dramatically that it induces new behaviors. Although knowing about past behaviors bolsters any threat assessment, not knowing about past behaviors is not an impediment to making a sound threat assessment of the current situation.

Consequently, the importance of this need-to-know comes from the insight it gives the threat assessor about the subject's previous behaviors toward this or similar targets.

Thus, previous situations are excellent barometers for assessing current situations. How the subject behaved in the past during similar situations is one of the best insights into how the current situation will play out.

Does the Subject Have a History of Violent or Threatening Behaviors, Including Any Criminal Behavior?

A generally held belief is that people who have been violent or threatening in the past will be violent in the future. While there is some truth to this, it is not that simple or superficial. The primary place to look for information about significant past violence will be criminal history records. Rather than taking a bare record at face value, continue the research and determine the extent of the violence, any weapons used, whether the violence was provoked or in self-defense, and the surrounding circumstances of the event. What inhibitors were in place or at risk at the time of the violence? How similar to the situation under assessment is the past violent situation?

Repetitive criminal or violent acting out will always be a concern because subjects who have successfully used violence to gain their needs and achieve their goals are confident in their ability to use violence. Not all violence results in arrest and prosecution. Take into consideration the real environment that the subject lives in every day. Remember the fine folks at the Buckhorn Lodge? Violence frequently occurs in the bar and the nearby mobile home park; however, nobody goes to jail, nobody reports the incidents, and no witnesses come forward. The same pattern also holds in many instances of domestic violence and child abuse.

Because of this reality, the threat manager needs to look more deeply than the criminal history. Look for law enforcement responses to current and past residences, field interview records, divorce documents, and civil records. When interviewing sources, ask about angry, explosive, or unpredictable behaviors. Look for aggressive or strange behavior that convinces others to shy away from contact with the subject. As always, look for patterns and circumstances similar to the situation under assessment.

All that being said, subjects who have no history of documented, verified past violence have carried out intended violence. Everyone is capable of violence under the right provocation. Although it is an important indicator, past violence is but one factor to consider within the entire context of a situation. As with knowing or not knowing about previous contacts, knowing about a subject's past history of violence greatly informs a threat assessment, but not knowing about previous violence does not undermine a current assessment. Everyone is capable of violence given the right provocations. That simple truth should undergird every assessment.

Consequently, the importance of this need-to-know comes from the insight it gives the threat assessor about the subject's previous behaviors, especially in situations similar to the one currently under assessment.

Thus, previous acts of violence provide a good, but not exclusive, indicator of the subject's potential for acting out violently in the current situation.

What Is the Subject's Knowledge About the Target's Current Situation?

Some subjects will have detailed knowledge of the life patterns and security measures of the target because of the nature of their relationship. This is true of current and prior intimates, such as spouses or employees in a workplace. The logistics of an act of targeted violence requires some knowledge to be successful. Those subjects who already have critical knowledge do not need to spend time or risk exposure to do research to discover vulnerabilities, learn schedules, or search out locations to carry out an attack. The results of this area of inquiry are an important factor in any protective response.

Often, determining the subject's knowledge of the target's current situation can be deduced by identifying the venue in which the situation resides. Intimate knowledge about the target can be deduced from domestic, workplace, or school relationships. Public figures, conversely, are generally protected from such knowledge about their affairs. How the subject behaves also offers clues into his or her knowledge about the target. Conducting target research suggests limited knowledge about the target; otherwise, the research would not be necessary. How successful that research is provides a measure of how much information the subject collected.

Consequently, the importance of this need-to-know derives from the knowledge that it gives the threat assessor about the subject's degree of information—or lack of information—about the current status of the target.

Thus, the threat manager should always look for evidence of how much information the subject has about the target because of the previous relationship or based on current knowledge of the subject.

Is the Subject Seeking Knowledge About the Target and the Target's Current Situation?

In contrast to prior intimates, some subjects will need to engage in research behaviors to gain the knowledge necessary to carry out an attack. Behaviors of concern include asking questions as to schedule and target location, stalking activities, and conducting surveillance. This is a critical step on the path to violence and any hint of research behavior should be cause for concern. The positive aspect is that the subject usually cannot engage in this type of activity without someone noticing. The question, then, becomes: Will that someone who does notice know to report it and to whom to report it?

To be in a position to capture this type of information requires training key staff in an organization. These staff members include perimeter security personnel, receptionists, parking attendants, groundskeepers, and others in position to observe research behavior. They need to know what suspicious behaviors are and to whom to report them. If the target is not part of an organization, development of sources sympathetic to the victim to report information will be valuable. The point is that research behavior is a key indicator. It should always be looked for and measures should be taken to ensure those persons in a position to know about it know how to report it.

A lack of evidence of research behavior cannot be taken as evidence of no such behavior. The threat manager has constantly to keep in mind that, in any situation, not everything that is going on is known. The subject may very well be collecting information or attempting to collect information without anyone noticing or, if noticed, no one reporting the behavior. Evidence of research behavior is one of those need-to-knows for which positive indicators should be taken quite seriously, while lack of evidence does not have the opposite effect. That is to say, not having evidence of research behavior does not mean that the behavior is not taking place.

Consequently, the importance of this need-to-know comes from the insight it gives the threat assessor about how actively or energetically the subject is trying to collect information—and what kind of information—about the target.

Thus, the threat manager should always look for evidence of research on the target by the subject.

Does the Subject's Behavior Indicate Mental Health Issues, Including Suicidality?

Obtaining official mental health records is difficult, if not impossible, without proper authority or a waiver from the patient. Rather than battle a bureaucracy, gather information on the subject's behavior. Look for behavior that indicates mental illness, such as delusions, hallucinations, uncontrollable impulses, and suicidality. When you find evidence of this behavior, focus on connections to the target and violence.

For example, a subject expresses a delusion that the governor is following him and is trying to kill him. In order to feel more secure, the subject defends himself by fortifying his residence against attack. When he hears on the news that the governor will be at his town for a public meeting, he tells a neighbor that he has a gun and always carries it. This information can be gathered without any confidential medical records. The subject is demonstrating behaviors indicating mental illness—specifically, delusions. The delusions have connections to violence and the subject is acting upon the delusions by carrying a gun. These are all indicators of potential violence.

When evaluating behavior of mental illness, also consider whether the subject is being treated by a mental health professional and whether he or she is taking prescription medication properly. The latter, unfortunately, is a rare occurrence in most threatening behaviors.

A complicating factor with the potentially dangerous and mentally ill subjects is the abuse of alcohol or street drugs, sometimes in combination with prescribed psychotropic drugs. This scenario can play out with many different combinations: alcohol and prescription drugs, alcohol and street drugs, prescription drugs and street drugs, alcohol only, and so on. Any of these combinations affects mentally ill subjects in dangerous and unpredictable ways. The effects can range from intensified symptoms, such as severe delusions, to psychotic events.

How the subject has acted in similar circumstances, as always, is the best indicator of how these substances will affect the subject's behavior.

Within this broad category of behavioral health, the threat assessor should also assess the subject's degree of mental disability or diminished mental capacity. The question is less about the subject's diagnosed mental illness and more about how functional the subject is—his or her ability to perform the necessary tasks to carry out an attack, and his or her cognitive ability. Do not be misled by a subject with low IQ or education. The key is to determine cognitive complexity, which, in simple terms, is to ask, "What are his or her street smarts?" A subject can have little education, but be extremely shrewd in criminal or violent behavior.

In general, when evaluating the mentally ill and the mentally disabled, rather than getting all wound up in diagnosis and mental records, focus on functionality and abilities. Does he or she have the physical and mental acuity to carry out the attack?

Pay particular attention to a history of suicide, which includes suicide attempts, threats, and verbal or written references to suicide. The research on intended violence in all venues indicates a strong link between past suicidality and violence. Keep in mind that the desire to live is the strongest human inhibitor and, without that, there are no limits on the risks a subject will take to meet an objective. This is also an important factor in determining a protective response.

When attempting to evaluate complex mental health behavior or interpret mental health records, it is best to consult with a mental health professional who specializes in the evaluation of dangerousness. This type of consultation would also be valuable in determining the impact of psychotropic medication or, more often, the lack of medication on the behavior of mentally ill subjects.

In making such determinations, we do not expect the threat manager necessarily to make a medical or psychological diagnosis of the subject's potential mental condition. Obviously, trained psychiatrists, psychologists, and other mental health professionals are best positioned to do exactly that, but threat managers do not need training in mental health in order to assess that a subject, even though clearly delusional, is capable of acting out whatever the delusion demands. The assessment, then, is not a medical or psychological diagnosis. Instead, the threat manager needs to assess the subject's physical and mental ability to get from point A to point B and beyond.

Consequently, the importance of this need-to-know derives from the insight it gives the threat assessor about the subject's current mental condition and state of mind.

Thus, the threat manager should always look for evidence of mental health disorders, especially suicidality, by determining how functional the subject is in terms of ability to plan and carry out an act of violence.

Does the Subject Possess, Have Access to, or Give Evidence of a Fascination With Weapons?

This is an area of inquiry that requires more than just determining if the subject has a gun, although that is important to know. Consider these examples: One subject has an old handgun that belonged to his father. He has never fired it and it is packed away in the garage. The other subject has several handguns—all for self-protection—along with thousands of rounds of ammunition, some of it exotic, such as armor piercing. The second subject constantly talks about the guns, along with violent themes. He wears gun logo clothing. He often mentions the guns as solutions to his disputes. He has brandished the guns in neighborhood disputes and practices with them back in the hills. His ex-wife claims that he has played Russian roulette while drunk or high on drugs.

If you are going to ask the simple gun possession question, the answer will be yes for both. But the situations are very different for assessment purposes. The inquiry is more than who possesses a gun; it is the persona of the subject, the attitude toward the weapons, and the relationship with violence that are important.

Consider also the use and purpose of the weapons based on the subject's conduct and the environment in which he or she lives. A hunter and sportsman would have a nonviolent, purposeful use for several high-power firearms and specialty knives. A subject who keeps a gun or a knife for protection hidden in every room in his apartment and in his vehicle could be a problem. In nineteenth century western America, the Colt was considered the "great equalizer." That still holds true today.

Yet, guns are not the only way to kill someone. Consider all weapons, not just firearms and knives. In a recent case in California, police arrested Nicholas Smit on multiple charges of attempted murder of the police detective who arrested Smit on marijuana charges. Police accused Smit of using a variety of weapons, including inflammatory devices, homemade bombs, a "punji trap" involving boards with upward pointing nails, flammable vapors pumped into an office, and a handmade gun, in a series of murder attempts stretching over a 7-month period. Fortunately, Smit's incompetence in the use of these myriad weapons doomed the attempts to failure.[14]

However, the threat manager should not overlook other weapons, such as poison, explosives, or clubs. Automobiles have also been used as lethal weapons. As with firearms, the issue is not simple possession; rather, it is the subject's attitude and persona toward the weapon and the relationship to violence.

Consequently, the importance of this need-to-know derives from its close association to the path to intended violence. Gaining access to a weapon—even seeking a weapon—places the subject clearly at the preparation stage along the path. As with many of the need-to-knows, answering this question requires positive evidence of weapon-seeking behavior. Lack of such evidence does not mean that the behavior is not taking place. It only means that the threat assessor has no information about it.

Case Illustration: The Lululemon Murder

On November 2, 2011, jurors in Montgomery County, Maryland, convicted Brittany Norwood of first-degree murder of fellow employee Jayna Murray at the Lululemon yoga store in Bethesda the previous March. The jurors accepted the prosecution's argument that the number and variety of murder weapons proved malice aforethought, even though the prosecutors offered no evidence or theory for Norwood's motive.

Montgomery State's Attorney John McCarthy argued that, because the attack was continuous and especially brutal, that was proof enough that the violence was premeditated. Norwood used a variety of makeshift weapons close at hand. Based on the physical evidence and the autopsy, prosecutors persuaded the jury that Norwood attacked Murray with, among other weapons, a hammer, knife, wrench, rope, and metal peg used to hold a mannequin. The coroner estimated that Norwood inflicted a wound on Murray every 3 seconds for 16 minutes. Murray sustained at least 331 injuries before she died.

Because of the variety of weapons used by Norwood, the jury opted for a first-degree murder conviction, discarding the defense lawyer's argument that Norwood "lost it" and, therefore, was not responsible for planning the murder. They accepted McCarthy's argument that "there were dozens of opportunities, multiple times, that she could have stopped this." The relentlessness of the attack and the choice of multiple weapons proved that what may have started as an act of impromptu violence ended in an act of intended violence. (*Source:* Dan Morse and Victor Zapana, "Woman Convicted of Killing Co-Worker at Bethesda Yoga Store, *Baltimore Sun,* November 3, 2011; "Medical Examiner: 'She Was Alive,'" *Bethesda Patch,* November 2, 2011)

Thus, the threat manager should always look for evidence of the subject's interest in and, especially, fascination with weapons of any sort.

Is the Subject Currently Seeking to Obtain a Weapon?

This is a critical corollary to the question about weapon possession. It includes a range of behaviors that signal the intent to use a weapon or lethal means for a purpose and are key steps on the path to violence. The behaviors to focus on include seeking a weapon; asking others about weapon availability; doing research on weapon use or other lethal means; seeking ammunition or other accessories, such as a holster or a rifle scope; practicing use of a weapon, such as going to a firing range or detonating prototype explosive devices; or altering an existing weapon. Behavior that furthers the intent to use a weapon for a specific purpose includes weapon practice and assembling other components to further the potential for success in an attack.

As with weapon possession, do not focus only on guns. Look for preparation of any means to an end result of death or injury. An ax is just an ax when it is in the woodshed and used to cut wood. It becomes a formidable weapon when moved into the house and hidden under the bed after a husband learns of a wife's infidelity.

As with many of the other need-to-knows, positive evidence of behaviors associated with seeking to obtain a weapon or the articles that can be used violently results in an assessment of high risk, but the lack of such evidence does not necessarily support a low risk assessment. The lack of such evidence means only that the threat manager does not have knowledge of such evidence—not that the behavior has not occurred. Because it is impossible to prove a negative (i.e., that the subject has not engaged in weapon-seeking behavior), the threat manager cannot assume that the behavior has not taken place.

Consequently, the importance of this need-to-know depends on positive evidence that the behavior has taken place. Lack of such evidence makes this need-to-know less important for purposes of the assessment. Obviously, answering the question becomes an important part of the subsequent fact finding. Still, the threat assessor needs to keep in mind one of the more frustrating parts of making an assessment: Not knowing about behaviors associated with seeking a weapon is not the same as not engaging in those behaviors.

Thus, the threat manager should always look for evidence of weapon-seeking behavior, but should not draw any strong conclusions from any lack of such evidence.

What Is the Status of the Subject's Inhibitors, Including Any Recent Losses?

Inhibitors are factors in people's lives that provide stability or are incentives not to act out violently. Key external inhibitors are home, personal relationships, careers, and financial stability. Key internal inhibitors are self-esteem and dignity. While these are typical inhibitors, they can be anything that the subject thinks is important enough to keep him or her from acting out violently in a specific situation. Be particularly focused on inhibitor losses or changes that are related to a subject's grievance or dispute. Also be aware of any inhibitor that is at risk due to a conflict or the actions of potential targets.

Generally, losses recent in time and related to the subject's grievance have the most potential for prompting violence. Also, pay attention when the subject's own actions result in the shedding of inhibitors. Always keep in mind: Those who have nothing to lose also have nothing to lose by acting out violently. Status of inhibitors should be an important consideration when choosing an intervention. In Chapter 7, we go into detail about the importance of inhibitors.

Consequently, the importance of knowing about the status of the subject's inhibitors, if any, derives from the insight it gives the threat assessor into the subject's current life situation. What does the subject have to lose by acting violently? Are those potential losses sufficient to act as a brake preventing violent behavior? Is the target involved in any activity threatening the subject's inhibitors, thus increasing the potential for violence? Answering these questions allows the threat manager to see the situation from the subject's point of view.

Thus, the threat manager should always inquire into the current state of the subject's inhibitors—or lack thereof.

Has the Subject Exhibited Controlling, Isolating, or Jealous Behaviors Toward the Target?

This is a pattern of conduct that is based on the subject's desire or determination to be in control of a person, an environment, or a situation. It is a common pattern in domestic violence and plays a strong role in bullying behavior in schools and workplaces. It also manifests itself in delusional behavior toward public figures wherein the subject believes that he or she has an interpersonal relationship with the public figure. Through these controlling behaviors, the subject demonstrates a need to dominate others in a particular social environment. When the subject perceives a loss of that control, the behavior can turn to threats or violence.

Consequently, the importance of this need-to-know comes out of understanding how the subject perceives the current situation related to the target, as well as assessing what the subject hopes or plans to happen. What does the subject hope to happen by his or her behaviors, including potential violence?

Thus, the threat manager should always inquire about the subject's perceived relationship with the target and how the subject uses that relationship to control or isolate the target.

Does the Subject Have a History of Abuse of Alcohol, Drugs, or Prescription Medicines?

While it is important to know if the subject is abusing these substances because it affects the subject's control over his or her behavior, the inquiry should also focus on the subject's behavior while under the influence. For example, is the subject happy, sad, angry, or mean when drunk? What are the circumstances that result in the substance abuse? Has the subject been violent while under the influence? Does he or she use the substances for courage or for preparation?

Be particularly aware of multiple substance abuse, such as combining alcohol and drugs, which is a dangerous mix. Also, as discussed in the mental health need-to-know, be concerned about the use of drugs or alcohol in combination with mental illness. As always, determine how the subject acted under similar circumstances in the past.

Consequently, the importance of this need-to-know derives from assessing the subject's behavior and association with mind-altering substances. Is the subject in control of his or her behavior or has the subject surrendered to substance abuse?

Thus, the threat manager should always look for evidence of substance abuse by the subject.

Does the Subject Have Any Relevant Medical Issues?

There are two main areas of inquiry on medical issues: medical issues that affect judgment and control, and medical issues that are, in effect, a loss of an inhibitor.

Medical issues that affect control and judgment typically are brain trauma or disease that results in risky behavior or lack of impulse control. Since the 1980s, scientists have correlated damage due to traumatic brain injury to the prefrontal cortex with psychopathic behavior and the inability to make socially acceptable decisions.

Look for information of a traumatic head injury—usually, vehicle or motorcycle accidents, industrial accidents, or injuries from a fight. Typically, the injury will be followed by distinct behavior and personality changes. While medical records will be difficult or impossible to obtain, this type of information can be found from family members, neighbors, or coworkers.

Prescribed medication (even when used properly) for some medical conditions can also affect judgment and impulse control and can even result in delusions and hallucinations. When there is evidence of potential violence that is affected by a medical condition, it is best to consult with a medical professional to assist in the assessment.

A medical issue can also, in fact, be a loss of an inhibitor. For example, if a subject is terminally ill, he or she may feel free to visit vengeance upon those who have wronged him or her because the subject has nothing to lose. Someone who has a debilitating disease may also take action now, while he or she is physically able.

A medical issue also can be an area of concern when intervention decisions are made. For example, a threatening employee needs medication to control the unpredictable effects of a prior brain injury. The administrative action intervention of termination of employment without allowing for medical benefits for a period of time may not be a wise choice.

Consequently, the importance of this need-to-know comes from determining the current physical state of the subject. Is the subject physically able to carry out an act of violence? Is the subject's current physical state driving him or her toward an act of violence?

Case Illustration: The Cancer

In the early 1990s, doctors and staff at Northwestern Hospital in Chicago successfully treated Bart Ross for cancer of the jaw. Although the treatment beat the cancer, it left Ross physically disfigured and in chronic pain. He sought relief through the courts, suing Northwestern Hospital in a series of lawsuits at the state and federal levels.

The courts consistently rejected Ross's claims by dismissing his various lawsuits. Frustrated, unemployed, and running out of money, Ross determined on a last resort. On the morning of February 28, 2005, after more than a decade of seeking justice against the hospital, Ross broke into the basement of the last judge who had held against him. The judge's husband accidentally discovered Ross, thus forcing Ross to kill the husband and the other occupant of the house, the judge's mother.

Ross then fled the house. He lived in his van for the next 2 weeks, apparently stalking other judges who had presided over his multiple suits. When a policeman pulled him over for having a broken taillight, Ross killed himself.

Ross's chronic pain and facial disfigurement provided him a constant motive for seeking revenge against the judicial system that refused to give him the one thing that obsessed him: justice against the hospital. (*Source:* Calhoun and Weston, *Threat Assessment and Management Strategies,* p. 27)

Thus, the threat manager should always look for evidence of medical conditions that may affect the subject's behavior.

Has the Subject Engaged in Any Final-Act Behaviors?

Final-act behaviors consist of actions that a subject takes that indicate he or she expects to die in the near future. These behaviors are end-game actions usually performed immediately prior to a major act of violence. At times, the actions are personal to the subject, such as burning down his or her house or making it uninhabitable, killing pets, or destroying personal articles. At times, they are symbolic acts, such as preparing a costume or a ritual cleansing. At other times, they are preparatory, such as writing a will, giving away property, or saying good-bye to family. In some cases, the actions are explanatory, such as writing a letter, social media postings, recording a message, or calling the news media. Information that a subject is exhibiting this type of behavior should always be cause for great concern and protective actions.

Again, evidence of such final-act behaviors is persuasive; lack of evidence is neutral. Many subjects expect to survive, even thrive, beyond their intended act of violence. They see no need for final acts. Yet, when the threat manager finds evidence of final-act behaviors, that evidence should be taken very seriously.

Consequently, the importance of this need-to-know derives from the insight it gives the threat assessor as to the subject's current expectations for the future. If the subject acts in such a way as to suggest that he or she does not see any future, then he or she may be preparing to end the target's future as well. In effect, the absence of a future becomes yet another lost inhibitor.

Thus, the threat manager should always look for evidence of the subject engaging in final-act behaviors.

Not All Need-to-Knows Are Created Equal

In theory, if threat management were similar to the disciplines of mathematics, chemistry, or architecture, for any given threat assessment, the threat manager could divide the number of knowns about the situation by the number of unknowns to produce a percentage that measures how informed the assessment is. For example, if 13 of the 20 need-to-knows are known in an assessment, the information quotient could be measured as 65%. If six of the need-to-knows are known, the information quotient for that assessment would be 30%.

As tempting as that procedure is, because it allows easy comparisons of how much is known across different assessments, it fails before the simple fact that, in any given threat assessment, not all of the need-to-knows have the same value. Threat management involves managing human behaviors amidst the uncertainties of life. For example, not knowing if the subject has a weapon is not nearly as valuable as knowing for certain that the subject recently purchased a handgun. Indeed, that fact alone may be enough to warrant assessing the situation as high risk.

Similarly, knowing that the subject chose to approach the target by writing a letter is indicative, but not conclusive, that the subject is acting like a howler. Other need-to-knows, such as a nonintimate threat or confirmation of the subject's inability to act out (because of incarceration or mental health commitment) would need to be determined before a low risk assessment could be made. Conversely, knowing that the subject chose to approach the target by engaging in suspicious behavior while physically near the target would support a high risk assessment because that is behavior clearly associated with potential hunters.

Not knowing the subject's criminal history is not nearly as important as confirming an arrest involving a violent crime under circumstances similar to the situation being assessed—and so, too, with mental health histories. Not knowing the subject's knowledge about the target is not as valuable as knowing for certain that the subject is currently seeking personal information about the target. Knowing that the subject has strong inhibitors suggests a potentially low risk assessment. Conversely, knowing that the subject suffered a recent loss of a vital inhibitor supports a high risk assessment.

The value of each need-to-know related to other need-to-knows in that particular situation, and each need to know's value derives from the situation itself, the answer to the question, and not from some consistent value inherent in the question itself. Trying to determine if a subject recently acquired a weapon is not that important if the subject is known already to own weapons or if the subject recently resigned from the U.S. Army's Special Forces. Knowing that the subject is in a long-term marriage suggests a strong inhibitor, but the value of that knowledge diminishes if the subject turns out to be terminally ill and the target is the hospital that did not save him. Thus, the value of each need-to-know has to be reevaluated within the context of each situation and in relation to what else is known about the situation.

Interestingly, low risk assessments require knowing about more of the need-to-knows than high risk assessments generally require. Emergency situations, which are the highest risk, are self-evident. As hunters approach the breach and attack stages along the path to intended violence, they act in ways clearly identifying themselves as hunters. Howlers, though, are much more difficult to spot, especially because the threat assessor has to distinguish them from hunters. This requires knowing as much as possible about the subject, the subject's relationship to the target, the subject's past behaviors, and the subject's knowledge about the target. In other words, distinguishing howlers from hunters requires gathering information on as many of the need-to-knows as possible.

Case Illustration: The Plane Crash

Beth Johnson knew immediately after the telephone call that her daughter was in a high-risk, emergency situation. The call came from her ex-husband. "I've got her, and you're not going to get her," Eric Johnson told her. In the background, Beth Johnson could hear her daughter saying, "Mommy, come get me, come get me." Beth Johnson immediately filed a missing person report with the Bedford, Indiana, police department, but already she was too late. Eric Johnson, who had recently gotten his pilot's license, flew his rented plane into his ex-mother-in-law's one-story house. His daughter was strapped into the passenger seat. He and his daughter were killed.

> High-risk situations need only a few of the need-to-knows to have confidence in the assessment. (*Source:* Associated Press, "Pilot Crashes Into Ex-In-Law's House," March 6, 2007)

The individual value of each need-to-know also varies depending on the venue in which the situation under assessment occurs. Threats have more value in domestic disputes and workplace violence than they have in public-figure cases. Leakage appears to increase in value in school settings compared to other venues. Abortion providers who engage in controversial or high publicity activities put themselves at greater risk than providers who practice quietly and without fanfare. We discuss in greater detail the unique and common elements among the various venues for violence in Chapter 9.

The value of a need-to-know may dramatically increase in combination with certain other need-to-knows. For example, weapon acquisition, in combination with seeking current information on the target's location, is a volatile combination. These are both hunter behaviors in the preparation stage along the path to violence. Recent loss, in combination with final act behaviors, is another serious combination.

The values of the need-to-knows are situation dependent. They have to be assessed within the context of the situation currently being addressed. Their value changes among different situations and across time. If the initial situation under assessment includes a personal approach by the subject to the target, that fact may decrease in value for later assessments if the subject's behavior indicates a backing away from the initial approach—say, for example, if the subject leaves the state or becomes incapacitated for some reason.

Generally, information indicating that a subject is moving toward a target with intent to do harm, with lethal means at hand, carries the most weight for assessing the situation as a high risk.

Final Thoughts on Gathering Information for Assessment

The timing of when the information is received is an issue of concern. Obviously, the most important thing to know is what the subject is doing now. Past behavior has value for the assessment, particularly behavior under the same or similar circumstances, but the fresher the information is, the better. Also keep in mind that just because you learned today about an alarming behavior that occurred a month ago, it is new information, it is relevant information, but it is not fresh information. There is a tendency to treat new information as fresh information, resulting in an over-reaction.

In addition, an ancient, old-school dinosaur saying among detectives is that "it's not the facts that put an investigation together, it's the glue." The glue is the recognition of the significance of each fact along with the skill, logic, and insight of the investigator that fits and holds the pieces of the investigation together. This is also true for threat assessments. Anybody can compile facts; maybe even a computer can do that. The true skill and art of threat assessment is recognizing the relevance of the information for this case at this moment in time. Doing that provides the glue that transforms pieces of information into a threat assessment.

Summary

In this chapter, we described the 20 factors needed to assess any given situation thoroughly. Some of these need-to-knows inhere in any situation. They can be used to make initial, though not well informed, assessments. The unknown need-to-knows can then be used to guide further fact finding. As each need-to-know becomes known, new and increasingly better informed assessments can be made.

Although it is tempting to use the proportion of knowns compared to the unknowns to gain a numeric value for how informed any assessment is, that should not be done because the individual need-to-knows vary in value depending on the situation and the venue in which the situation occurs. Not every need-to-know is equal to every other need-to-know in every situation.

Notes

1. In their book *Just Two Seconds: Using Time and Space to Defeat Assassins,* Gavin de Becker, Tom Taylor, and Jeff Marquart (Studio City, CA: The Gavin de Becker Center for the Study and Reduction of Violence, 2008) argue that trained physical protectors can disrupt an attack once the attacker has launched the assault. Although they make an excellent argument, only a fool would wait until the last moment to quell an assault if proper threat management could avoid it, including informed assessments.
2. de Becker, G. (1997). *The gift of fear: Survival signals that protect us from violence* (New York, NY: Little, Brown, and Company), 42–53.
3. For examples of this phenomenon, see Calhoun, F. S., & Weston, S. W. (2003). *Contemporary threat management: A practical guide for identifying, assessing, and managing individuals of violent intent* (pp. 75–76, 142–143). San Diego, CA: Specialized Training Services.
4. ASIS/SHRM. (2011). Workplace violence prevention and intervention: An American national standard. Alexandria, VA: ASIS, p. 3.
5. Meloy, J. R. (2000). *Violence risk and threat assessment: A practical guide for mental health and criminal justice professionals* (pp. 13–14). San Diego, CA: Specialized Training Services.

6. Scalora, M. J., Zimmerman, W. J., & Welles, D. G. (2008). Use of threat assessment for the protection of the United States Congress. In J. R. Meloy, L. Sheridan, & J. Hoffman (Eds.), *Stalking, threatening, and attacking public figures: A psychological and behavioral analysis* (pp. 425–434). New York, NY: Oxford University Press.

7. Turner, J. T., & Gelles, M. (2003). *Threat assessment: A risk management approach* (pp. 41–47). New York, NY: Haworth Press.

8. Cawood, J. S., & Corcoran, M. H. (2009). *Violence assessment and intervention: The practitioners' handbook* (pp. 112–124). Boca Raton, FL: CRC Press.

9. Calhoun, F. S., & Weston, S. W. (2001). *Defusing the risk to judicial officials: The contemporary threat management process* (pp. 113–146). Alexandria, VA: National Sheriff's Association; Calhoun, F. S., & Weston, S. W. (2003). *Contemporary threat management: A practical guide for identifying, assessing, and managing individuals of violent intent* (pp. 113–144). San Diego, CA: Specialized Training Services; Calhoun, F. S., & Weston, S. W. (2009). *Threat assessment and management strategies: Identifying the howlers and the hunters* (pp. 21–104). Boca Raton, FL: CRC Press.

10. See, for example, White, S. G., & Meloy, J. R. (2008). *Workplace violence threat assessment: Case studies using the WAVR-21*. Presentation at the Association of Threat Assessment Professionals' Threat Management Conference, August 21, 2008.

11. Calhoun, F. S., & Weston, S. W. (2003). *Contemporary threat management: A practical guide for identifying, assessing, and managing individuals of violent intent* (pp. 136–137). San Diego, CA: Specialized Training Services.

12. As an example of potential leakage, Anders Breivik, who killed over 70 people in Norway on July 22, 2011, maintained a 1,500-page diary on the Internet. See Englund, W. (2011, July 11). Diary reveals suspect's preparations, ideology. *Washington Post.*

13. Calhoun, F. S., & Weston, S. W. (2009). *Threat assessment and management strategies: Identifying the howlers and the hunters* (pp. 31–36). Boca Raton, FL: CRC Press.

14. Flaccus, G. (2010, July 7). Nicholas Smit to be charged for Hemet police booby traps. *Huffington Post LA.*

Case Study
Knowing What
You Need

6

Memo to: Chief Executive Officer
From: Security Assessment Branch
Subject: Threat Assessment of Mitch Randall

The Facts

On August 17, a law enforcement officer (LEO) on the Louisiana Joint Terrorism Task Force contacted this office. The LEO reported that on August 16, a Texas correctional officer, who works part-time at a Louisiana bar, reported inappropriate comments directed at this company by a regular patron.

The bartender overheard a subject who identified himself as Mitch Randall tell another customer that Randall's wife and mother died on the same day 2 weeks earlier. Randall spoke at length about how this company caused his wife's death because the company had fired Randall 2 years ago, thus causing him to lose his family health insurance. Randall stated that he intended to get revenge on this company. The bartender stated that Randall had arrived and left driving a 10-year-old pickup truck.

Randall's company personnel file reveals that he worked for the company for 10 years and was terminated in October last year. The cause of the termination was erratic behavior, coming to work intoxicated, with three refusals to obtain a fitness for duty evaluation from a medical professional. The file notes that Randall's former supervisor swore out an arrest warrant in November of that year against Randall for threatening and harassing phone calls to the supervisor at work. The warrant is for a misdemeanor charge. The supervisor still works for the company.

Randall's last known address is across the state line in Texas, approximately 90 miles from the company headquarters. Texas law enforcement does not extradite for misdemeanor charges.

The Assessment

Attachment A summarizes the critical information known about Mitch Randall at this time. Based on what is currently known about Randall's behavior related to the company, the Security Assessment Branch assesses Randall as posing a potential risk of violence toward the company and toward his former supervisor at this time. Not only is Randall a disgruntled former employee who was terminated, but he also blames the recent death of his wife on that termination and the subsequent loss of his family health insurance. Randall is familiar with the physical layout of the company and with the company routines. He has a history of previous threats and still has a warrant out for his arrest in Louisiana. His behavior indicates anger over the loss of his wife and mother. He also continues to abuse alcohol. He has the means to travel; however, he has chosen not to approach the company thus far, as far as we know.

Recommended Protective Response

Security Assessment Branch recommends maintaining increased physical security around the company until more information can be obtained and assessed. Randall's employee badge photograph and vehicle description should be distributed to security officers. His former colleagues should be instructed to report to Security immediately if they see him near the company. A personal security briefing should be given to his former supervisor.

Plans should be developed to have Randall arrested for trespassing if he enters company property. The misdemeanor warrant could possibly be served at the same time, if he does show up.

This information should be passed on to the company's regular law enforcement contacts.

Recommended Fact Finding

As Attachment A indicates, several of the "need-to-know questions" remain unanswered. Corporate security should try to obtain the answers. Security should do an in-depth interview with the bartender to determine the exact words used by Randall and the context of the conversation. Security should attempt to have the bartender continue to pass on information if Randall continues to frequent the bar. If possible, the person to whom Randall made the threat should be identified and a decision made whether or not to interview that individual, depending on the individual's relationship to Randall.

Recommended Threat Management Strategy

Corporate security should arrange to interview Randall when sufficient information has been gathered and assessed. The interview should start out as a fact-finding approach in order to gain insight into Randall's feelings and what he actually meant by the threat. If appropriate, during the interview, he should be warned of the consequences to him personally if he should approach the company or his former supervisor. The company should arrange with local law enforcement to arrest him for trespassing if he attempts to get on company property. It might also be possible to serve the outstanding misdemeanor warrant on him the next time he visits the bar where he made the statements. The company should also contact the bartender in order to open direct communications with him should Randall continue frequenting the bar.

Local law enforcement contact in the jurisdiction of the company premises should be made aware of the outstanding warrant. Agreements should be made to use this criminal justice intervention in the event that Randall approaches company assets.

Attachment A: Known Risk Factors About Mitch Randall

Need-to-Know Questions	What Is Known About Randall
1. How did the subject choose to approach the target?	Randall leaked his intentions to harm the company by talking to someone at a bar and was overheard. At this time, he does not know that we know of the threat. He has chosen not to approach the company thus far.
2. What about the situation indicates the subject's identity and physical proximity to the target? In other words, who and where is the subject?	Unknown
3. What about the situation indicates whom or what the subject is targeting? In other words, who is the target?	Randall expressly stated an intent to get "revenge" on the company for his wife's death.
4. What about the situation indicates the type of venue being targeted and what about the venue gives insight into the subject's intent, motive, and ability?	Randall is a disgruntled former employee of the company who has expressed an intent to harm the company because of his termination.
5. What about the situation indicates whether or not the intimacy effect is in play? In other words, what is the nature of the relationship between the subject and the target?	Randall is familiar with the company and his former supervisor, who continues to work here.
6. What about the situation relates to the subject's choice of context, content, and circumstances?	Randall openly expressed his intention in a public place while drinking. The timing of his behavior is related to the deaths of his wife and mother.
7. Is the target currently accessible to the subject?	Company security has been increased, but the company is accessible to Randall.

8. Does the subject have the ability and motivation to take advantage of any current accessibility to the target?	Randall has the ability and motivation to approach the company, although so far he appears not to have done so, as far as we know.
9. Is there a known history of previous contacts with the target or other targets by this subject?	Randall threatened his former supervisor a month after he was terminated.
10. Does the subject have a history of violent or threatening behaviors, including any criminal behavior?	Randall threatened his former supervisor a month after he was terminated; however, he did not carry out any violence.
11. What is the subject's knowledge about the target's current situation?	Randall has in-depth familiarity with the layout of the company.
12. Is the subject seeking knowledge about the target and the target's current situation?	Unknown.
13. Does the subject's behavior indicate mental health issues, including suicidality?	Potential despondency based on the recent deaths of his wife and mother on the same day.
14. Does the subject possess, have access to, or give evidence of a fascination with weapons?	Unknown.
15. Is the subject currently seeking to obtain a weapon?	Unknown.
16. What is the status of the subject's inhibitors, including any recent losses?	Randall lost his job 2 years ago and his wife and mother 2 weeks ago. He is currently unemployed.
17. Has the subject exhibited controlling, isolating, or jealous behaviors toward the target?	Unknown.
18. Does the subject have a history of abuse of alcohol, drugs, or prescription medicines?	Part of the reason for Randall's termination was coming to work intoxicated. He continues to drink.
19. Does the subject have any relevant medical issues?	Unknown.
20. Has the subject engaged in any final act behaviors?	Unknown.

The Denouement

On August 18, two corporate security supervisors interviewed the bartender and confirmed Randall's threatening statement. The bartender did not know who the other patron was and had not seen him since that evening. The bartender agreed to contact one of the supervisors should Randall continue to frequent the bar or make threatening statements again.

On August 21, the two supervisors went to Randall's house to interview him. Initially, Randall refused to open his front door, but after the supervisors spoke to him through the closed door for 30 minutes, he agreed to let them inside the apartment. The supervisors reported that the apartment was unkempt, with trash and empty beer cans littering the living room. Randall himself appeared unwashed and unshaved. He also smelled of alcohol.

During the interview, Randall at first denied making any threats toward the company. After finally admitting to the statements, he claimed that he made them after drinking too much and feeling sorry for himself over the loss of his wife and mother. He claimed that he had no intention of taking any action against the company or his former supervisor. He denied owning any weapons, but would not allow the supervisors to search his apartment. According to the supervisors, Randall's demeanor was passive and subdued. They assessed his denial of intending any harm as credible.

The supervisors contacted local law enforcement, informed the police of Randall's comments, and asked them to keep a liaison with Louisiana law enforcement to report any relevant behavior by Randall.

Based on the results of the interview, the Security Assessment Branch revised its threat assessment to low risk. Enhanced security measures were returned to normal.

In September, Texas law enforcement passed on a report that Randall was under investigation for an arson at his residence that destroyed the building. They suspected some type of improvised explosive, but were waiting for lab results. They believed that he was now living in his vehicle somewhere along the Texas–Louisiana border. The bartender was contacted. He stated that another bar patron told him that he had seen Randall and he looked "real bad." He looked like he was on methamphetamine.

On September 14, the former supervisor reported that he had received a telephone message from someone who he thought might have been Randall. The phone message was rambling and ended with the statement, "See you soon."

Reassessment

Due to the potential for possession of explosives, the loss of a critical inhibitor (his home), Randall's apparent physical deterioration, and his physical movement toward the company by living along the state border, the Security Assessment Branch reassessed Randall as a high risk of violence toward the company and the former supervisor.

Protective Response

Enhanced security was reinstated and emergency planning was begun with local law enforcement. An all-out effort with Texas and Louisiana law enforcement was started to locate Randall. Protection was provided for the former supervisor pending further developments.

Louisiana law enforcement found Randall living in his car. Officers arrested him on September 28 for the old warrant. The search incident to his arrest discovered explosives linking him to the arson. The interview after the arrest confirmed his intention to mount an attack on the company. Randall was having trouble getting all the equipment he needed and was stalled by his drug and alcohol addiction and lack of money. At the time of his arrest, his plan was devolving from explosives to a Molotov cocktail. Randall also stated that he intended to set fire to the company building as soon as he got out of jail.

Randall could not afford to make bail. Company attorneys presented all the information that company security had compiled to the district attorneys' offices handling the arson prosecution in Texas and Louisiana. Prosecutors charged him with the arson, possession of improvised explosives, and the prior threat. Six months later, prosecutors gained a conviction for these crimes. The judge sentenced Randall to 5 years in the state penitentiary. He is currently serving that sentence.

Company security arranged with prison authorities to alert the company of any change in Randall's status.

Lessons Learned

1. Assessments evolve based on the information available at any given time. Although the initial assessment, based on what was known at that time, rated Randall as a high risk of violence, information gained during the interview with him revised that assessment to low risk. New information and changes in Randall's life changed the situation back to high risk. Threat assessors need to reassess situations continuously, based on what is known.

2. Enough information was known based on the bartender's report and Randall's personnel file to support an initial assessment. This assessment supported the protective action taken and resources allocated for fact finding.

3. As Randall's inhibitors toppled, he continued to focus blame on the company and his former supervisor for his troubles. Especially in the workplace venue, threateners can carry a grudge for years. That requires security to monitor and reassess the situation as new developments or life changes occur.

4. Threat managers also need to switch threat management strategies and employ multiple strategies as the situation changes. The

initial strategy of interviewing Randall worked at first, but once his inhibitors fell, the situation became critical.

5. Simply because one has the warrant or other reason to have the subject arrested does not mean that arrest is the best tactical move at that time. The subject can make bail or plead the charges down. Consideration should be given to waiting on the arrest until it is the best move to lower the risk or gain a tactical advantage.

6. Major factors in the success of this case were a preexisting relationship with law enforcement and not holding back any information that would be useful to both law enforcement and prosecution authorities.

7. The protective response included contingency planning and taking measures to ensure that information on Randall's conduct continued to flow to the threat assessment team.

8. The team did not become married to the interventions implemented. Threat managers must be willing to change tactics when necessary, always remembering that they do not control everything. Life will intrude on the best plans: In this case, people died, houses burned, addictions affected behavior, and grievances festered. All of these critical factors are not in the control of the threat manager. The key is in knowing what he or she needs to know for each situation and taking measures to know if these things are happening.

Inhibitors and Their Impacts

7

Inhibitors consist of those influences in an individual's life or life situation that exert a positive influence on the individual's behavior or that encourage or control the individual to maintain good behavior. For most people, inhibitors consist of interpersonal attachments to other people, family relations, good employment, financial stability, home, religious beliefs, self-esteem, and a strong sense of self-worth or dignity. Inhibitors encourage appropriate behavior or discourage bad behavior. Individuals fear losing their inhibitors, so they tend to act in ways that do not put their inhibitors at risk. In effect, inhibitors comprise anything the individual values or treasures.[1]

Inhibitors usually consist of relationships, assets, or benefits that the individual feels loath to lose. Thus, they act as a brake on the individual's behavior. People with strong inhibitors in place are far less likely to engage in impulsive or illegal activities because doing so puts the inhibitors at risk. Inhibitors can be anything in a particular individual's life that he or she does not want to give up or sacrifice. In that respect, inhibitors can be uniquely tied to an individual's personal quirks or idiosyncrasies. What seems unimportant to most people may, in fact, assume enormous importance to one person. Consequently, in determining a subject's inhibitors, the threat management team should approach the question with a broad-minded attitude and not just assume that what is important to the vast majority of people must, *ipso facto*, hold the same importance to the subject under assessment.

Inhibitors exist at some level in all our lives. Anyone who has raised an adolescent child or grandchild knows that a powerful influence can be maintained over the child's behavior by controlling his or her ability to use a cell phone for calls or texting or a computer for social networking. A law enforcement officer knows that an off-duty bar fight will result in employment discipline or termination; therefore, he is more likely to walk away from a perceived insult. In both these situations, the inhibitors control the individual's behavior because the individual perceives the cost of losing the inhibitor as too high or the potential loss as too much to bear. Inhibitors encourage individuals to follow the rules of behavior, whatever those rules may be.

Consequently, for the threat manager assessing a subject, identifying and exploring the status of the subject's inhibitors offers tremendous insight into the state of the positive influences operating on the subject. Identifying a stable set of inhibitors strongly suggests that the subject poses a lower risk of acting violently or inappropriately toward the target. Conversely, subjects with weak inhibitors—or, worse, inhibitors that are toppling due to the grievance or dispute—indicate a potential for a higher risk of acting violently or inappropriately toward the target. The assessors should also pay close attention to any recent loss of a key inhibitor, such as the death of a loved one; employment termination, including expulsion or suspension from school; relationship breakup; home foreclosure; or loss of self-esteem or dignity. Combined with the other need-to-knows, and seen in context with those other need-to-knows, inhibitors provide an excellent barometer for assessing the subject's potential risk.

A recent loss of something valued appears to precede many acts of intended violence. In our last book, we termed this the "last straw syndrome."[2] We defined it as a penultimate event that pushes the subject toward an act of violence, almost as though the loss of that last inhibitor released the subject to act out. Usually, a last straw is the loss of something the subject holds dear—but that something is highly personal to the subject. Thus, the loss may be the death of a loved one, or the loss of a job, or a foreclosure on a home, or the denial of child visitation. But the loss may also be a perceived disgrace or insult. Due to mental illnesses, the loss could also be something irrational, but nonetheless greatly important to the subject.

Case Illustration: "A Real Stand-Up Guy"

The *Huffington Post* quoted someone who knew Andre Turner as saying that Turner "seemed like a real stand-up guy." Robert Young, who lived across the street from Turner, told the online news service that "everything looked completely normal over here." Young continued, "I never had an inkling he'd do something like that. But who knows what happens in somebody's mind? People say, 'He lived in that nice house, in a nice neighborhood, what could be wrong?'"

Several things went wrong. Turner bought his nice 5,000 square-foot, five-bedroom house in a nice neighborhood not too far from the Hidden Valley Golf Club in 2004, at the height of the housing boom. He paid $711,000 for it new. In 2008, Citibank sued Turner over his credit card debt, obtaining a judgment against him for more than $5,000. In 2009, a similar amount went to Cavalry Portfolio Services, a debt collection agency. By the end of 2011, the Riverside County assessor's office valued Turner's nice house in the nice neighborhood at $543,000. Turner put it up for sale in November 2011 for $590,000—over $120,000 less than he had paid for it. The bank began foreclosure proceedings.

In the fall of 2011, Turner received a reprimand from his employer, Southern California Edison, for missing an audit deadline. On Friday, December 16, Turner spent the day working. Toward the end of the day, he took his pistol and went hunting for managers. Coworkers later reported that "he did not like management." Turner killed two supervisors and wounded two others and then killed himself. In between the shootings of the four managers, Turner "calmly walked past several coworkers and had brief and calm conversations with them," according to a statement posted by Lt. Holly Francisco of the Los Angeles Sheriff's Office.

Turner's world had crumbled and his inhibitors were rapidly falling. In effect, he could no longer stand up to his problems. (*Sources:* Andrew Dalton, "Andre Turner, So Cal Edison Shooter, Seemed 'Like a Real Stand-Up Guy,'" *Huffington Post,* December 18, 2011; Robert Jablon, "Andre Turner, So Cal Edison Shooter, Received a Verbal Reprimand Before the Shooting," *Huffington Post,* December 20, 2011; "Pictured: Boss Killed by Office Worker Who Went on Deadly Shooting Rampage Because He 'Did Not Like Management,'" *Daily Mail Reporter,* December 18, 2011)

We feel that inhibitors are so powerful that, among all the need-to-knows, they warrant their own chapter. We will discuss the following here:

- The power of inhibitors
- The tendency of inhibitors to topple like dominoes, with one inhibitor knocking over the next in a sequence of decline—frequently, rapid decline
- How the threat manager can use inhibitors to exert a positive influence on a subject
- What to do when the target or the organization associated with the target strips a subject of his or her inhibitors
- Strategies for propping up a subject's inhibitors

Inhibitors and their absence act as a scale balancing an individual's positive and negative behaviors. When an individual has inhibitors, the scale tilts toward appropriate behavior. But the lack or loss of inhibitors can tip the scales toward negative or inappropriate behavior. Consequently, any threat assessment must include a sensitive determination of those influences that the subject deems important to him or her and then assess the current status of those treasures.

Case Illustration: The Avenging Beer Thief

For years, Omar Thornton believed himself the victim of racial taunts by coworkers and management at the Hartford Distributors Corporation in Manchester, Connecticut, where he worked as a beer truck deliveryman.

According to his girlfriend and his best friend, Thornton truly believed himself a victim of racism.

In the summer of 2010, Hartford Distributors hired a private detective to find out if Thornton had been pilfering beer from his truck. The detective videotaped Thornton handing over beer to his best friend's girlfriend. Management scheduled a disciplinary meeting for the morning of August 3. When Thornton left for work that morning, Kristi Hannah, his girlfriend, reported, "He gave me a weird hug. It was really long. And a kiss and said good-bye. He looked at me hard and told me he loved me."

At the disciplinary meeting, management gave Thornton a choice between resigning or termination. He chose to resign and then excused himself to get his lunch pail from his truck. He had two handguns hidden in the pail. Returning to the warehouse, Thornton began methodically shooting coworkers. According to Hannah, the eight people that Thornton killed that morning had all been among his perceived tormentors. "Every one of [the victims] was a person I heard Omar mention," Hannah told a news reporter. "He didn't go around randomly shooting people. He knew these were the people who harassed him."

After killing the eight coworkers, Thornton called his mother to tell her he loved her. He then called 911. When the police dispatcher answered, Thornton calmly said, "This is Omar Thornton, the shooter in Manchester." He promised the state trooper that he was done killing coworkers and then went on to justify his murders as revenge for the racism that he believed permeated the company. "Uh, you probably want to know the reason why I shot this place up," Thornton said to the trooper. "This place here is a racist place." Later during the 4-minute call, Thornton complained, "Treat me bad. I'm the only black driver they got here. Treat me bad all the time."

Before first responders could get to him, Thornton killed himself. His forced resignation proved the last straw for all the torment that Thornton believed he had suffered at the hands of management and coworkers.

The teamsters union that represented Thornton later reported that it had never received any complaints of racism from Thornton. Perhaps Thornton felt avenging racism a better motive for the shootings than resigning over a few pilfered six packs. (*Sources:* Matthew Lysiak and Corky Siemaszko, "Kristi Hannah, Girlfriend of Omar Thornton, Recalls Gunman's Goodbye, Racism Concerns," *New York Daily News,* August 4, 2010; Ray Rivera, "In 911 Call, Killer of 8 Spoke of Wanting to Kill More," *New York Times,* August 5, 2010; Matthew Lysiak and Leo Standora, "Rampage Murderer Omar Thornton Caught on Video Giving Friend Beer," *New York Daily News,* August 7, 2010)

The Power of Inhibitors

Inhibitors can exert a powerful influence on the individual favoring them. Individuals with a steady job, money in the bank, reasonable mortgage on the house, a spouse and children, and a good reputation in the community tend to be upstanding citizens very unlikely to engage in illegal or inappropriate behaviors.[3] As a result, they are the type of individual least likely to come to the attention of a threat manager. Thus, the power of inhibitors runs both ways: Their presence leads to avoiding problematic behavior; their absence contributes to such behavior.

When evaluating inhibitors, look for quality, not just quantity. A home, family, and career may at first look like a stable set of inhibitors. Further fact finding, however, may uncover domestic violence, pending layoffs, or a house in foreclosure. No one suspected the turmoil that Andre Turner was going through.

Case Illustration: The Breakup Rampage

At 8:00 p.m. on March 25, 2006, Aaron Dunn stepped out onto Laguna Boulevard in Davis, California, and began firing his 12-gauge shotgun at anyone who happened to be nearby. Dunn knew none of his victims and held no grudge toward any of them. He had recently split from his wife, a loss of an inhibitor serious enough to turn him to violence. He compounded that loss by taking methamphetamines, which further loosened any controls over his behavior. By the time that police incapacitated him, Dunn had killed two men and wounded seven others.

The loss of inhibitors, compounded by the uninhibiting effects of drugs, can lead to fatal results. (*Source:* Associated Press, "Alleged Gunman in California Spree Charged," April 4, 2006)

Inhibitors act like rudders. They keep the individual steady and on course. Losing them sets the person adrift in unfamiliar, even frightening waters. Although we cited examples of different types of inhibitors earlier, in fact no standard list of inhibitors exists for all potential subjects. Different subjects can have their own peculiar or individualized set of positive influences or things they treasure. Clues from their past behavior may help to identify what those influences may be in a particular case.

What does the subject hold onto over time? What does he struggle to keep? The threat manager should keep that very much in mind, for identifying what the subject values improves the threat manager's ability to evaluate the potential for violence and possibly manage the subject away from potential risk. Not only can the unique inhibitors be exploited positively, but identifying them also allows the threat manager to avoid any steps that might inadvertently damage or destroy the inhibitor.

Identifying inhibitors unique to a specific subject requires keeping an open mind and an active imagination. This is the time for a good threat manager to exercise a great amount of empathy. The question is not what we think is valuable, important, or, in extreme situations, worth killing or dying to keep. Rather, the question is what does this subject, at this time, consider potentially worth killing or dying for?

Subjects suffering from some mental illness or delusion may value something rational people would not think about or recognize. Obsessive subjects may become emotionally invested in something that most people would not waste time or energy worrying about. What is important to one person may be inconsequential to someone else or even to most people. The rule here is to avoid the "any reasonable person test" and, instead, to ascertain through the subject's behaviors what this subject at this time considers important or valuable.

Case Illustration: The Importance of Tattoos

As indicated by his final actions, Steven Kazmierczak valued his girlfriend, Jessica Baty, enough to mail her his most treasured possessions. Prior to killing five students and wounding 15 more at a Northern Illinois University science class on Valentine's Day, 2008, Kazmierczak mailed Baty a package containing two textbooks, his cell phone, and a note stating, in part, "'You've done so much for me. You will make an excellent psychologist and social worker someday." She received another package from him containing a gun holster and ammunition. He called her on the day of the shooting and asked her not to forget him. Then he went on his rampage.

In the months leading up to the shooting spree, Kazmierczak began covering his arms with tattoos. The images that he had inked into his flesh included a skull pierced by a knife, a pentagram, and the image of a macabre character from the "Saw" horror movies. A few weeks before the rampage, Kazmierczak abruptly stopped taking Prozac, which psychologists later speculated may have prompted the shooting because abruptly ending taking the tranquilizer can exacerbate the underlying mental illness.

According to one report, immediately prior to going into the lecture hall, the former graduate student at the school (he had transferred to the University of Illinois at Champaign several months before) listened to Marilyn Manson's "The Last Day on Earth" while sitting in his white Honda Civic. When the song ended, he walked into the lecture hall wearing a black T-shirt emblazoned with an image of a red AK-47 assault rifle and the word "Terrorist." He used to joke about wearing the T-shirt to an airport. Kazmierczak clearly valued these images and his fixation on violence.

What becomes important to a particular subject can be unique and specific to that subject. (*Sources:* Associated Press, "Victims of Campus Shooting Mourned," February 18, 2008; Marilyn Elias, "Before Tragedy Struck at NIU, Signs Were There," *USA Today,* February 19, 2008; Steve Schmadeke, "NIU Killer Tried Suicide 4 Times, Magazine Says," *Chicago Tribune,* July 9, 2008)

Inhibitors, too, come in all shapes and sizes. They are the things in an individual's life that the individual treasures. Hence, they can be intensely personal and unique to the individual. Kazmierczak valued two particular textbooks enough that, as a final-act behavior, he mailed them to his girlfriend. He also found some level of comfort in tattoos depicting violent themes. His abrupt halt to taking Prozac lifted the one inhibitor controlling his mental illness. Inhibitors are whatever exerts some control on the individual's behavior, including whatever the individual values and tries not to lose—not what society or reasonable individuals consider valuable.

A subject's inhibitors need not make sense to any rational person or reasonable determination. What matters is how the subject perceives his or her inhibitors. Individuals suffering some mental illness often focus on delusions or fantasies that become highly personal to them and may not make sense to anyone else. Even individuals who do not suffer a mental illness may latch onto something—tangible or not—that no one else would think would act as an inhibitor. As a result, the threat management team needs to consciously examine what the subject views as an inhibitor in his or her life, rather than what normal inhibitors occupy the subject's life.

Clearly, the most important inhibitor is the subject's sense of dignity or self-worth. Individuals who perceive themselves as treated with the respect they deserve feel good about themselves and good about the world. Even as other inhibitors disappear, a subject's sense of dignity can frequently keep the subject from acting rashly or inappropriately. Conversely, subjects frequently resort to violence to protect their perceived dignity or self-worth. If someone feels insulted, he or she may conclude that violence is the only recourse to alleviate the insult. Omar Thornton tried to retain his dignity by justifying his killings as avenging racism, thus avoiding the shameful end of being fired for petty theft—better to be a noble champion than an ignoble thief.

Case Illustration: The Price of Disrespecting the Mob

In January 2003, New York City police charged Joel Cacace, presumed to be the acting boss of the Columbo crime family, with ordering four killings, including the 1987 mistaken assassination of George Aronwald, an administrative law judge. According to the police, Cacace ordered his hit men to kill former prosecutor William Aronwald, the judge's son.

According to the police informant, Cacace accused the son of "disrespecting" organized crime. The hit men mistook the judge for the son and mistakenly shot him to death at a laundry in Queens. (*Source:* Associated Press, "Reputed N.Y. Boss, 12 Others Charged," January 22, 2003)

This simple fact—that a subject's sense of dignity and respect acts as the single most important inhibitor—offers a profound lesson for how the threat manager should handle the subject. Taking care to treat the subject respectfully and overtly protecting the subject's dignity is an effective strategy for managing the subject away from potential violence. Thus, for example, during a job termination meeting, simply ensuring that the fired employee receives respect and courtesy helps take the sting out of the procedure. Most individuals find it difficult to maintain anger at someone who is treating them with dignity and deference.

Case Illustration: Not Liking How Other Men Treated Him

Although store employees thought Bernard Allen was acting strangely, they nonetheless did not hesitate to sell him an 8-inch knife for $41.60. As Allen left the Mesa, Arizona, store in April 2008, he took the knife out of its package and slipped it into his clothes. Allen walked into the adjoining shopping mall and went to the restroom nearest the food court. As he entered the men's room, Issaruh Jackson accidentally bumped into him. When Jackson turned his back to Allen, Allen stabbed him in the back. As he plunged the knife in, witnesses heard Allen state, "You disrespected me." The wound proved fatal.

Allen's history of mental illness no doubt compounded the situation. When police arrested him, he told the officers that he suffered from schizophrenia. He confessed to having stabbed another individual in the neck the day before, this time using a pocket knife. Allen told police that "he simply didn't like the way other men treated him." (*Source:* Associated Press, "Man Fatally Stabbed in Ariz. Mall," April 2, 2008)

In some cases, there is a connection or symbiotic relationship between an inhibitor and the subject's grievance on the path to intended violence. The subject's job, relationships, or business is each an inhibitor until each is lost. The loss of the inhibitor then evolves into a grievance against the former supervisor, the wife, or the bank that canceled the business line of credit. Abner Thornton, who apparently did not like managers under any circumstances, faced the loss of his home and his credit rating, and then received a reprimand from those hated managers. At that point, he determined to take everything out on them. In other cases, such losses may even turn into a grievance against society in general without a specific target. Instead, the subject may lash out at everyone or anyone, or at least anyone who comes in range of the subject's wrath.

Interpersonal disputes frequently affect inhibitors and can evolve into grievances. The dispute itself becomes larger and more important to the subject than whatever issue started the controversy. We hypothesize that with some subjects it comes down to winning (or at least not losing or appearing to lose) the dispute. To the subject, it is more than a disagreement; it is a battle between right and wrong, good and evil, life and death. This is a recognizable pattern in interpersonal violence, workplace violence, and litigious disputes.

Case Illustration: Shooting at Seal Beach

Scott Dekraai worked on the water in Seal Beach, California. Friendly and outgoing, he was popular among residents and visitors. But that personality did not extend to his marriage. After a whirlwind courtship, Dekraai married Michele Fournier in 2003 in Nevada. According to one of her friends, Fournier claimed that Dekraai held a gun to her head shortly after their wedding.

The abuse continued. "He threatened her innumerable times, innumerable times," said a friend of Fournier's, "This was not a one-time thing." According to court papers filed in their divorce and child custody cases, Dekraai was described as mentally unstable and suffering from bipolar disorder. He had threatened to kill himself or someone else. As to seeking custody of their son, Fournier complained that Dekraai was "almost manic when it comes to demanding absolute right to control our son and make unilateral decisions." That mania continued for over 4 years, from the time they filed for divorce in early 2007 until October 12, 2011.

Dekraai and Fournier divorced in early 2007. That same year, Dekraai suffered debilitating leg injuries in a boating accident that also killed one of his mates. A doctor later diagnosed him with posttraumatic stress disorder because of the accident. His injuries left him with a severe limp and chronic pain—pain so bad that Dekraai expressed the wish that his legs had been amputated. He later married the caregiver whom his employer had hired for him because he could not drive. Unfortunately, that new inhibitor did little to offset Dekraai's obsession with gaining sole custody of his son.

Dekraai and Fournier began arguing over who should have custody of their 8-year-old son. Dekraai's "violence started to escalate, escalate, escalate and she was scared to death of him," a neighbor told news reporters. In September 2011, Dekraai went to the upscale hair salon where Fournier worked and threatened her with physical harm. Fournier told a friend that she feared that Dekraai would one day kill her. On October 11, the former couple had yet another court hearing to determine custody of their son. The judge ruled against giving Dekraai sole custody. Dekraai demanded a full-scale trial to resolve the issue.

The next day, Dekraai called Fournier at her work. They got into another stormy argument. After hanging up, Dekraai donned a bullet-proof vest and armed himself with three firearms. He then drove to the beach and went to the nearby hair salon.

Once inside, Dekraai allegedly began firing and killed Fournier and six others inside the salon and then killed a man seated in a parked car outside the salon. Dekraai later told police that he thought the man was an undercover policeman reaching for a weapon. Police arrested Dekraai in his car a block away from the salon.

Police described the rampage as the worst mass killing in Orange County's history. (*Sources:* Paul Bentley, *Mail Online,* October 16, 2011; Adam S. Levy, "Who Is Scott Dekraai? A Closer Look at the Hair Salon Killer," *Radar Online,* October 13, 2011; Amy Taxin, Thomas Watkins, Brian Melley, Anthony McCartney, and Noaki Schwartz, *HuffPost Social News,* Nancy Wride & Paige Austin, "Jekyll and Hyde Profiles of Suspected Salon Killer," *Belmont Shore Naples Patch,* October 12, 2011; Laura Matthews, "Ex-Wife's Attorney Saw No Indication Scott Dekraai Was Violent," *International Business Times,* October 13, 2011; Amy Taxin, "Scott Dekraai, Ex-Argued Before Salon Shootings," *San Francisco Chronicle,* November 3, 2011; Nicole Santa Cruz, Tony Barboza, and Joel Rubin, "Suspect a Haunted Man: A Bitter Custody Fight and His Involvement in a Fatal Accident at Sea Weighed on Scott Dekraai, Many Say," *Los Angeles Times,* October 14, 2011; "Seal Beach Shooting: Victim Predicted Ex-Husband Would Kill Her," *Los Angeles Times,* October 13, 2011; "Seal Beach Shooting: Suspect Had Been Ordered Not to Carry Guns," *Los Angeles Times,* October 13, 2011.)

In intimate violence cases, the subject's remarriage is typically a positive sign that the subject has moved on with his or her life. However, in the Seal Beach case, Dekraa did not want his ex-wife back. Instead, he wanted control over their son or, just as importantly, he did not want her to have any control. This is an example of that need-to-know factor regarding a history of controlling behavior. Notice that Dekraa litigated the issue for years to prevent the ex-wife from having even minimal custody rights because he wanted the control or, to describe it more as he probably saw it, he wanted her to have no control or custody rights. The battle was now on and he had to win or, at the very least, feel that he did not lose to her. He saw the court decision denying him sole custody as a loss too much to bear. The new wife was not enough of an inhibitor. Even the welfare of the son did not stop him. He simply could not lose to the ex-wife.

The Domino Effect

Inhibitors are best visualized as dominoes standing front to back in a row. As long as each remains standing, each inhibitor reinforces the others and helps control the subject's behaviors. But when one key domino topples, it can risk tipping its neighbor over, which, in turn, risks toppling all of the dominoes. Subjects falling in a downward spiral often begin losing everything important to them. They lose their employment, their homes, their family, their health, their hold on reality. As these inhibitors fall, the controls preventing the subject from acting out violently tumble as well. Indeed, the very loss of the inhibitors acts as a strong motivation for retaliating violently.

Think about people you have known who have fallen on difficult times. It could start with a marriage breakup, drug dependency, or the loss of a job. When one key inhibitor falls, such as a marriage, it typically affects others such as finances, home, and mental health. We have all seen the downward spiral in a person's life when the inhibitors start to fall. As tragic as the spiral itself is, it risks breeding more tragedies as the individual decides to take others down with him or her.

Inhibitors exert a profoundly positive influence on individuals. Losing one's inhibitors exerts an equally profound negative influence. An individual's inhibitors do not just disappear on their own. We all know that life's randomness can happen to people due to no fault of their own. Deaths in the family, layoffs, accidents, or illness can all have an effect on people's behavior. To us, the loss seems unavoidable or, at the least, no one's fault. However, to the subject, it could become the motivation for a grievance against an individual or organization that the subject perceives has inflicted an injury.

In some cases, the individual engages in behaviors that disrupt or topple his or her own valuables. In late July 1999, Mark Barton of Atlanta, Georgia, lost $50,000 in day trading on the stock market. Guilty over the loss of his life savings and thus stripped of his most powerful inhibitor, he determined on a drastic course of action. He began disinhibiting himself. On Wednesday, July 27, he killed his wife. The next day, Barton murdered his two children. On Friday, July 29, he returned to the two day-trading companies where he had lost his money and killed a total of 12, wounding another 12. As long as Barton kept his stock market losses under control, he behaved normally. But his loss of his savings stripped him of his most important inhibitor. That loss prompted him to destroy the other important inhibitors in his life: his wife and children. He then took his revenge on those whom he perceived had caused all his losses.[4]

Often, those subjects who destroy their own inhibitors do not take responsibility for their own actions. Typically, they blame others or convince themselves that fate has forced them to take drastic actions. Charles Whitman justified killing his wife and mother as the only way to spare them the humiliation that his subsequent actions at the clock tower would cause. Barton, too embarrassed to admit his stock losses, killed his wife and children for similar reasons. In both cases, they excused their own brutality to suit their needs. Unable to take responsibility for their own actions, they seemingly held their victims responsible.

Inhibitors tend to topple much like dominoes, with one domino knocking over another and so on until all of them have fallen. An employee starts drinking too much. That causes poor work performance, which leads to discipline actions and job loss. With no income, the individual defaults on his mortgage. Homeless, his marriage falls apart. His drinking increases, which leads to loss of child custody or visitation rights. Ultimately, all of these losses result in diminished self-esteem, the most important of all the inhibitors. At that point, the individual has nothing left to lose.

Case Illustration: The Man Who Disinhibited Himself

Walter Garcia and Damaris Quiles lived together in the Los Angeles area for several years and had a son. But by January 2008, their relationship had deteriorated and Quiles obtained a restraining order to keep Garcia away. Frustrated and unable to cope with the breakup of their relationship, Garcia went to Quiles's home early on the morning of January 10. As usual, they began to argue outside the house. Quiles's mother heard the commotion and went outside to intervene.

That interference made Garcia even angrier. He pulled a knife and stabbed his former girlfriend and then turned the knife on her mother, killing them both. Once police arrived at the scene, they wisely locked down the nearby elementary school that Garcia's son attended out of concern that Garcia might try to come for the 6-year-old boy. He apparently made no attempt to do so.

Instead, overcome by the sudden loss of his loved ones, Garcia drove to the Colorado Street Bridge, a 150-foot high span over the Arroyo Seco. Locals refer to it as the "suicide bridge" because of the dozens of people who have jumped from it since its construction in 1913.

Having disinhibited himself of his girlfriend and her mother, and with nothing now left to lose, Garcia jumped to his death before police could talk him out of it. (*Source:* Associated Press, "Man Kills 2, Jumps From Bridge to Death," January 11, 2008)

Using Inhibitors Positively

In various situations, inhibitors can be used to manage a subject away from an act of intended violence. Sometimes, simply reminding a subject of all the things that he or she stands to lose by acting inappropriately or by continuing on the course of action that he or she has currently set acts to put a brake on problematic behaviors. In other situations, pointing out to the subject the potential loss of something that he or she holds dear—of which the threat manager has control—also serves to change the subject's behavior. In workplace and school settings, the threat management team can use the institution's administrative actions—its discipline process—to encourage or direct appropriate behaviors by the subject.

Similarly, courts and law enforcement can bring to bear the power of the law to deal with problem subjects that come to their attention. This can involve a "carrot and stick" type of combination of rewarding good behavior while punishing problematic behaviors. In effect, the threat manager should be attentive to positive and negative ways to use a subject's inhibitors to manage the subject away from violence.

Doing so requires an imaginative and creative approach to managing the subject. The threat manager needs to identify the most important inhibitors that the subject holds dear, always understanding that the subject may have very idiosyncratic treasures. At the same time, the threat manager has to take care to avoid any action that might upend or put the subject's inhibitors at unnecessary risk. This demands a delicate touch.

Case Illustration: The Gatekeeper

Sheriff's deputies in a rural California county responded several times to neighbor disputes along a private road. The deputies determined that one particular resident caused the problems because he considered himself the gatekeeper of the private road. He routinely challenged anyone who drove along the roadway, demanding to know who they were and if they had a right to be on the road. Over time, he had challenged all of the other residents and their visitors, thus making himself a source of contention with his neighbors. He also became more aggressive and rude during his encounters with those he considered trespassers, making statements that he was a military veteran who had killed people.

The neighbors became both alarmed and weary due to his behavior. They began calling the sheriff's office when he persisted in his aggressive challenges. When confronted by sheriff's deputies, the gatekeeper adamantly defended his right to regulate who came on the private road. He also forthrightly admitted that he possessed firearms and knew how to use them.

The sheriff became concerned about this entire situation and asked a veteran resident deputy to see if he could de-escalate the situation. Like many longtime deputies in rural areas, the deputy was adept at working through problems without using traditional law enforcement tools, such as arrest and prosecution. The deputy knew that he could probably support a criminal charge or some type of restraining order, but he doubted that those actions would make the situation better. He decided on a different approach.

The deputy went to the gatekeeper's house and sat down with him on his porch to talk over the problem. The deputy found out that the man lived on a small military pension and that his wife had died of cancer a year ago. Since that time, the gatekeeper had become increasingly isolated and reclusive. In discussing the situation with the gatekeeper, the deputy determined that the gatekeeper did not know any of his neighbors. Consequently, the gatekeeper treated everyone using the road as a stranger and potential trespasser. During the discussion, the deputy observed that the man had four dogs, all dachshunds. The dogs constantly crawled on and off the gatekeeper's lap and around his feet the entire time that the deputy talked to him.

The deputy implemented a two-pronged approach to solve the problem. He brought to the man's attention that if he continued his behavior he faced arrest. The gatekeeper did not seem concerned about that until the deputy pointed out that he would have to take the dogs to the animal shelter if he arrested the gatekeeper. This eventuality shocked the gatekeeper. He became very subdued and then agreed that maybe he had been wrong in his approach. He promised to be less suspicious and aggressive.

The deputy then loaded the man and his dogs into his squad car and introduced him to all the other residents on the private road. On the way back to the gatekeeper's house, the gatekeeper thanked the deputy and commented that all the neighbors seemed like nice people. The deputy followed up with the neighbors over the next several weeks and found out that the problem had stopped. Now the gatekeeper gave them a friendly wave when they drove by. (*Source:* Authors' personal knowledge)

Disinhibiting a Subject

In certain situations, actions taken by the threat management team can act to disinhibit or strip away a subject's inhibitors, thus actually increasing the risk of violence. This is the synergy of the threat management process. For example, terminating a problem employee or expelling a problem student actually takes away the inhibitor of having a job or an education. This is not to say that a problem employee or student should never be fired or expelled. Often, that is the only way to deal with an unruly subject. In doing so, the threat management team needs to be ever mindful of the consequence and countermeasures of the disciplinary actions being taken. Arrangements should be made to keep in touch with the subject or, at the least, to maintain a general awareness of the subject's future actions.

Many times in active cases, the threat manager will have to balance interventions against the subject's inhibitors. It is a balance between the risk of employing the intervention versus the potential loss of inhibitors. We call this the *intervention/inhibitor dichotomy*. Consider the stereotypical actions of an abused wife who bails out her husband from jail so that he can go to work the next day. She is balancing the safety provided by the criminal justice intervention against propping up the inhibitor of her husband keeping his job. While doing so, she feels that she is propping up the entire family by keeping the paychecks coming in.

Threat managers will be confronted with the intervention/inhibitor dichotomy in many cases. Should a mentally ill and potentially violent employee be terminated, thus removing the inhibitors of the job and the medical benefits that provide him both counseling and medication? Should a threatening student be expelled from school, thereby removing the inhibitor of the school structure and access to counseling while also leaving him at home alone and unsupervised during the day? Should a client at the unemployment office be denied service due to the client's unruly and angry behavior, even though getting the client a job would end the problematic behavior? These are difficult, seemingly impossible situations to resolve. They can only be tackled on a case-by-case basis, taking into consideration all the known need-to-knows and other factors influencing the situation. No standard formula exists for handling these types of cases.

Case Illustration: Protecting Inhibitors

A sergeant from the Department of Corrections was forced to retire due to an injury. He always had a great deal of emotional investment in his job and was very proud of being a peace officer. After his retirement, he stayed in touch with his coworkers and joined an organization of retired correctional officers. He became addicted to pain medication due to his injury and also suffered from depression due to job loss. His behavior resulted in trouble in his marriage and, after a night of drinking in combination with the pain medication, he attacked his wife while she was sleeping, beating and choking her. His wife called the police. The officers arrested him. She went to a battered women's shelter and filed for divorce.

The subject was forced to plead guilty to a misdemeanor criminal charge because of the overwhelming evidence. The wife was contacted by the District Attorney's Office for her input on appropriate sentencing for his crime. One of the options under discussion was the cancellation of the subject's privileges as a retired peace officer, including his authority to carry a concealed weapon. The wife was very aware of his pride connected with being a peace officer and his strong identification with his prior career. The subject had not attempted to contact her or cause her any trouble since the night of the assault. In consultation with the threat manager, the district attorney and the wife decided not to pursue this option and agreed that it was best to attempt to preserve his dignity and self-esteem. Instead, as conditions of probation, he was restricted from possessing a firearm for 1 year and required to participate successfully in an addiction treatment program. (*Source:* Authors' personal knowledge)

We have no easy answers to these questions, other than to emphasize that the threat manager must always balance the risk of lost inhibitors versus the potential gain of increased safety when making intervention recommendations, always keeping in mind the intervention synergy. In making these decisions, we again remind the threat manager that the purpose of an intervention is to control the subject's actions and make the situation better—not to punish the subject or to satisfy a target's desire for revenge or retribution.

Propping Up a Subject's Inhibitors

In certain situations, helping the subject may also help resolve the problem behavior or diminish the risk of violence. Some threat managers, particularly our brothers and sisters in law enforcement, may find this a difficult concept to embrace. A mentally ill subject whose barrage of threats disrupts the local neighborhood can best be controlled long term by access to the mental health system and social service programs than by a series of arrests for misdemeanor crimes. Indeed, the subject may perceive an arrest as an escalation of the dispute, thus compelling him or her to escalate the problematic behavior and thereby taking another step toward violence. The threat management team should be mindful of the dictum that individuals who need help should get the help that they need.

Using such resources as employee assistance programs, counseling, employment assistance, or social service programs as well as employing tactics like cutting through bureaucratic red tape, overtly respecting the subject's dignity, and other strategies available to the threat management team can help resolve issues confronting the subject. We recognize that some subjects' perceived problems can never be resolved by the threat manager. In these situations, the threat management team should take care never to promise more than it can deliver. Increasing a subject's frustrations or being caught in a lie increases the potential for future problem behavior.

In some cases, beginning a dialogue with the subject or simply listening to his or her grievance may have an impact on the subject's behavior. This is particularly true when the subject exhibits anger directed toward government organizations or large bureaucratic institutions. As we stated before, treating a subject with respect and keeping in mind the dignity domino can have very positive results. The dignity domino is the most important one to keep standing.

Summary

In this chapter, we discussed the power of inhibitors to control an individual's behavior. People fear losing things that they hold dear—whatever those "things" may be. Conversely, losing something that one treasures frequently prompts inappropriate behaviors and pushes a subject onto the path to intended violence. As a consequence, understanding the power of inhibitors is a crucial part of the threat management process.

We also discussed the tendency for inhibitors to act like dominoes once they begin to topple. Frequently, the loss of one inhibitor leads to the loss of other inhibitors as the subject falls into a downward spiral ending with nothing left to lose. At that point, subjects tend to lash out at those they blame for their losses.

Perhaps the most important lesson from studying the influence of inhibitors is recognizing ways in which the threat management team can use that influence to encourage positive behavior on the part of the subject. The power of inhibitors should not be lost in the threat management process.

At the same time, the threat management team needs ever to be mindful that actions taken in dealing with the subject may unavoidably put the subject's inhibitors at risk. This is not to say that those actions should not be taken—problem employees should be terminated, abusive spouses should be compelled to stay away—but taking these measures should always be done with a conscious recognition that an important inhibitor has been taken away.

Finally, the threat management team should also look for ways to prop a subject's inhibitors up. Most importantly, the dignity domino should be bolstered whenever possible.

Notes

1. Behavior-controlling medications also act as inhibitors because they offset the effects of mental illnesses.
2. Calhoun, F. S., & Weston, S. W. (2009). *Threat assessment and management strategies: Identifying the hunters and howlers* (pp. 134–142). Boca Raton, FL: CRC Press.
3. The exception to this is domestic violence, especially when it is impromptu and emotionally driven. Individuals caught up in an angry moment do not have enough rational control to consider the cost of losing their inhibitors.
4. Calhoun, F. S., & Weston, S. W. (2003). *Contemporary threat management: A guide for identifying, assessing, and managing individuals of violent intent* (p. 81). San Diego, CA: Specialized Training Services.

The Toppling Inhibitors   8

Robert Hawkins, who killed himself at the age of 17, spent most of his teen years in and out of the juvenile justice system in and around Omaha, Nebraska. He became a ward of the state in 2002 after threatening to kill his stepmother. He admitted to one social worker that he felt over-whelmed by court hearings and school. He also confessed that he had once tried to kill himself. In January 2006, Hawkins swallowed 30 Tylenol pills trying to kill himself. He told other social workers that he was satanic and admitted that he often acted without considering the consequences of his actions. Hawkins smoked marijuana daily and sold drugs to his high school classmates to pay for his joints. He had a felony drug conviction and a disorderly conduct charge dating from 2005. In December 2007, he faced additional charges of contributing to the delinquency of a minor. In August 2006, social workers released him from state custody after case-workers, his therapist, and his family agreed that it was not worth keeping him in custody another 9 months until he turned 19 because of his lack of cooperation.[1]

After his father and stepmother kicked him out of their house, Hawkins befriended two brothers. Their parents let him move into their house in 2006. "He didn't cause a lot of trouble. He tried to help out all the time," Debora Maruca-Kovac, the mother, told reporters, "He was very thankful for every-thing. He wasn't a violent person at all."[2]

In November 2007, Hawkins's girlfriend broke up with him. A week later, he was fired from his job at McDonalds. On the night of December 4, 2007, he showed Maruca-Kovac his AK-47 semiautomatic rifle. She thought little of it. The next day, at around 1:00 p.m., Hawkins called her to apologize. He thanked her for everything she had done for him and said that he was sorry. He explained that he had gotten fired from his job. Maruca-Kovac pressed him to come home so that they could talk about things. "It's too late," he replied, and then he told her that he had left a note explaining everything. Maruca-Kovac found the note. Hawkins had written that he was "sorry for everything" and stated that he would no longer be a burden to his family. "Now I'll be famous," the note read.[3]

Shortly after the phone call, Hawkins went to the Von Maur department store at a mall in Omaha. He took the elevator to the third floor. As soon as he stepped out of the elevator, Hawkins began firing his AK-47. He killed eight random shoppers and wounded another five people before turning the rifle on himself. When police arrived at the scene, they found his body lying next to the AK-47.[3]

Lessons Learned

1. Robert Hawkins, a troubled youth, continued to spiral downward with one inhibitor toppling after another over a period of many years. What finally appears to have broken him was the breakup with his girlfriend and getting fired from his job.
2. Hawkins never had the fundamental inhibitors in place that a young man his age would normally have. He did not have a stable home life or family support. Any stability in his life was temporary and fragile. At the same time, what few inhibitors he did have began to topple. He lost his girlfriend and then his job. All of these factors simply compounded to push him into desperate straits.
3. Hawkins had no delusions about his condition and status in society. At the end, he exerted his dignity domino by proclaiming, "Now I'll be famous," probably envisioning dying defiantly in a gun battle with police rather than the ignoble suicide that actually happened.
4. Inhibitors are often fragile things that can disappear or topple seemingly all at once. When they do begin falling altogether, the result can be feelings of despair leading to desperate actions, especially in a person with mental health issues such as past suicidality.
5. Hawkins both planned and engaged in an act of opportunistic violence by going to the third floor of the mall department store and shooting people at random. The wonder is that he did not target his former girlfriend or the family that had befriended him. He preferred strangers instead. In his note, he stated his desire to be famous. Individuals do not get famous by killing a former girlfriend. They have a better chance of infamy by killing eight people during a public act of violence at a well-known location. Yet, 5 years after his shooting spree, the name Robert Hawkins is hardly a household name. Even after his death, his inhibitors failed to serve him.
6. In the end, Hawkins engaged in several final-act behaviors. He displayed his weapon the night before using it and placed a phone call to say good-bye. During the call, he explicitly told Maruca-Kovac that he had left a note, thereby ensuring that she would find it. Both the phone call and the note were intended to announce and explain his subsequent behavior.

Notes

1. Associated Press. (2007, December 27). Files: Mall gunman was satanic, suicidal; Associated Press. (2007, December 6). Mall gunman called quiet and depressed.
2. Associated Press. (2007, December 6). Mall gunman called quiet and depressed.
3. Associated Press. (2007, December 6). Mall gunman called quiet and depressed; CNN. (2007, December 6). Police: nine killed in shooting at Omaha Mall, including gunman.

Differences Among the Various Venues of Violence

9

Acts of intended violence end in the same result, but different motives and purposes spawn that violence depending on the social setting in which the assault occurs. The similarity of the end results tends to overshadow the very real differences among the different venues of violence. By venue, we mean the setting or target of the violence. Workplace violence differs from attacks on public figures, which differ from violence toward intimates, which differs again from violence targeting gathering places, which differs from violence against symbolic or representative targets. Understanding these differences—and recognizing them when they emerge from a subject's behavior—gives the threat manager a much fuller understanding of the situation under assessment and the subject's relationship with the potential targets. In other words, not all grievances evolve or develop in the same context and circumstances. The differences emerge from the social setting or venue in which the act of violence occurs.

Yet, regardless of setting, subjects intent on committing an act of intended violence must traverse the path to intended violence:

- Begin with a grievance
- Develop the idea that violence is the only alternative open to them
- Research and plan how to implement the violence
- Make preparations
- Breach the target's security
- Attack

The path to intended violence comes into play in every act of targeted, premeditated violence, regardless of who or what the target may be. Whether the violence occurs in a domestic setting, or a workplace, or toward some ideological entity, or against a public figure, following the path to intended violence makes up the one constant in intended violence. When Jared Loughner opened fire at Congresswoman Gabriel Giffords's political event at a Tucson, Arizona, shopping center, he moved from grievance to attack. When Scott Dekraai killed his wife and seven others at the hair salon where she worked in Seal Beach, California, he, too, took all the steps from grievance to attack. Every case illustration and case study we have presented in this book have involved subjects who followed the path to violence.

The concept of the path to intended violence is a powerful one, perhaps the most important idea for understanding and assessing potential acts of intended violence. We believe that it is, in effect, a universal, integral part of committing intended violence. Its potency derives from its focus on observable behaviors engaged in by the subject associated with planning and preparing for a violent act. Hence, threat assessors should always look for evidence of any behaviors engaged in by the subject related to the stages along the path to violence. This holds true regardless of target or target setting.

But understanding this crucial concept does not mean that all targets and all target venues are the same or that the differences among them are unimportant. As crucial and universal as the path to intended violence is, threat assessors also need to identify the potential target venue or venues and incorporate the unique aspects of that particular venue into the threat assessment. Target venues each have their unique and different aspects. Different targets or different physical locations attract violence for different reasons. Understanding those differences plays a key role in any threat assessment. We also believe that a subject's threatening behaviors manifest themselves in different ways in different venues. Gathering information about these behaviors comes from examining the circumstances and context of the relationship between the subject and target. That relationship was one of the need-to-knows described in a previous chapter.

Experts in the field of threat management often overlook this conceptual dynamic. Researchers have tended to conclude that their findings in researching one venue for violence must somehow hold true for violence in all venues. In two early studies of approach behavior toward celebrities and approach behavior toward members of Congress, Park Dietz and his associates concluded that subjects who made threats toward these two similar types of targets (both are public figures) were actually less likely to approach the target.[1] Researchers at the Secret Service looked into violence against public figures and concluded that "persons who *pose* an actual threat often do not *make* threats, especially direct threats."[2] Threat assessors subsequently applied these findings to other types of targets, as though public figures represented all types of targets. This resulted in a perceived, though significant, diminishment in the value of threats as preincident indicators of intended violence across all venues. Ultimately, the findings convinced Dr. Reid Meloy to conclude that "threats are not that big a deal," regardless of target type or venue.[3]

Yet, as Debra Jenkins's research into the *intimacy effect* found, the value of threats as a pre-incident indicator of potential violence escalates as the degree of intimacy or interpersonal knowledge between subject and target increases.[4] This finding, important enough in and of itself, had the added effect of introducing the idea that differences existed among the various venues of intended violence. Recognizing these differences could be used to identify factors and features in subject behaviors in each venue. Those differences had a direct bearing on improving any threat assessment conducted in the context of each venue.

In other words, the path to intended violence may be universal, but the individual context in which that violence plays out may have very specific, unique attributes that will further inform the threat assessment. For example, because of the *intimacy effect*, we know that threats toward public figures are not good pre-incident indicators. Threats toward domestic partners, however, are excellent pre-incident indicators of future violence. The difference is not within the path to intended violence, but, rather, within the setting or venue in which the threats are delivered.

In this chapter, we look at the differences among several venues of violence and ask what it is about that particular venue that attracts subjects intent on an act of intended violence. This focus on setting distinctly shifts this part of the assessment away from the subject—instead looking at unique attributes of the target or the target venue, including how the subject relates to that target or target venue. To many practiced threat assessors, this may seem an unusual, even radical approach, almost as though it holds the target responsible for any violence directed toward it. What we are here bringing forward is the concept that the setting and relationships in which an act of intended violence may occur exert independent influences on the subject's behavior and the potential act of violence. The circumstances and context in which the subject's behavior occurs directly affect those behaviors. Identifying those influences and incorporating them into each threat assessment helps further inform each assessment.

In this chapter, we focus on several different venues in which intended violence frequently occurs:

- Intended violence against public figures
- Intended violence against intimates
- Intended violence at workplaces committed by current or former employees
- Intended violence at gathering places, such as iconic locations, shopping malls, or other places where people come together
- Intended violence against representative targets, usually ideologically or politically symbolic, such as violence against abortion clinics and abortion providers, churches, religious groups, or other targets selected for their emblematic value

When making threat assessments for each of these venues, we identify salient features about that setting that differ from the other venues. We then ask how those differences play into better assessing the subject's potential for committing an act of intended violence.

These venues are not exclusive of each other. Domestic violence frequently spills over into workplaces, churches, courthouses, or any other place in which the subject may find the target. Churches and synagogues may be targeted as a gathering place, but also as representative of something repugnant to a subject's beliefs or biases. Jared Loughner targeted Congresswoman Gabriel Giffords as a public figure, but found her and the other victims gathered together at a shopping center. Consequently, in determining target venue, the threat assessor has to understand what attracts the subject to that target or target location. Is he or she seeking an intimate partner, a public figure, workplace revenge, or simply a target-rich environment or some symbolic victim? Knowing this gives enormous insight into the subject's intent, motive, and ability to carry out any violence.

Our list of venues is not meant to be definitive or all inclusive. We do not examine, for example, robberies or run-of-the-mill bank or store holdups that result in violence. Even though these types of intended violence compose the vast majority of incidents of workplace violence, the motive for committing them is not the act of violence itself. Rather, violence is but a tool for achieving the true motive, which is enriching the robber or making an escape. We keep our focus on those acts of violence for which the motive is to commit the violence. In these venues, the attack is the sole and only goal of the attacker. That, we think, is a significant, defining difference between violence during robberies and holdups compared to the violence wreaked by a disgruntled employee, enraged spouse, or misguided crusader.

Some experts in the field would define almost any act of violence as a type of workplace violence. The national standards for preventing and intervening in potential violence recently promulgated by ASIS and SHRM seem to treat all acts of intentional violence as incidents of workplace violence.[5] After all, Congresswoman Giffords was working when Loughner shot her; schools, courthouses, shopping malls, houses of worship, reproductive health care clinics, and other scenes of violence are workplaces for somebody, if not always the subject or the target.

Yet, that approach strikes us as too broad and too indiscriminate. Granted, people working at shopping malls occasionally become victims of individuals who go to the mall intending to commit violence. But the victims are not targeted because they work at the mall; rather, they are targeted because they and their customers happen to be at the mall at that particular moment. The subject goes there, not because he or she has a grievance against the employees, but rather because malls are places where people gather. The subject wants a crowd, not a particular business or workplace. That, it seems to us, is a significant difference from more traditionally understood workplace violence.

Similarly, some subjects target abortion clinics and their employees because of their ideological opposition to the procedures done at the clinics.

True for the doctors, nurses, and staff, the clinic is their workplace. Doctor Tiller frequently described himself as just a guy trying to make a living.[6] But for the subject, the clinic and the people working there represent something that he or she loathes. Churches and synagogues are worksites, but they also represent symbols that some subjects find offensive. Although they are technically workplaces, the ideological element of the motive distinguishes these acts of violence from more traditionally understood workplace violence. The subject intends the violence as a statement of his or her personal beliefs.

These differences do not strike us as particularly subtle or hard to fathom, yet they provide crucial insights into the subject's motive and intent. Although Scott Dekraai's assault on the Seal Beach hair salon can be understood as an incident of workplace violence for the employees and customers, his motive and intent are best understood as domestic violence that happened to spill into his wife's workplace. The violence occurred at her workplace because she happened to be there. His threats and other pre-incident indicators are best assessed through the lens of domestic violence rather than workplace violence. Domestic violence, as we shall demonstrate, centers around intimacy and control; traditionally understood workplace violence tends to stem from a sense of injustice and injury. These are very different grievances.

Violence at public gathering places involves seeking target-rich environments where the subject feels assured that he or she will rack up a high body count, somehow confusing his or her personal worth by the attention received from the number of other people that he or she can kill. The issue, then, is what attracts that subject to that target at that locale—not necessarily what inheres in that target or locale. Did Loughner go to the Tucson shopping center because it was a workplace, a place where people gathered, or the place at which he knew he would be able to find Congresswoman Giffords? Answering that question provides the context for assessing the potential for intended violence.

The Concept of Social Ecosystems

An interesting way to think about the various venues for intended violence treats each venue as an independent, though frequently overlapping, type of human social ecosystem. An ecosystem, according to the online Encarta Dictionary, is "a localized group of interdependent organisms together with the environment that they inhabit and depend on." Applied conceptually to the venues for intended violence, each venue serves as a localized grouping where individuals—organisms, if you will—interact with each other in both positive and negative ways. Individuals work and play with their domestic partners and families, interact with their fellow employees or fellow students, invest their emotions and support with public figures, share their sociopolitical views with churches or political movements that appeal to them, and gather together at various places, such as shopping malls, churches, and sports stadiums. In each of these human ecosystems, the interaction between the individuals within the system helps define the peculiar nature of that ecosystem.

Within each venue social ecosystem, there are some consistent elements. Usually, for example, some type of recognized hierarchy exists: Ministers oversee churches, principals and teachers oversee students and schools, managers oversee workplaces, parents oversee children, and judges oversee courtrooms. Behavioral norms also exist. Conduct expected in a workplace is different from that expected in a school, which is different from that expected within a family at home. Competition between groups and individuals results in some kind of pecking order among the individuals. Recognized indicators of success or failure influence each individual within the social ecosystem.

As a result, individuals become part of different, often overlapping ecosystems throughout the course of their lives. Individuals form domestic relationships. They go to work and school. They support or admire various public figures. They believe in shared political or religious philosophies. They gather at the same places, such as shopping malls or houses of worship. All these different relationships help shape and define the particular individual within the ecosystem. And how that individual relates to each ecosystem varies from one setting to the next. People assume slightly different demeanors and feel differently about themselves, depending on where they are: at home, at work, at church, at the movies, at political rallies.

In effect, each ecosystem is an element affecting the case dynamics. The subject's interaction with the target, bystanders, and the system or setting itself deeply influences how events unfold. Those interactions are unique to each ecosystem. They depend on which ecosystem is in play. By understanding the flow of those systemic dynamics, the threat manager can better assess and understand the potential for violence.

The ecosystem or venue for potential violence must also be considered from the point of view of the subject. Why has he or she chosen that venue for a potential act of intended violence? If the target is an individual, what is the relationship between the subject and the target? Is the target closely identified with a particular venue? Is the venue chosen because of its connection to a unique grievance? Did the subject choose that venue because the people who frequent that venue meet the subject's criteria for a target of violence? This latter one is typical when the violence is toward a particular group, such as gays or Jews. Subjects also choose venues because they meet the criteria of being most vulnerable to attack. The point here is that each venue for intended violence offers its own attraction for spawning the violence. Understanding that attraction helps the threat manager fully assess the potential risks.

Case Illustration: Furrow's Choice

Buford Furrow, a longtime member of the hate group Aryan Nations, detested Jews and others different from him. In the summer of 1999, he broke up with his long-term girlfriend, Debbie Matthews, the widow of Aryan Nations leader Robert Matthews, who had been killed in a shoot-out with the FBI in 1994.

The breakup prompted Furrows to leave the couple's home in Washington state. Determined to act, Furrows drove his van to Los Angeles. He had loaded the van with weapons, including hand grenades and ammunition. He made it into the San Fernando Valley. He parked his van a block from the North Valley Jewish Community Center, which hosted a day-care center for Jewish children. Furrow now had a specific target: anyone at the center.

On August 10, 1999, Furrows walked into the community center and began firing. He later confessed to police that he fired 70 rounds, although he managed to wound only five people, including three children. Fleeing the center, Furrow happened to run into Joseph Ileto, a postman of Filipino descent, as Ileto was delivering the mail—another target of opportunity who was different from Furrow. Furrow fired and killed the postman.

Furrow spent the rest of the day getting a haircut and shopping for baseball caps. That night, he hired a taxicab to drive him to Las Vegas, where he surrendered and confessed to the FBI the next day.

Because of the confession, Furrow avoided the death sentence and got life in prison instead. Ten years later, he announced to a reporter from his cell in the federal penitentiary in Terre Haute, Indiana, that he had renounced his white supremacist beliefs. "My mind was filled with sickness and unfortunately I acted on it," Furrow wrote to the reporter, "But, I am now a 'model' inmate who has shunned criminal activity and spend my day with exercise, art, and learning prison civil law. I can't change the past, but I can damn sure change the future, and my future will never include Neo-Nazi activity again."

"I feel deep remorse for my crime," Furrow continued in his letter. "About 5 yrs. ago I threw away my racist books, literature, etc. and took up a new leaf. I now publicly renounce all bias toward anyone based on race, creed, color, sexual orientation, etc. and am a much happier person. I feel a life based on hate is no life at all."

Furrow's two targets attracted him for different reasons. The Jewish Community Center offered a gathering place for Jewish children and their teachers. In essence, the center represented a Jewish ecosystem for Furrow to exploit his hatred of Jews. After leaving the center, he chanced to run into Mr. Ileto, a non-White and, therefore, a different race from

Furrow. Furrow killed him over that difference. (*Sources:* James Sterngold, "Supremacist Who Killed Postal Worker Avoids Death Sentence," *New York Times,* January 24, 2001; Corina Knoll, "White Supremacist Buford Furrow Says He Has Renounced His Views, Newspaper Reports," *Los Angeles Times,* September 6, 2009)

The concept of ecosystems also extends to the target's behavior when threatened. Does he or she remain in the same ecosystems, such as workplace, school, church, or gym? This may also be the reason why violence occurs at certain venues: because, simply put, that is the ecosystem where the target can be found.

Differences in the characteristics of different venues mean that information about threatening behaviors, approaches, or other potential indicators of future violence may come to the attention of either the target or authorities by somewhat different methods. Those venues that are insulated by physical security, such as government organizations and large corporations, will most likely receive information from perimeter security, the mailroom, or some other peripheral source. In venues such as schools and workplaces, the information may come from other students or coworkers. In most venues, subject behavior that is out of the recognized norm will come to the attention of someone. Normal behavior in one venue may appear abnormal in another.

Our approach to understanding the different social ecosystems is defined by the following axioms:

- The path to intended violence exists in all acts of premeditated, targeted violence, regardless of the target or venue of the violence.
- The venue, the ecosystem, the target, and the location or setting of the act of violence all have unique characteristics that have an impact on the behavior of the subject, the target, bystanders, and responders.
- The grievance on the path to intended violence is strongly related to the venue in which the violence occurs.
- The subject's behavior along the path to intended violence should be assessed within the context of the venue in which it occurs.
- Indicators of potential future violence may present differently due to the characteristics of the individual venues.

The separate influences that each venue for violence imposes on the act of intended violence have been little understood up to now. We offer our thoughts here in the hope that they will stimulate more research leading to a deeper understanding of this particular, yet vital dynamic.

The Role of Motive in Distinguishing
the Venues for Intended Violence

Attacks on public figures have received more attention from researchers than, perhaps, any other venue for intended violence. Over the course of the last 30 years or so, researchers have significantly improved our understanding of how and why public figures attract violence. Yet, what emerges from these studies in comparison to what we know about the motives for other types of intended violence is the rather startling fact that motive may not be a distinguishing feature for understanding the differences in the various venues for violence. Using the research on public figure violence as a benchmark, we can begin to see that we need to look elsewhere for signs of distinguishing features among the different venues.

In groundbreaking work conducted by James Clarke in the early 1980s, Clarke identified and defined four types of U.S. presidential assassins, which he labeled

- Psychotic assassins, driven by severe emotional and cognitive distortion of reality
- Nihilist assassins, who believe that "the condition of their lives is so intolerably meaningless and without purpose that destruction of society and themselves is desirable for its own sake"
- Neurotic assassins, who seek acceptance, recognition, and status through the act of violence
- Zealots, who pursue political ideals and world changes through their act of violence[7]

Although Clarke focused exclusively on presidential assassins, his approach contributed significantly to the broader study of public figure assassins. In particular, Clarke's greatest contribution lay in his willingness to understand the rationale behind the seemingly irrational act of assassination. He stripped through all the psychobabble of previous studies to get to the underlying motives prompting the decision to kill the president. By making the motives available, Clarke allowed for objective understanding of what, before, had seemed an incomprehensible act.[8]

Yet, these same motives also appear in other venues. School shooters and workplace violence perpetrators can also be psychotic, nihilistic, neurotic, and zealous. Subjects such as Scott Roeder, who embark on violent crusades in support of their personal beliefs, certainly qualify as zealots, even if their target is not generally considered a public figure.

Almost 30 years later, Robert T. M. Phillips, a psychiatric consultant to the Secret Service, devised his own typology. Based on his case experiences, Phillips identified five types of presidential stalkers or assassins:

- The resentful type seeks retribution against the president for some perceived injury or insult.
- The pathologically obsessed type wants retribution or personal gain by attacking the president.
- The infamy seeker wants to become famous at the president's expense.
- The nuisance type tries to help the president or wants help from the president.
- The attention seeker hopes to see the president or be seen with the president.

Phillips, who uses his typology when consulting with the Secret Service on active cases, believes that it allows him to categorize individuals under Secret Service assessment "based on motive, the presence or absence of delusions and/or active psychosis, and the intent to do harm."[9] Yet, the categories devised by Phillips can also easily be applied to subjects in other venues for violence. Subjects who engage in workplace violence frequently feel resentful toward their supervisors. Domestic violence frequently results from a pathologically obsessed spouse. School shooters and subjects who engage in violence at gathering places often seek infamy. Nuisance types and attention seekers appear across all the venues for violence.

Both Clarke and Phillips focused solely on presidential assassins. But what of other public figures? An earlier study by Secret Service researchers went beyond those who sought to assassinate the president. The Exceptional Case Study included 83 American attackers of public figures reaching back to the 1930s, including assassinations and attempted assassinations of U.S. presidents, other Secret Service protectees, other national political figures, celebrities, members of Congress, federal judges, business executives, and state and city officials. Robert Fein and Bryan Vossekuil identified eight major motives prompting attacks on public figures:

- Seeking notoriety or fame
- Bringing attention to a personal or public problem
- Avenging a perceived wrong or retaliating for a perceived injury
- Ending personal pain through being removed from society or being killed
- Saving the country or the world; fixing a world problem
- Developing a special relationship with the target
- Making money
- Bringing about political change[10]

As with Clarke and Phillips, Fein and Vossekuil stressed the importance of focusing on the subject's motive in order to put the subject's behavior within the context of the subject's goal for committing the violence. Yet, the eight motives they identified also prompt violence in other settings. They are not exclusive to violence against public figures.

We have already discussed Dietz and colleagues' two breakthrough studies discounting the importance of threats as pre-incident indicators of potential future violence toward members of Congress and Hollywood celebrities.[1] Seventeen years later, Louis B. Schlesinger and V. Blair Mesa looked in depth at 21 cases of stalking, attacking, or attempting to attack nonpolitical public figures. They identified three "red flags" as useful indicators of a person dangerously obsessed with a public figure:

- All 21 celebrity stalkers "seemed to have crossed the line from being loyal fans to being obsessed with their celebrity victims, and the level of obsession was apparent to others in at least half the cases."
- Most of the celebrity stalkers "had unrealistic or delusional expectations of the celebrity."
- "Half the offenders were angry about some personal behavior of the celebrity, which seemed to have served as a trigger for the violent acting out."[11]

All of these studies focused on determining the range of motives prompting acts of violence against public figures. But in some ways, that focus creates a distortion. Having unrealistic or delusional expectations, being angry, seeking notoriety, bringing attention to a personal problem, and avenging a perceived wrong also compel acts of violence in other venues, such as school violence, domestic disputes, workplace violence, and violence in gathering places. Omar Thornton, the petty beer thief, justified murdering eight coworkers as a crusade to stamp out racism at the beer distributorship. Paul Hill, who shot an abortion provider and his escort at a Pensacola, Florida, abortion clinic, saw himself as an avenging martyr destined to save the lives of the unborn.

Consequently, although we recognize the vital importance of understanding a subject's motive, we believe that a particular motive may not be exclusive or unique to any particular venue. Instead, the connections between the subject, the grievance, and the characteristics of the venue provide the best lens to view the potential for future violence.

Why Public Figures Attract Violence

Public figures attract violence because they occupy positions of public prominence. That simple fact holds true regardless of whether the public figure is a politician, head of government, business leader, or celebrity. Those who would harm a public figure are driven to do that harm by the figure's public status. That distinction, oddly enough, has never been explicitly identified in the research studies conducted to date. Although it may seem like we are showing a keen awareness of the obvious, sometimes the obvious is easily overlooked.

As a direct result of their prominence, public figures usually do not know or are not able to recognize their assailants, even though the subject may feel a profound emotional or sexual attachment to the public figure. As a practical matter, public figures, unlike victims of workplace or domestic violence, are poor sources of information regarding their attackers. Identifying a subject intent on violence against a public figure requires the threat manager to seek other sources of information. For example, the mailroom supervisor at a government facility can provide more information on who is angry at the government than can a top government official working at that facility.

Public figure prominence also results in the subject narrowing the act of violence to a single target: the public figure. In other venues for violence, the subject may seek target-rich environments, thus gaining the sought-after notoriety by large body counts. But with public figures, the subject almost always directs the violence toward a single target. This does not mean that the subject may shift from target to target or that other people are harmed during the attack, but it remains true that at any one time, subjects targeting public figures only target one at a time. Loughner's attack on Congresswoman Giffords is the exception to the rule.

Case Illustration: Which Target?

On the morning of March 31, 1981, John Hinckley ate an Egg McMuffin at the McDonald's near his hotel, two blocks from the White House. While eating his breakfast, he tried to decide what he wanted to do. His choices consisted of going to New Haven and killing himself on the Yale campus, where Jodie Foster was going to college; killing Senator Ted Kennedy; firing randomly in the chambers of the U.S. Senate; or assassinating President Ronald Reagan. He chanced to read in that morning's *Washington Star* that President Reagan would be making a noontime speech at the Washington Hilton, not too far from Hinckley's hotel.

Convenience won out and Hinckley took a taxi to the Hilton. Although he debated among several targets, in the end he settled on just one.

(*Source:* James W. Clarke, *On Being Mad or Merely Angry: John Hinckley, Jr., and Other Dangerous People.* Princeton, NJ: Princeton University Press, 1990, pp. 3–4)

Subjects who target public figures usually do not have firsthand information on the target's routines, habits, work, living arrangements, and so on. Certainly, subjects targeting public figures do not have direct information to the extent that a domestic partner, coworker, or student has information on spouses, coworkers, and campuses. As a result, lack of detailed personal information requires the subject to engage in overt research and contact behavior about the public figure, which is frequently how the subject comes to the target's, or the target's security's, attention. However, we are coming to realize that the availability of information about public figures is changing due to the use of social media. As celebrities and other public figures use these methods to keep their fans informed of their activities, location, and future plans, the need for overt research has diminished, thus reducing the opportunities for identifying a threat.

Subjects who target public figures usually engage in acts of intended violence, with impromptu violence toward public figures rarely occurring. This factor does not hold true for other venues for violence, which frequently become the stage for both intended and impromptu acts of violence. Consequently, threat managers with responsibility for assessing the risk to a public figure usually need to focus their attention only on those behaviors associated with intended violence.

This is not to say that public figures are not victimized by impromptu violence. When they are, it is almost always a different venue for violence, usually domestic violence. The late singer Whitney Houston suffered abuse from her husband, Bobby Brown. But Brown directed his violence toward her not because she was a celebrity, but rather because they were in a domestic relationship. Similarly, singer Rihanna's boyfriend, Chris Brown, assaulted her because of their domestic relationship—not her celebrity status.

Howlers make up a higher proportion of subjects attracted to public figures than to other venues of intended violence. Because of the *intimacy effect*, their threats diminish in value as pre-incident indicators of violence. Although all reported incidents need to be taken seriously, threat managers overseeing public-figure security should keep in mind this higher proportion of howler interest in the public figure.

Finally, for the practicing threat manager, the lesson here is to recognize when a protectee gains public prominence. Andy Warhol's "15 minutes of fame" teach us that anyone, at any time, may suddenly gain public acknowledgment and be propelled into the world of public figures. Once there, the new celebrity may attract the attention of those individuals, for whatever motive, who find themselves inappropriately attracted to celebrities or what they may represent.

Deeply intertwined with whatever other motive the subject may have to attack a public figure is the desire to be recognized, to be important, to be somebody. Because of our news cycle society, assassins well understand that anyone who attacks a public figure will instantaneously become famous. This is enormously attractive to certain people. This trait is shared with those who commit high-profile, high body count, or attention-getting crimes of violence. For those who crave recognition or fame, such as John Hinckley, attacking a public figure will achieve that end.

In today's world, infamy does not come from killing your neighbor, your mother, your wife, or your children. It does come from attacking a celebrity, committing violence at a public location, or killing large numbers of people in strange or unusual ways.

Guidelines for Assessing Threats to Public Figures

As a result of these distinctions in threatening situations toward public figures, we suggest that any threat assessment involving a public figure keep the following factors in mind:

- Public figures attract violence and threatening situations because of their public prominence and how they are personified by the media or their own public relations.
- The subject usually has limited information on the public figure's real personal life and routines beyond what is reported in the media. Therefore, some type of research and contact behavior is necessary to locate and gain access to the target.
- The public figure is a poor source of information about the subjects who may pose a threat to him or her.
- Howlers make up a higher proportion of subjects targeting public figures than in other venues of violence.
- The predominant motive in public figure violence is to gain notoriety or infamy.
- Direct threats are a poor predictor of future violence directed toward public figures.

Although each situation under assessment needs to be assessed on its own evidence and in its own context, threat managers assessing situations involving public figures should keep these attributes very much in mind when making the assessment. They lend context to each situation under assessment.

Why Intimate Partners Attract Violence

Two aspects of domestic violence distinguish this form of violence from the other venues. First, the degree of intimacy between subject and target is at its fullest in the domestic setting. The intimacy is both physical and personal. The subject needs to conduct little research into the target's routines and habits because the subject is already very familiar with those routines and habits. The attacker usually has ready access to the target. That intimacy also puts the *intimacy effect* very much into play, thus increasing the value of threats as a pre-incident indicator of domestic violence.[12]

Second, the desire for control over the target spawns most instances of domestic violence. Patricia Tjaden and Nancy Thoenes, who, more than anyone, analyzed the results of the Department of Justice's nationwide Violence Against Women survey conducted in the mid-1990s, concluded:

> Violence perpetrated against women by intimates is often accompanied by emotionally abusive and controlling behavior. The survey found that women whose partners were jealous, controlling, or verbally abusive were significantly more likely to report being raped, physically assaulted, and/or stalked by their partners even when other sociodemographic and relationship characteristics were controlled. Indeed, having a verbally abusive partner was the variable most likely to predict that a woman would be victimized by an intimate partner. These findings support the theory that violence perpetrated against women by intimates is often part of a systematic pattern of dominance and control.[13]

The authors also cited other research showing that

> [W]ife assault is more common in families where power is concentrated in the hands of the husband or male partner and the husband makes most of the decisions regarding family finances and strictly controls when and where his wife or female partner goes.[14]

A host of other factors also stood out, such as that unmarried, cohabitating couples had higher rates of domestic violence than married couples; that lower income brackets had higher rates than upper income families; and that the lower a woman's educational level was, the higher the rate of violence.[14] But, by far, the aggressor's controlling behavior contributed the most to increasing the risk of domestic violence.

Others with practical experience dealing with domestic violence also cited controlling behavior as a distinguishing characteristic of this venue. The Danvers, Massachusetts, Police Department issued a list of 11 factors related to domestic homicide. Among them, the department cited "ownership of the battered partner" and "centrality of the partner" to the abuser's life, both symptoms of controlling behavior.[15] Similarly, the Nashville, Tennessee, Police Department listed its own factors contributing to domestic assaults. The department subtitled the list "Threats, Power Misuse, and Control." It included using emotional abuse; using privileges, such as treating the target as a servant and acting like the "master of the castle"; economic abuse, coercion, and threat; and using intimidation.[16] The American Judges Foundation, giving advice on handling domestic violence in the courtroom, pointed to "possessive and punitive behavior" as one of many indicators of potential problems.[17]

Case Illustration: The Controlling Police Chief

Tacoma, Washington, Police Chief David Brame insisted that his wife, Crystal, weigh herself ever day in front of him. He monitored the mileage on her car and demanded that she account for any trips she took outside the house. When Crystal left him and filed for divorce in late February 2003, Brame began threatening her. The threats attracted enough attention that Tacoma's director of human affairs recommended to city leaders that they take Brame's badge and gun away from him. City Attorney Robin Jenkinson rejected the advice, saying that the chief's divorce was none of the city's business.

The next day, Brame happened to see Crystal parking her car in a shopping center. He had both their children in his car. Brame parked his car, telling the children to stay put so that he could talk to their mother. When Crystal saw him approaching her, she retreated back to her car, but he beat her there. He sat in the driver's seat as they talked. Witnesses heard them begin to argue, raising their voices. Brame pulled his service pistol and shot Crystal behind the left ear and then shot himself in the head.

Crystal died a week later, just as Brame's casket was being lowered into his grave. (*Source:* Blaine Harden, "Tacoma Murder Case's Revelations Shake City," *Washington Post,* May 5, 2003; Sean Robinson, "David Brame's Life, Career Crumble When Wife Seeks a Way Out," *News Tribune,* May 11, 2005)

Incidents of domestic violence tend to be as much impromptu violence as intended violence. Brame was not looking for his estranged wife when he saw her driving into the shopping center parking lot, but he took advantage of accidentally running into her. Because of the intense emotions involved between intimate partners, normally benign situations can easily escalate into violence.

In addition, incidents of domestic violence easily slip into the target's workplace, the courthouse, and, increasingly, the target's church. In these situations, the wife or girlfriend (usually) may leave the couple's home seeking sanctuary at a friend's house or a shelter or some other location where the husband or boyfriend (usually) does not know where to find her. But he does know where she works. He also knows when she is scheduled to go to court because he is scheduled to be there at the same time. And, as several incidents over the past few years suggest, he knows when she will be at her church. The subject uses that knowledge to plot his attack. The assault itself becomes the last full measure of control over her.

Case Illustration: Disturbing the Sanctity of the Sanctuary

Kevin Collins loved Jamika Williams. They had a 10-month-old daughter and life seemed good until Williams refused to marry him. In early February 2006, Collins trailed Williams to the Zion Hope Missionary Baptist Church in Detroit, Michigan, to beg her to become his wife. She refused again. Outraged, Collins grabbed at her, scratching her neck. He fled the church. Williams reported the assault to the police, but failed to follow up with prosecutors to get a warrant. Collins remained free.

On Sunday, February 26, Collins again went looking for Williams. This time, he carried with him a sawed-off shotgun. Williams made it to the church in time for the 11:00 a.m. service, which Williams usually attended with her mother, Rosetta Williams. That Sunday, however, Jamika felt "uneasy." She stayed home. Instead, Rosetta went to church with her sister, Leeyeng Williams, and her goddaughter. They went to take their usual seats in the balcony, but as they emerged from the stairs they saw Collins. "He was there—waiting for us," Leeyeng remembered, "I was stunned."

Collins confronted Rosetta, demanding to know where to find Jamika. Rosetta refused to tell him. Collins began yelling and cursing at her. A man intervened, telling Collins to leave. Collins headed toward the balcony stairs. At the entrance, he suddenly turned back and began blasting away with the shotgun. The first two shots hit Rosetta in the legs; the third shot killed her and wounded her goddaughter. Collins fired another shot at the man who had intervened, grazing him with pellets. Collins fired a last shot at the pulpit and then fled the church.

Several blocks from the church, Collins approached a car parked along the street. He pushed himself into the passenger side and began grappling with the driver, Victoria Davis. She screamed for help. Her husband responded to her cries. Collins shot him. He died the next day.

Collins fled that scene and remained on the loose for over 5 hours. A police officer saw him walking along a street about a mile from the church. Collins ran behind a building and turned the shotgun on himself before the officer could get to him. The officer found him with a hole in his chest.

"The sanctity of our sanctuary has been disturbed," Zion Hope Church Pastor Curtis Grant said of the church shooting. (*Sources:* Associated Press, "2nd Victim Dies in Mich. Church Shootings," February 27, 2006; Joe Swickford, Patricia Montemurri, and Zachary Gorchow, "Another Family Grieves in Detroit Church Shootings: As Second Victim Dies, Kin of First Criticize Police," *Detroit Free Press,* February 28, 2006)

Guidelines for Assessing Threats to Domestic Partners

As a result of these distinctions in threatening situations toward domestic partners, we suggest that any threat assessment involving potential domestic violence keep the following factors in mind:

- The *intimacy effect* is very much in play in domestic violence, meaning that threats of violence are very good pre-incident indicators of future violence.
- Because of their current or prior intimacy, the subject has detailed knowledge about the personal habits and routines of the target. Little target research needs to be done.
- Domestic violence appears to center on issues of control and dominance. The risk of it occurring increases in direct proportion to the subject's perception of losing that control and domination.
- Getting the target out of the violent relationship is not enough. Simply leaving the relationship does not abate the risk. Instead, it may increase the risk of violence moving over into the target's workplace, the courthouse, or the target's church.
- Typical intimate violence target behavior, such as returning to an abusive subject, hiding or minimizing threatening behavior, and suffering silently, continues to challenge intervention methods.

Although each situation under assessment needs to be assessed on its own evidence and in its own context, threat managers assessing situations involving potential domestic violence should keep these attributes very much in mind when making the assessment. They lend context to each situation under assessment.

Why Gathering Places Attract Violence

One phenomenon of intended violence involves subjects who choose places where people gather and then randomly kill as many people as possible, usually then committing suicide or challenging the police to kill them. Shopping malls, churches, schools, sporting events, neighborhoods, and other places where people flock provide the setting for these types of incidents. The randomness of the target selection—essentially targets of opportunity—distinguishes gathering place intended violence. The subject is not after specific individuals, but rather just a large body count.

The desire for notoriety usually motivates these subjects, although a recent loss of one or more inhibitors may also spawn violence. Indeed, recent loss of inhibitors affects all the venues for violence. In March 2006, Aaron Dunn, distraught over a recent breakup with his wife and doped up on methamphetamines, went to Laguna Boulevard in Davis, California, armed with a 12-gauge shotgun. He began firing indiscriminately, killing two men and attempting to kill seven others. Police wounded him, bringing his rampage to an end. Dunn knew none of his victims. They just happened to be at the place that he chose for his shooting spree.[18]

There also seems to be an act of egotism involved, as though the subject is proving that his or her life is worth the lives of multiple others. This egotism also extends to the subject's belief that his or her particular problem, which may seem fairly common to other people, demands a grandiose solution. On February 11, 2007, Sulejman Talovic talked to Monika Ibrahimovic over the telephone. Both were Bosnian immigrants. The two had never met in person, but Talovic felt close enough to Ibrahimovic to confide to her that "tomorrow would be the happiest day of his life." He also stated that "she would never forgive him," but did not explain what she would never forgive him for. The next day, Talovic went to the Trolley Square Mall in Salt Lake City, Utah, where he killed five people and wounded four more before police shot him 15 times, killing him. Talovic knew none of his victims; they just happened to be at the place where he chose to launch his attack.[19] Apparently, what made Talovic happy was taking as many victims as he could before police killed him.

Churches and church functions also provide a venue for gathering-place violence. In early May 1956, 400 worshippers gathered at the St. Dumitru Romanian Orthodox Church in New York City for a midnight service ushering in the Eastern Orthodox Easter. Tony Sava, from a room across the street, began firing into the crowd. He managed to kill the church warden and wound five other people before breaking off the attack. The next day, Sava went to the Criminal Courts Building in New York City and surrendered. When asked the inevitable "why," Sava cried out, "Long life, liberty" and then mumbled something about doing it "for America." He then explained that all he really intended to do was "scare the people" gathered at the church.[20]

Case Illustration: The Wedgwood Baptist Church Massacre

Every Wednesday, around 150 students attending the Wedgwood Baptist Church gathered in the evening for the "See You at the Pole" service during which the students affirmed their faith and expressed their concerns for the problems of society by praying around the school's flagpole. Inside the sanctuary, other students gathered for choir practice.

On this Wednesday, September 16, 1999, Larry Ashbrook decided to make an appearance. Ashbrook's father had died 2 months before, leaving his house to his son. But Ashbrook had trouble making the mortgage payments. He had no steady job and was a source of trouble for his neighbors; on one occasion he exposed himself to two women across the street when he thought they were laughing at him. One neighbor explained that she always knew when Ashbrook was home because she could hear him kicking doors open and slamming them shut.

Armed with pistols and a pipe bomb, Ashbrook began firing into the crowd of teenagers. He reloaded several times, then lit the pipe bomb and threw it to the front of the sanctuary. After killing seven and wounding another seven, Ashbrook sat in a rear pew and shot himself in the head.

When police searched Ashbrook's house, they found considerable damage. Holes dotted the walls, the toilets had been broken, and concrete was poured down the drains.

Ashbrook was not a member of the Wedgwood Baptist Church, but he knew people would be gathered there on Wednesday evenings. (*Source:* Jim Yardley, "Gunman Kills 7, and Himself, at Baptist Church in Fort Worth," *New York Times*, September 16, 1999; Yardley, "Deaths in a Church: The Overview; An Angry Mystery Man Who Brought Death," *New York Times*, September 17, 1999)

In some cases, the rampage combines targeted and opportunistic violence. The subject may begin by first killing family members and then going after random victims. However, the reverse may also be true: The goal is the mass murder in a public place and the killing of family is the ego-driven final act behavior. Charles Whitman killed his mother and then his wife in order to spare them the shame of his next violent act: shooting 43 people from the clock tower at the University of Texas.[21] Similarly, Mark Barton killed his wife and then his son and daughter before killing nine and wounding 10 at the day-trading places where he had lost his life savings.[22] Both Whitman and Barton sought to kill as many people as they could. Killing their respective families constituted part of their final-act behaviors.

Shopping malls, schools, and other places where people gather may also represent opportunities to gain notoriety for the subject. Robert Hawkins, who killed eight at a department store in an Omaha, Nebraska, shopping mall, bragged to his friend, "Now I'll be famous."[23] For Hawkins, the department store offered him a venue for notoriety.

Guidelines for Assessing Threats to Gathering Places

As a result of these distinctions in threatening situations toward gathering places, we suggest that any threat assessment involving potential violence against a gathering place keep the following factors in mind:

- Violence against gathering places involves an increased use of opportunistic violence, although targeted violence may also be present.
- The subject using violence against gathering places usually seeks notoriety or fame based on a large body count or the connection to the well-known location.
- Violence against gathering places also seems to involve an act of egotism on the part of the subject. The subject believes that his or her personal grievance or loss demands a public exhibition of violence.

Although each situation under assessment needs to be assessed on its own evidence and in its own context, threat managers assessing situations involving gathering places should keep these attributes very much in mind when making the assessment. They lend context to each situation under assessment.

Why Workplaces Attract Violence

Several attributes of workplace violence distinguish it from other venues of intended violence. These incidents involve interpersonal relationships, which again puts the *intimacy effect* into play, but not at the same level of intimacy as domestic relationships. In general, workplace violence has a higher incident of leakage than other forms of violence. In schools, students frequently confide in fellow students about their plans to commit violence. One student even warned a favorite teacher not to come to school on the day that she and her three other conspirators planned to shoot up the school, thus allowing police to intervene before the elaborate plans were carried out.[24] Fellow workers frequently seem unsurprised when a fellow coworker turns violent. He or she may not have explicitly warned others of the upcoming assault, but his or her behavior in the days leading up to the attack indicated, if only in hindsight, that something was brewing.

Case Illustration: Leakage at School

High school student Evan Ramsay felt singled out and targeted for teasing and other mistreatments. He decided to avenge himself against those other students, particularly the school jocks, who caused the mistreatment. He told friends about his plans, even sought out one friend to tutor him in how to load and use the shotgun he intended to use.

On the day Ramsay picked to attack, at least a dozen fellow students gathered on the balcony overlooking the front hallway of the school. One even brought a video camera to record the event, but in the excitement of the moment forgot to turn it on.

Ramsay hid the shotgun in his pant leg while riding the bus to school. Upon entering the front door, Ramsay began shooting. He killed one other student and the school principal before police subdued him. (*Source:* Calhoun and Weston, *Contemporary Threat Management,* p. 47)

The ecosystem of a workplace or school provides countless opportunities for the development of a grievance. Some people are successful and some people fail. Some people are promoted and some people are fired. Some people are popular and some people are outcasts. The official and unofficial social structures are fertile ground for resentment and unmet expectations.

Workplace violence also frequently combines targeted and opportunistic violence. The subject seeks out supervisors or others who he or she believes caused the grievance, but also takes the opportunity to kill anyone else who happens to get in the way. Sometimes, by luck or happenstance, the subject cannot find the target or targets, but instead takes out his or her wrath on bystanders. This distinction makes workplace violence all the more horrific because of its seemingly indiscriminate nature.

Case Illustration: The Plastics Killer

Residents of the little town of Dixon, Kentucky, seemed divided in their opinions of Wesley N. Higdon. Some described him as "a good kid." Others, though, called him a troublemaker and said they were not surprised when he killed himself and five others at the plastics factory where he worked. "'He was the kind that got in trouble all the time," Rhonda Carter, who knew Higdon from high school, told a reporter. "He was always mischievous. He was kind of weird. When they said he was the shooter, I was not shocked."

In late June 2008, Higdon got into an argument with his supervisor. Whatever the issue, it infuriated him so much that he called his girlfriend, Teresa Ventura, and threatened to kill the supervisor and himself. Ventura chose not to call the police or warn anyone because Higdon had made those kinds of statements before. She did not believe that he really meant it, any more than he had meant the previous threats.

This time, he carried out the threats. After phoning Ventura, Higdon shot his supervisor outside the plastics plant and then went inside and randomly shot four fellow employees before killing himself.

(*Source:* Associated Press, "Kentucky Plant Gunman Known As Friend, Troublemaker," June 27, 2008)

Individuals who engage in workplace violence also seem to feel a greater sense of being wronged; they excuse their violence—both to themselves and to the world—as a legitimate act of revenge for some hurt or insult their victims did to them. Omar Thornton, immediately after his supervisors fired him for stealing six packs of beer, told the police dispatcher that he went on his shooting rampage, killing eight coworkers, because he was avenging the racial discrimination he had suffered working at the beer distribution warehouse. Although we continue to endorse Dr. James Gilligan's observation that all violence is a search for justice, in workplace settings that search seems to become particularly obsessive.[25] Bart Ross, for example, who went hunting for Judge Joan Lefkow, but ended up killing the judge's husband and mother, felt betrayed and maltreated because Judge Lefkow had dismissed his federal court case against Northwestern University Hospital. Although the hospital doctors and staff cured Ross's throat cancer, the cure left him disfigured and in constant pain. When the court refused to give him his desired justice, he claimed it for himself.[26]

As Ross demonstrated, hunters going after judicial officials frequently exhibit a profound sense of injustice. Their issues generally revolve around specific court cases in which they believe justice had not been met. As we argued in *Defusing the Risk to Judicial Officials,* five attributes distinguish attacks on jurists:

- Judicial officials are attacked because they represent—even personify—a system of justice.
- The motive prompting the attack is usually anger or revenge at that system.
- Target and assailant know each other through their involvement in that system.
- The judicial official openly resides in the same community as the attacker and can be easily found for attack.
- The judicial process entails bringing into the courtroom—often forcibly—individuals most likely to pose a risk to the judicial officials.[27]

Other forms of workplace violence bear similar traits. Employees and former employees frequently target supervisors and others who represent the company or organization; employees know each other. Disgruntled employees seek revenge against some perceived injustice committed by the employer. As Omar Thornton demonstrated, bringing an employee into the worksite in order to administer a disciplinary action exposes the worksite and its employees to the risk of violence.

Incident after incident demonstrates the role of vengeance in workplace violence. Joe Jackson killed three and wounded one at a Chicago law firm because he believed that the firm had cheated him out of patenting his invention—a toilet stashed under the driver's seat for long-haul truckers.[28] Grant Gallaher, a Baker City, Oregon, postman, became enraged when his supervisor asked him to deliver more mail. He returned to the post office after his shift, striking the supervisor with his mail truck. He went inside the post office looking for the postmaster. When he could not find him, Gallaher went back to the parking lot and shot the supervisor several times, killing her.[29] Some perceived insult or injustice prompts the subject's anger and the anger then gets translated into violence. The violence serves as the subject's justice.

We could go on with other examples, but the point seems clear. Workplace violence carries a heavy strain of revenge, of the subject seeking justice—a justice distorted by their own demands.

Case Illustration: Pursuing Justice

Jason Burnham complained to his mother that coworkers teased him at the Indianapolis factory where he worked. She advised him to ignore the teasing, but he could not. In mid-January 2007, Burnham took a .380 caliber handgun to work and sought out his tormentors. He shot two men and two women, wounding them. Police caught him in the cafeteria standing next to a vending machine. He offered no resistance when officers disarmed him. He told the officers that he had targeted the victims because of the teasing. "It was over respect," Burnham told the police, as though that justified his actions.

"There was some type of confrontation that was brewing all week, and it just came to a head and he got fed up and started shooting people," the Indianapolis police chief told reporters. (*Source:* Associated Press, "Four Hurt in Indianapolis Workplace Shooting," January 11, 2007)

Guidelines for Assessing Potential Workplace Violence

As a result of these distinctions in threatening situations toward workplaces or coworkers, we suggest that any threat assessment involving potential workplace violence keep the following factors in mind:

- The violence is interpersonal becausee the subject and the targets know each other from working together, thus bringing the intimacy effect into play.
- Leakage frequently occurs, either by an explicit threat or warning from the subject or by suspicions aroused among coworkers based

on the subject's behavior. Fellow workers are the best barometers for assessing an individual subject's potential for violence.
- Workplace violence frequently combines targeted and opportunistic violence; thus, it is not enough to assess the risk to a particular target. Rather, the risk to the workplace and all employees needs to be assessed.
- The most common motive for workplace violence is the search for justice, but it is a justice very specific and personal to the subject.

Although each situation under assessment needs to be assessed on its own evidence and in its own context, threat managers assessing situations involving potential workplace violence should keep these attributes very much in mind when making the assessment. They lend context to each situation under assessment.

Why Representative Targets Attract Violence

Some targets attract violence because they represent or symbolize something to the subject. Buford Furow, for example, went to the community center intending to shoot as many targets as he could—not because he knew it to be a child care center, but rather because the sign informed him that the target was a *Jewish* community center. For him, the target offered a way to express his fervent anti-Semitism. The fact that many of his victims were children also meant that they posed little risk to him personally.

Case Illustration: The Fence Jumper

Brian Patterson, bearded and wearing blue jeans and a white T-shirt, jumped over the wrought-iron fence surrounding the White House and ran across the north lawn toward the front entrance. As he ran, he repeatedly yelled out, "I am a victim of terrorism." It was midafternoon on a spring day in 2006.

Secret Service guards hustled to intercept him. "I have intelligence information for the president," Patterson told them. "I'm not afraid of you." The guards corralled him and he eventually knelt to the ground as they took him into custody. The incident was at least the fourth time Patterson had climbed the fence. For him, the White House represented sanctuary from the terrorists who he believed pursued him. (*Source:* Nedra Pickler, Associated Press, April 9, 2006)

Representative targets differ from other venues due to the symbolic value they hold for the subject. As a result, the subjects tend to engage in

opportunistic violence rather than targeted violence. What is most important to the subject is the symbolic value of whatever the target represents,
rather than the target and its victims.

In some cases, violence at iconic locations, such as courthouses or
bridges or the Hollywood sign, puts the violence on a larger, grander stage.
The location itself provides the notoriety that the subjects seek. Osama
bin Laden targeted the World Trade Center precisely because of its symbolic value. Al Qaeda had no interest in the people working in the twin
towers; the terrorists sought a high body count at a high-profile location
as a way to thumb their collective noses at the United States. Similarly,
Timothy McVeigh blew up the Murrah Federal Building because it symbolized to him the hated authority of the federal government. Violence
against representative targets tries to transfer the symbolic value of the
target to the attacker.

Case Illustration: Attacking Republicans

Matthew DePalma attended the CrimethInc. Convergence in Waldo,
Wisconsin, in July 2008. That event inspired him to begin planning to use
Molotov cocktails to attack the Xcel Energy Center in St. Paul, Minnesota,
during the Republican National Convention. DePalma described his
plans to an FBI informant.

In preparation for his attack, DePalma obtained enough materials to
assemble five arson cocktails before the FBI arrested him and prosecutors
charged him with possessing unregistered firearms.

For DePalma, the convention symbolized something he opposed.
He did not intend to target any particular victim. The congregation
of Republicans alone invited his violence. (*Source:* Associated Press,
"Michigan Man Accused of Planning Anti-GOP Attack," September 4,
2008)

Guidelines for Assessing Potential Attacks
Toward Representative Targets

As a result of these distinctions in threatening situations toward representative targets, we suggest that any threat assessment involving potential representative violence keep the following factors in mind:

- Violence against representative targets results from the target's symbolic value to the subject, rather than from some interpersonal dispute or interchange.

- The violence tends to be opportunistic rather than targeted. The subject seeks a high body count to deliver a message but not any particular individual target.
- Violence against representative targets tends to be acted out on a larger, grander scale, with the subject seeking to make some kind of profound statement by attacking the larger target, rather than just the individuals who happen to be there.

Although each situation under assessment needs to be assessed on its own evidence and in its own context, threat managers assessing situations involving potential violence against representative targets should keep these attributes very much in mind when making the assessment. They lend context to each situation under assessment.

Summary

In this chapter, we discussed the differences between several different venues for violence. We proposed that social ecosystems influence acts of violence by preying on the subject's motive and intent. Understanding the currents and interplay within each ecosystem gives the threat management team profound insight into the subject's purpose.

Although previous research on acts of intended violence tends to generalize across target venues, we believe that each venue offers distinct opportunities that attract subjects for different reasons. Violence against public figures, for example, has completely different objectives from those for domestic violence. While domestic violence tends to be about intimacy and control, workplace violence tends to be about assuaging personal injustice or insult. Violence targeting gathering places offers the subject a chance for infamy, while violence against representative or symbolic targets attracts the subject by the allure of whatever the target represents.

Keeping these distinct attributes very much in mind while conducting a threat assessment will help the threat assessor root the assessment within the context of the potential violence. Keeping context in mind by identifying which venue may be involved helps narrow the focus of the assessment. It also forces the assessor to ask the crucial questions: What is the target? Why this target?

Notes

1. Dietz, P. et al. (1991, September). Threatening and otherwise inappropriate letters to members of the United States Congress. *Journal of Forensic Sciences, 36*(5), 1466; Dietz, P. et al. (1991, January). Threatening and otherwise inappropriate letters to Hollywood celebrities. *Journal of Forensic Sciences,* 187 (1991, September).

2. Vossekuil, B., & Fein, R. (1998). *Protective intelligence and threat assessment investigations: A guide for state and local law enforcement officials* (p. 14). Washington, DC: National Institute of Justice.

3. Meloy, J. R. (2000). *Violence risk and threat assessment: A practical guide for mental health and criminal justice professionals* (p. 161). San Diego, CA: Specialized Training Services. To be fair, Meloy seems to have backed off from his discounting of the value of threats. See Meloy, J. R., Sheridan, L., and Hoffmann, J. (2008). Public figure stalking, threats, and attacks: The state of the science. In J. R. Meloy, L. Sheridan, and J. Hoffman (Eds.), *Stalking, threatening, and attacking public figures: A psychological and behavioral analysis* (p. 6). New York, NY: Oxford University Press.

4. Jenkins, D. M. (2009).When should threats be seen as indicative of future violence? Threats, intended violence, and the intimacy effect. In F. S. Calhoun & S. W. Weston (Eds.), *Threat assessment and management strategies: Identifying the hunters and howlers* (pp. 151–199). Boca Raton, FL: CRC Press.

5. ASIS & SHRM (2011, September). Workplace violence prevention and intervention: American national standard.

6. Authors' personal knowledge.

7. Clarke, J. W. (1982). *American assassins: The darker side of politics* (pp. 166–222). Princeton, NJ: Princeton University Press.

8. Calhoun, F. S. (1998). *Hunters and howlers: Threats and violence against federal judicial officials in the United States, 1789–1993* (pp. 33–35). Washington, DC: U.S. Marshals Service.

9. Phillips, R. T. M. (2008). Preventing assassination: Psychiatric consultation to the United States Secret Service. In J. R. Meloy, L. Sheridan, and J. Hoffman (Eds.), *Stalking, threatening, and attacking public figures: A psychological and behavioral analysis* (pp. 370–383). New York, NY: Oxford University Press.

10. Fein, R. A., & Vosssekuil, B. (2000). Protective intelligence and threat assessment investigations: A guide for state and local law enforcement officials (p. 19). Washington, DC: National Institute of Justice.

11. Schlesinger, L. B., & Mesa, V. B. (2008). Homicidal celebrity stalkers: Dangerous obsessions with nonpolitical public figures. In J. R. Meloy, L. Sheridan, and J. Hoffman (Eds.), *Stalking, threatening, and attacking public figures: A psychological and behavioral analysis* (p. 101). New York, NY: Oxford University Press.

12. Jenkins, D. When should threats be seen as indicative of future violence? Threats, intended violence, and the intimacy effect. In F. S. Calhoun & S. W. Weston (Eds.), *Threat assessment and management strategies: Identifying the hunters and howlers* (pp. 185–191). Boca Raton, FL: CRC Press.

13. Tjaden, P., & Thoenes, N. (2000). *Extent, nature and consequences of intimate partner violence: Findings from the National Violence Against Women Survey* (p. iv). Washington, DC: National Institute of Justice.

14. Tjaden, P., & Thoenes, N. (2000). *Extent, nature and consequences of intimate partner violence: Findings from the National Violence Against Women Survey* (p. 33). Washington, DC: National Institute of Justice.

15. Danvers, Massachusetts, Police Department. Assessing whether batterers will kill. http://sww.danverspolice.com/domvio14.htm

16. Metro Nashville Police Department. Domestic abuse: Symptoms of abuse—Threats, power misuse, and control. http://www.telalink.net/--police/abuse/symptoms.htm

17. American Judges Foundation. Domestic violence in the courtroom: Understanding the problem. Knowing the victim. http://aja.ncsc.dni.us/domviol/booklet.html

18. Associated Press. (2006, April 4). Alleged gunman in California spree charged.

19. Associated Press. (2008, January 30). No motive found for Utah mall gunman.

20. Feinberg, A. (1956, May 8). Sniper surrenders in church slaying, *New York Times*.

21. Calhoun, F. S., & Weston, S. W. (2003). *Contemporary threat management: A guide for identifying, assessing, and managing individuals of violent intent* (pp. 11–12). San Diego, CA: Specialized Training Services.

22. Georgia killer's notes show a troubled man, July 30, 1999, CNN U.S. http://articles.cnn.com/1999-07-30/us/9907_30_atlanta.shooting.06_1_gladys-barton-debra-spivey-barton-note?_s=PM:US

23. Associated Press. (2007, December 6). Mall gunman called quiet and depressed; CNN. (2007, December 6). Police: Nine killed in shooting at Omaha mall, including gunman.

24. Associated Press. (2001, November 28). Fourth student charged in Massachusetts plot.

25. Gilligan, J. (1997). *Violence: Reflections on a national epidemic* (pp. 11–12). New York, NY: Random House.

26. Dardick, H., & Sadovi, C. (2005, March 11). Decade of despair boiled over to paranoia. *Chicago Tribune*.

27. Calhoun, F. S., & Weston, S. W. (2001). *Defusing the risk to judicial officials: The contemporary threat management process* (pp. 27–48). Alexandria, VA: National Sheriffs Association.

28. Johnson, C. K. (2006, December 9). Police: Shooter thought he was cheated over invention. *Chicago Tribune*.

29. Cockle, R. (2006, April 8). Union says postal worker upset over request to deliver extra mail. *Oregonian*.

Case Studies on the Different Venues for Violence

10

Rather than focus on one detailed case study illustrating the concepts from the previous chapter, here we offer five brief case studies illustrating the five venues for violence discussed in Chapter 9. The "Lessons Learned" section compares and contrasts the examples in order to exemplify the differences among the various venues.

Why Public Figures Attract Violence: The Reluctant Public Figure

Tony Hayward did not want status as a public figure known—and reviled—around the world. Events thrust him into the world spotlight. On April 20, 2010, a tragic accident occurred on BP's Deepwater Horizon oil rig off the coast of Louisiana. An explosion killed 11 crewmen and released millions of gallons of oil into the Gulf of Mexico. As BP's chief executive officer (CEO) at the time, Hayward stood up for his company as its public spokesman.

And he did an abysmal job of it.

After a series of very public gaffes, he earned the nicknames "Captain Clueless" and the "Bumbler from BP." Two months after the explosion, newspapers published photographs of Hayward, adorned with baseball cap and sunglasses, taking part in a yacht race around the Isle of Wight, rather than helping slough the oil off the gulf. During one interview, he complained, "I would like my life back." Hauled before the U.S. Congress, Hayward refused to answer questions some 65 times, responding to one question saying, "I can't answer that because I wasn't there." He also minimized the ecological damage to the gulf from all the oil spewing out from the deepwater well. "I think the environmental impact of this disaster is likely to be very, very modest," he told one interviewer, adding that the spill was "relatively tiny" compared to the "very big ocean."[1]

These performances and faux pas earned Hayward the wrath of the public around the world. And, as so often happens when a public figure becomes notorious, it brought him personally to the attention of those angry at BP or the perception of BP as portrayed by the media. He and his family—his wife and two teenage daughters—began receiving death threats, hate mail, and other "nasty" telephone calls at his private residence near Sevenoaks, Kent, England. British police put him under 24-hour protection.

On July 26, BP's board of directors replaced Hayward with a new CEO. But even that step further stoked the fires of the outraged public. Hayward's publicized retirement package included a seven-figure payoff, 1 year's continued salary, and an estimated £584,000 annual pension. The settlement prompted one charter boat crewman no longer able to work in the gulf to say, "Will people be angry? Hell, of course. It's going to be galling and a slap in the face for the fishermen who have lost everything."[2]

Timing being everything, Hayward's abrupt departure also outraged the families of the 270 victims killed in the Lockerbie terrorist bombing of December 1988. Congress had summoned Hayward and other BP executives to testify that week on what, if any, role BP had in arranging for the release of Abdelbaset al-Megrahi, the only man convicted in the terrorist attack. "It's the chance to finally get some answers from BP and Mr. Hayward," Frank Duggan, president of Victims of Pan Am 103, Inc., announced, "and it doesn't look like he is going to be there."[2] Hayward could not even handle his departure from BP without controversy. Having had his 15 minutes of fame, the reluctant public figure faded from the public eye.

Why Domestic Partners Attract Violence: "If I Can't Have Him/Her..."

Josh Powell owned his two sons, Charlie, 7, and Braden, 5. During a camping trip in December 2009, Powell's wife, Susan, disappeared. For the next 2 years, police considered Powell the sole "person of interest" in her disappearance, but they never found the body or any other evidence to support an arrest. Powell moved the boys into his father's house, but lost custody of them when authorities discovered child pornography and videotapes of women and young girls in the father's possession. A judge ordered the boys into the custody of their maternal grandparents. Utah police also found "incestuous" sex images on Powell's computer, but by then he had moved to Washington state. They forwarded the pictures to police there.[3]

Powell fought back. In early February 2012, he petitioned the court to grant him custody of the two boys. During a child custody hearing, a psychologist recommended that Powell undergo "intensive" psychosexual evaluation. The judge agreed, but he also allowed Powell to have supervised visitation with the two boys. Powell arranged for the boys to visit him the following Sunday, February 5.[4]

Prior to their arrival, Powell began his final preparations. He donated the boys' toys to charity and sent e-mails saying good-bye and "I'm sorry" to his friends and his attorney. In a voice mail to his family, Powell said, "I am not able to live without my sons and I'm not able to go on anymore."[5]

Elizabeth Griffen-Hall, a Washington social worker, took the boys to Powell's house around lunchtime that Sunday. Powell greeted them at the front door, but did not let Griffen-Hall into the house. She heard him tell Charlie, "I've got a big surprise for you." Moments later, she heard Braden cry out. Then, she smelled gasoline. She called 911, but the dispatcher told her that they only responded to "emergencies, life-threatening situations first." Griffen-Hall responded, "Well, this could be life threatening." Through the window, she saw Powell. "I saw Josh for just 1 second. His eyes caught mine," she told a reporter. "He had a look in his eyes that was just kind of sheepish and then he slammed the door." Moments later, an explosion knocked her down.[4]

Afterward, police determined that Powell first bludgeoned his sons with a hatchet, hitting them each in the head and neck. The blows did not kill them, but certainly contributed to their deaths. He then set off a gasoline explosive device that he had rigged in the home. All three died of smoke inhalation before the fires consumed them.[5]

A friend of Powell's, John Hallewell, tried to explain Powell's motive: "I don't think it could have been for revenge," he said. "I think it was more a case where he thought he was in a corner and didn't have a way of keeping the kids, and thought, 'If I can't have them, nobody's going to.'"[5]

Why Gathering Places Attract Violence: "Thank God, This Is a Sunday..."

Robert Bonelli, Jr., at 25 years old, had a "lurid fascination" with the 1999 Columbine High School shootings. His journal recorded his admiration for Eric Harris and Dylan Klebold, as well as a "morbid lust for weapons, for blood, for homicide, for suicide," according to the New York district attorney who prosecuted Bonelli in May 2006. The prosecutor charged Bonelli with wounding two people and firing more than 60 rounds from an assault-style rifle at a shopping mall in Kingston, New York.[6]

On February 13, 2005, Bonelli purchased armor-piercing ammunition from a nearby Walmart. Several hours later, dressed all in black, he went to the Kingston shopping mall where more than 300 shoppers had gathered. He began firing, mostly into the floor of the Best Buy. Bullet fragments hit Thomas Silk in the wrist and knee. Private Thomas Haire, a recruiter for the National Guard, was shot in the left knee, crippling him for life. At trial, the prosecutor played 911 tapes made from inside the mall. The sound of gunfire played in the background of each call.[6]

Police officers subdued Bonelli, placing him under arrest. He confessed that he had planned for the police to kill him. Silk took a contrary view. "Had he wanted to commit suicide 'by cop' he could have picked a police station instead of a crowded mall," the victim told the court. "He did not want to die; he wanted to terrorize." Clearly, Bonelli went to the mall because he knew that many people would be there. It offered him a target-rich environment.[6]

On the day of the shootings, Bonelli told the police officer who arrested him, "Thank God this is a Sunday, because if it was Monday, it would be a school."[6]

Why Workplaces Attract Violence: An Eye for an Eye

Dr. Bradley Schwartz had reached the top. He had a successful pediatric medical practice called "Arizona Specialty Eye Care," pulling in over a million dollars a year by 2001. Indeed, the practice was so successful that Schwartz decided to hire a partner. He offered the job to Dr. Brian Stidham in 2001. Together, they expanded the practice.[7]

Yet, Schwartz also had problems. He was a womanizer, and police later estimated that he had had over 50 affairs with the mothers of his patients. "If patients came in, he would tell our techs, 'Here comes a GLM'—good looking mother. And if there was a good looking mother, the techs knew to give them extra time," the office manager, Laurie Espinoza, remembered.[8]

By late 2001, Schwartz had developed chronic back pain and began prescribing himself Vicodin. Four weeks after Stidham joined the practice, agents with the Drug Enforcement Agency raided the practice. Nine months later, prosecutors indicted Schwartz for false prescriptions. He lost his medical license and was ordered into a drug rehabilitation program. His partner, Stidham, gave 30 days' notice and began planning to open his own practice. Schwartz's life was falling apart.[8]

A year later, Schwartz got his license back and he set about trying to rebuild his practice. But Stidham's success rankled, and Schwartz developed an almost obsessive hatred for his former partner. He accused Stidham of taking away his patients. One of his girlfriends remembered Schwartz's attitude toward Stidham: "How dare he? The only reason this guy has any patients? Anybody knows about him? Is because I brought him here." Increasingly, Schwartz blamed Stidham for abandoning him, taking his staff and some of his patients, and destroying his once successful practice.[7]

On the night of October 5, 2004, Dr. Stidham left his office, set the burglar alarm, and headed toward his car. As he crossed the parking lot, someone attacked him with a knife, stabbing him 15 times and leaving him for dead. Schwartz had an ironclad alibi. At the time of the murder, he was on a date with a woman he met on an online dating site. They were having dinner at a Thai restaurant.[8]

But as police continued their investigation, they pieced together enough evidence to show that Schwartz paid Ronald "Bruce" Bigger, a fellow drug addict and former patient, $10,000 for the murder of Dr. Stidham. In May 2006, a jury convicted Schwartz of conspiring to kill Dr. Stidham, though the jury claimed that it could not reach a verdict on the first-degree murder charge.[7]

Why Representative Targets Attract Violence: "A Man Who's Dangerous, Who's Not Rational, and He Has Weapons"

Jacob Robida, dressed all in black, went to Puzzles Lounge in New Bedford, Massachusetts, late on the evening of February 1, 2006. He ordered a drink. When the bartender brought it to him, Robida asked if Puzzles was a gay bar. A website offering resources for gays and lesbians listed Puzzles as a place to go. The lounge had proved popular with the local gay community.[9]

Robida finished his drink shortly after midnight and ordered another one. He wandered over to the back of the bar. Two men were playing pool. Robida shoved one of the men to the ground, pulled a hatchet from under his sweatshirt, and began hitting the man on the head. Nearby patrons tackled Robida, sending the hatchet skittering across the floor. Robida pulled a pistol. He shot both pool players and then another man coming out of the bathroom, striking him in the chest. Robida then fled from the bar.[9]

"Obviously, we have a man who's dangerous, who's not rational, and he has weapons," Paul Walsh, Jr., the local prosecutor, warned.[9]

Robida went home, bleeding from the head according to his mother. He left the house and drove to West Virginia, where his former girlfriend lived. He somehow got her to join him. Police suspected that he abducted her. As they crossed into Arkansas, a policeman pulled them over for a traffic stop. Robida shot and killed the officer and then fled the scene. Other officers took up the chase. The pursuit went on for 20 miles before Robida pulled over. He exchanged fire with police and then shot his companion, killing her. He then put the gun to his head and killed himself.[10] A search of his room uncovered a homemade poster of a Nazi swastika and a small arsenal of firearms, swords, and knives. Anti-Semitic graffiti adorned the walls. Police also found a note Robida that had addressed to his mother. It said, in part, "I had to go out by my means."[11]

Robida was 18 years old.

Lessons Learned

Each of these different venues for violence offers its own attraction for the violent acts. Understanding their differences and why subjects seek the violent act helps the threat manager better assess the subject's intent and motive.

1. In the four cases that resulted in violence, the perpetrators followed the path to intended violence, including grievance, ideation, planning, preparation, breach, and attack. In the public figure case, which did not result in violence, the target was subjected to howler-type behaviors—that is, threats and inappropriate contacts communicated from a distance for the purpose of causing fear and expressing anger.

2. Those who wrote BP's CEO wanted to cause fear and convey their message of outrage over the oil spill and Hayward's insensitive reaction to it. Josh Powell intended to assert the ultimate power and control over his children. Robert Bonelli hoped to gain attention through an act of violence at a location chosen for that purpose. Dr. Schwartz sought personal justice and revenge. Jacob Robida attacked individuals whom he believed to be part of a group that he professed to hate.

3. Tony Hayward did not seek public figure status; events thrust it upon him. For threat managers, the lesson here is to anticipate when and evaluate why a protectee gets targeted for threats and threatening incidents. Has the protectee done something to attract public attention, thus making the protectee a temporary public figure? How are his or her actions presented in the media? Hayward's own actions and statements further estranged the public and incited the angry response. Threat managers need to evaluate not only what the public figure does, but also how the public perceives those actions.

4. Unlike public figure violence, which is about threatening and inappropriate contact inspired by public attention, domestic violence centers on issues of control and power within the relationship. Josh Powell wanted complete control over his two sons. When the court took them from him, giving custody to the boys' maternal grandparents, Powell became enraged. He decided that if he could not have the boys, no one would.

5. Violence at gathering places seems to emerge from the subject's obsession with becoming important and being somebody, with doing something so horrific and memorable that in his or her mind it earns the subject a place in history.

6. Workplaces attract violence out of the subject's sense of being mistreated, of suffering some injustice. Schwartz blamed Stidham for

taking away his medical practice, when in fact Schwartz's addiction and mistreatment of his authority to prescribe medicine was his own undoing. In his reality, he sought personal justice against his former partner.

7. Robida went to Puzzles because it was a well-known hangout for gays and lesbians. The lounge represented something to him that inspired him to commit violence. Therefore, any patron in the bar personified the characteristics of the group that he wanted to target with violence. Robida did not target them as individuals. Rather, in his mind, their presence in the bar identified them as gay, thus making them his desired target.

Notes

1. Bracchi, P. (2010, July 26). Captain Clueless walks the plank…but is he just a scapegoat? *Mail Online*; Helman, C. (2010, May 18). After the spill: Big oil plots its comeback. *Forbes*.

2. Barrow, B., & Bates, D. (2010, July 26). BP blunderer's golden good-bye: Hayward exits with £10 million pension pot as he's replaced by an American. *Mail Online*.

3. Flegenheimerm, M., & Raftery, I. (2012, February 5). Man whose wife disappeared dies with sons in explosion. *New York Times*; Matthews, L. (2012, February 10). Josh Powell explosion: Dad had a "sheepish" look, "incestuous" images found. *International Business Times*; Caulfield, P. (2012, February 7). Final voice mail released in Josh Powell murder–suicide explosion. *New York Daily News*.

4. Matthews, L. (2012, February 10). Josh Powell explosion: Dad had a "sheepish" look, "incestuous" images found. *International Business Times*.

5. Caulfield, P. (2012, February 7). Final voice mail released in Josh Powell murder–suicide explosion. *New York Daily News*.

6. Holl, J. (2006, May 19). Man sentenced to 32-year prison term in mall shooting. *New York Times*.

7. Associated Press. (2006, May 3). Ariz. eye surgeon convicted of conspiracy; Paisley, I., Aguiar, L., & Halderman, J. (2007, October 25). An eye for an eye. CBS News.

8. Paisley, I., Aguiar, L., & Halderman, J. (2007, October 25). An eye for an eye. CBS News.

9. Henry, R. (2006, February 2). Teen shoots up Mass. bar, police say. Associated Press.

10. Jacob Robida entry, Murderpedia, http://murderpedia.org/male.R/r/robida-jacob.htm; Associated Press. (2006, February 7). Prosecutor: Teen in gay attack left note.

11. Jacob Robida entry, Murderpedia, http://murderpedia.org/male.R/r/robida-jacob.htm

On Cutbacks, Silos, Bunkers, and Myopic Management Strategies 11

In this chapter, we present a number of disparate concepts we see currently emerging in the field of threat management. Budget cuts at the state and local government levels are severely impacting any threat manager's ability to intervene effectively. Threat management teams—not only in law enforcement, but also in the mental health and private industry sectors—have enclosed themselves in silos, cutting themselves off from effective information sharing and communication with other entities. They have also hunkered down into bunkers, effectively blinding themselves to the larger issues presented by individuals who intend to act violently.

Finally, we perceive a growing tendency to apply threat management strategies in a nearsighted fashion. Each of these trends works to the detriment of successful threat management. Consequently, we intend to use this chapter as a clarion call for more intelligent uses of intervention strategies and a warning against building silos, establishing bunkers, and pursuing myopic threat management strategies.

Diminishing Access to Intervention Strategies

Since the publication of our previous book in 2007, the United States, indeed the entire world, suffered the worst recession since the Great Depression. Its impact has yet to go away. Among many disastrous consequences, the Great Recession reduced tax base funding available to state and local governments. The resulting budget pressure reduced funding for core programs.

Case Illustrations: Cutting Back

A budget shortfall of $1.8 million forced the Klamath County, Oregon, sheriff to abruptly end construction on two needed pods at the county jail, thus increasing the problem of overcrowding.

In late 2011, Pennsylvania state police faced laying off up to 500 troopers because of budget cuts.

Alameda, California, police and firemen watched helplessly as a man drowned. Budget cuts in their training programs resulted in none of them being certified for water safety. Had they tried to save the man, they could have been sued. (*Sources:* B. Franklin, "Klamath County Budget

Shortfall," Klamath News.net, January 5, 2012; Jan Murphy, "Facing Budget Cuts, Pennsylvania State Police Forecast Possibility of Laying Off 500 Troopers," *Patriot News,* December 11, 2011; Stephen C. Webster, "Budget Cuts Force California Police and Firemen to Watch Man Drown," *Raw Replay,* June 1, 2011)

We have described a range of intervention strategies starting with the least intrusive and confrontational—do nothing at this time—to the most confrontational—arrest and prosecution. The following graphic illustrates the array of threat management strategies available to threat management teams.

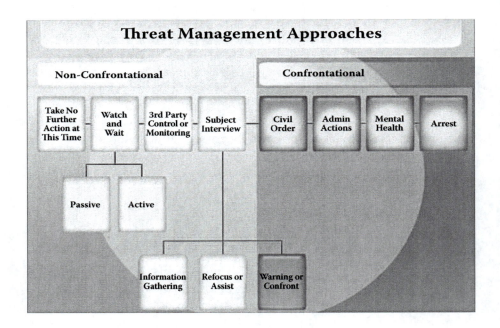

The economic downturn and the resultant reduction in funding for state and local services has had a profound impact on several of these strategies, thus limiting the options currently available for threat managers. The loss in funding hit the strongest interventions—arrest and prosecution and mental health commitments—especially hard. It compelled many law enforcement agencies to adopt a back-to-basics philosophy, causing them to reduce or eliminate specialized units that formerly focused on threat assessment and mental health commitments. Threat crimes compete for investigative attention with crimes generally perceived as more urgent, such as homicide or robbery. In effect, threat crimes draw attention only after the threat has been carried out. In addition, across the country, law enforcement agencies reduced or even eliminated specialized training in threat assessment because budget reductions typically begin with training.

At the prosecution level, many jurisdictions downsized or eliminated specialized units targeting domestic violence. Staff reductions require prosecutors to take a more selective approach to deciding which cases to prosecute, forcing them to plead down many cases to lesser charges. In the fall of 2011, the Topeka, Kansas, City Council repealed the city's ordinance prohibiting domestic violence after the Shawnee County district attorney, citing budget shortfalls, transferred enforcement of those laws to the Topeka Police Department. The district attorney claimed that a 10% budget cut forced him to suspend prosecution of misdemeanor cases, over half of which had been domestic battery cases the year before. The City Council also cited budget concerns for the city's inability to enforce the laws.

As a result, at least 20 accused abusers were released from prison.[1] The game of chicken ended after a month when the district attorney blinked first by agreeing to prosecute cases of alleged domestic violence once again. "My office now retains sole authority to prosecute domestic battery misdemeanors and will take on this responsibility so as to better protect and serve our community," District Attorney Chad Taylor said in a statement. "We will do so with less staff, less resources, and severe constraints on our ability to effectively seek justice."[2] Budget concerns disrupted the enforcement of the law.

Even when a prosecution succeeds, jail and prison crowding result in reduced sentences, early release, or placing more subjects on unsupervised probation. The strategy of third-party control relies heavily on the probation and parole systems, both now severely understaffed. Some jurisdictions choose to eliminate special units that previously monitored domestic violence offenders and mentally ill subjects.

Case Illustrations: Setting Up for Failure

In February 2011, *USA Today* reported an increase in the number of felonies by individuals on probation or parole, blaming it in part on cuts to programs that help former inmates stay out of prison. The director of the Pew Center's Public Safety Performance Project, Adam Gelb, warned that state budget cuts put successful criminal justice programs at risk. "The [financial] hole is so deep," said Gelb. "Programs for convicted felons are an easy target." Carl Wicklund, executive director of the American Probation and Parole Association, blamed the fiscal crisis for "pushing more people out of prison" with fewer people to supervise them and fewer dollars to support drug treatment, housing, and job assistance. "We're setting these people up for failure," Wicklund says.

The Thurston County, Washington, District Court Probation Office website begins with this simple announcement: "Due to budget cuts, the Probation Office can be reached by phone from 8:30 a.m. to 3:30 p.m."

In Minnesota in 2010, some counties saved money by leaving probation officer positions unfilled, or by cutting positions. Those officers left on the job ended up with more people to supervise. They complained that higher caseloads endangered their ability to ensure public safety. "It gets frustrating. You get into this business because you want to help people. You want to help people change their lives," said Patrick Guernsey, a Hennepin County probation officer for 17 years. "And what's going to end up happening is people are going to fail."

At the federal level, the Southern District of New York faced budget cuts of 10% to 15% in 2012, possibly forcing the court to fire more than 15% of nonjudicial staff in the clerk, probation, pretrial services, and district executive offices. The effect of these layoffs could keep the court from funding narcotics testing and treatment during bail investigations, Chief Judge Loretta Preska testified before a six-member task force studying the effects of the budget cuts. She further stated that cuts in the probation department could prevent carrying out random searches to find child pornography on a convicted sex offender's computer. The chief U.S. probation officer, Eileen Kelly, estimated that funding cuts would leave her short two dozen probation officers. That would disrupt postconviction supervision and work and education programs. She complained before the task force that judges would not change the sentencing they doled out because of budgetary constraints. "I don't think that judges are going to sentence people based on finances," Kelly said. (*Sources:* Kevin Johnson, "Budget Cuts Slice Programs for Ex-Inmates," *USA Today,* February 8, 2011; www.co.thurston.wa.us/distcrt/probation.htm; Rupa Shenoy, "Budget Cuts Hurt Probation Efforts," Minnesota Public Radio, January 4, 2010; Adam Klasfield, "Federal Judges Worry Over New York Budget Cuts," Courthouse News Service, December 8, 2011)

After many years of underfunding and lack of crucial resources, the Great Recession slammed into mental health facilities again. Local governments significantly reduced (in some cases even eliminated) the number of mental health crisis beds. That compelled law enforcement to take mentally ill individuals to hospital emergency rooms for treatment. Overcrowding there resulted in releasing these patients without adequately treating their underlying mental health conditions. Once they were back on the street, the cycle continued.

Increasingly, mental health facilities will be unable to treat all but the most severely mentally ill. According to the National Alliance on Mental

Illness (NAMI), two thirds of the states slashed funding for mental health services in the past 3 years. "State mental health cuts are a national crisis," the executive director of NAMI, Michael Fitzpatrick, complained. "Some states are trying to hold the line or make progress, but most are cutting deep." The cuts created a domino effect impacting emergency rooms and the court system because people needing help go to those two services when they cannot get mental health care. "Mental health cuts mean that clinics, crisis centers, and hospitals close," Fitzpatrick explained, "Where services remain, staff is cut, wait times for appointments are stretched, and when people finally are seen, it's for shorter amounts of time."[3] Consequently, threat managers found it extremely difficult to use mental health commitments to manage a subject simply because most mental health facilities lacked sufficient resources to afford new patients. Again with California the lead example, the Supreme Court recently ruled that overcrowding in the state prison system's mental health unit violated the prisoners' Eighth Amendment rights not to be subjected to cruel and unusual punishment.[4]

Mental health counselors in Massachusetts argued that budget cuts there contributed to the murder of two mental health counselors in that state in separate incidents in January 2011. On January 8, a client kidnapped a mental health counselor from a group home in Revere and brutally murdered her. On January 20, a homeless 19-year-old with a history of mental problems stabbed a shelter worker to death in Lowell. "If you have one woman [counselor] and five men with mental health problems, it screams to me of mental health cuts," Barry Sanders, a Massachusetts counselor with 20 years' experience, said, referring to the January 20 murder. "Having these kinds of staffing levels is like playing the odds—rolling the dice with someone's life." According to Laurie Martinelli, executive director of the Massachusetts chapter of the NAMI, "It's been devastation. Complete and utter destruction and devastation. The entire mental health system is shredded."[5]

Case Illustration: The Untimely Death of Linda Carol Clark

Police frequently responded to Linda Carol Clark's home in Folsom, California, due to mental health issues. In March 2010, the neighboring El Dorado County Sheriff's deputies used their peace officer authority to take Clark to the emergency room under a mental health hold. While overworked staff at the hospital made arrangements to transfer Clark to a mental health facility, they left her unsupervised. She took the opportunity to hijack an ambulance. Responding officers took up a low-speed chase after the ambulance.

Clark evaded police efforts to stop the ambulance. Finally, she turned into a private drive, effectively cutting herself off from escape. Police cars barricaded her in. She put the ambulance into reverse and plowed into the police cars blocking her exit. An officer stepped in front of the ambulance just as she put it into drive and began moving forward. Fearing for his life, the policeman fired five times, hitting her once and killing her.

Carla Jacobs, writing in the *Sacramento Bee,* used Clark's death as her lead example to uphold her claim that "California has become a killing field for people with mental illness." (*Source:* "Coroner Identifies Woman Killed as Linda Clark of Folsom," www.news10.net/news/story.aspx?storyid=78411&catid=2, March 30, 2010; Carla Jacobs, "Looking at Laura's Law: Mentally Ill Are Dying for Lack of Care," *Sacramento Bee,* April 13, 2010)

At the civil court level, staff reductions resulted in long waits to obtain restraining orders and other civil actions that had been routine in the past. Again in California, for example, drastic state budget cuts severely weakened the judiciary. In San Francisco alone, those cuts have forced the courts to lay off 40% of their employees and close 25 of 63 courtrooms. Across the state, the courts face budget cuts of $350 million in operations and $310 million in construction budgets.[6] Because of these draconian measures, the court estimated that it will soon take hours to pay a traffic ticket, months to obtain copies of court records, and as long as a year and a half to get a divorce. Only criminal cases will go to trial.[7] Amidst all of this, trying to get a restraining order or other court process quickly to use in a threat situation will no doubt become nearly impossible. As California goes, so, ultimately, do most of the other 49 states.

Even if a target succeeds in getting such an order, it hardly matters now that the Supreme Court effectively gutted such court orders of any authority. In *Castle Rock v. Gonzales,* the Court granted local police departments complete discretion over enforcing temporary and permanent restraining orders.[8] That discretion extended to *not* enforcing court-ordered restraining orders. Given the budget impacts on police departments nationwide, it takes little imagination to envision many departments exercising that discretion to save money and resources.

At the risk of mimicking Chicken Little sounding the alarm that the sky is falling, we believe that threat managers need to be aware of the reality of the current economic situation because of the impact upon the availability of various intervention strategies. It does no good to depend on a particular intervention in theory when the reality on the street dooms it to failure.

For example, in a typical criminal threat case resulting in conviction, after a term of incarceration the subject would be placed on probation. The threat manager would then work with the probation department to impose strict conditions on the probation—specifically, measures designed to keep the subject away from the target. Depending on the circumstances of the case, these conditions might include stay-away orders, drug and alcohol testing, mandatory mental health counseling, anger management classes, and other conditions aimed at improving the subject's ability to deal with society. Also depending on the circumstances of the case, the threat manager could arrange for the subject to be placed in a specialized probation caseload—for example, domestic violence offenders—that would provide closer supervision. The threat manager would also stay in close contact with the probation officer to share information as necessary.

In 2002 and before, an experienced threat manager would have all these intervention tools available as a matter of course. In the current environment, the availability and effectiveness of the same interventions may not exist due to the following circumstances:

- The threshold for the evidence needed to begin a prosecution may be higher due to the reduction in staff and case priorities at the prosecutor's office.
- If the prosecutors do file the case, they may be more likely to plead it down to a lesser offense to avoid the cost of a trial.
- If convicted, the subject could serve little or no time due to overcrowding in prisons and jails.
- If the subject did serve prison time, he or she typically would have no access to drug treatment or mental health services.
- Upon release from jail or prison, the subject may be placed on unsupervised probation due to staff reductions.
- If placed on supervised probation, the subject would have little or no interaction with the probation officer due to overwhelming caseloads.
- Few, if any programs remain available for drug rehabilitation or mental health services.
- If the subject should violate his or her probation, returning to prison or jail for any significant time would be unlikely due to overcrowding.
- If the subject simply disappeared and went "at large," he or she would likely be apprehended only if caught in the commission of a new crime, most likely one related to the original target.
- If the threat manager succeeded in keeping in contact and sharing information with the probation officer (and this would be no easy task), the threat manager would consciously have to maintain reasonable expectations, always keeping in mind the size of the probation officer's caseload.

In detailing these current realities, we in no way mean to criticize the men and women currently working under these budget constraints and trying to do the best job they can under the circumstances. In this situation, the threat manager has to be realistic about the availability of some of the traditional intervention options and adjust his or her tactics accordingly. Today's successful threat manager has to be more proficient in gathering information, establishing effective liaisons, and using less confrontational intervention strategies than his or her predecessor a decade ago. That requires considerable creativity, flexibility, and, more than anything else, patience. The job, always a difficult and challenging one, is now all the more difficult and challenging.

All of this being true, employing arrest and prosecution as an intervention strategy requires the threat manager to overcome many challenges. To succeed, the threat manager must know the law, including current case law, for threat crimes within the jurisdiction in which he or she practices. The threat manager must ensure that the subject's conduct meets all the requirements of those laws. The threat manager must properly document the subject's conduct and ensure that all the evidence is legally obtainable. The victim and any witnesses must be willing and available to testify. The threat manager must present to the prosecuting authority a strong, compelling case: no almost cases, no close cases, no good-enough cases. If the prosecutor needs more evidence or additional follow-up, the case manager will need to get it done without delay. Even if the threat manager can truthfully say that all of these requirements have been met, a prosecution may not be obtainable or successful. If that happens, the best threat managers will regroup, assess the dynamics of the case and the synergy of the intervention, and then develop another strategy to control the subject's behavior.

This same strategy can be useful when mental health commitments are difficult, if not impossible, to obtain. Know the law and the standards required for mental health commitments within your geographic area. Know the process that must be followed and provide all available information in writing to the mental health treatment center or law enforcement. Be realistic about the mental health system's legal ability to detain a mentally ill person. Be knowledgeable about alternative sources of mental health treatment, such as community-based programs and faith-based programs. And, as with criminal prosecution, be prepared to develop another strategy to control a mentally ill subject's behavior.

If some type of civil order seems the best strategy, the threat manager must know the standards required and the administrative process necessary to obtain the order. The threat manager needs to know where to go and how to fill out the paperwork. This includes designing a protective response ensuring the detection of and immediate response to any violations of that civil order. And, again, if the court denies a civil order or otherwise makes it unobtainable, the threat manager needs to be prepared to develop another strategy to manage the subject's behavior, always keeping in mind the case dynamics and intervention synergy.

Despite the challenges outlined here, we do not give up hope. By describing the challenges resulting from budget shortfalls and legal limitations, we do not intend to foster despair. Instead, as always, we seek a realistic approach to resolving life and death issues. Continuing to employ the full range of threat management strategies currently available offers the best chance of diverting problem subjects away from potential acts of violence.[9]

Information Silos (The Silent Silos)

As we illustrated in Chapter 2 in the Scott Roeder case, information silos could have a detrimental effect on information flow regarding threat management cases. The silo effect is a phenomenon occurring when system components fail to communicate with each other. Picture a row of silos symbolizing the lack of connection between different units and the inability of anyone within one silo communicating or even seeing others in other silos.

Whenever there are information silos, regardless of the reason for their existence, the result is thwarted communication, competition between organizations, redundancy, and a higher risk of system failures. Since September 11, law enforcement has implemented significant improvements to tear down information silos among law enforcement agencies related to terrorism at the federal, state, and local levels. While law enforcement has come a long way, significant barriers still exist to the passing of information due to organizational policies and the sometimes indecipherable requirements for top-secret clearances and the need to know. The desire for confidentiality also affects the flow of information related to personnel matters or legal settlements.

Our society itself is compartmentalized with individual ecosystems separating government from private companies, schools from churches, cities from states. Sensitive information very rarely flows between these different systems unless required by law.

Case Illustration: College Silos

A medium-sized public junior college has its own ecosystem that includes a governance hierarchy, a security force, defined standards of success and failure, and a process and procedures for managing students. While located within the boundaries of the city, it operates independently.

A male student begins to act inappropriately in class, exhibiting signs of both mental illness and drug abuse. Other students are concerned about his behavior. As a result, they shy away from him, but do not report their concerns to school authorities for fear of getting him in trouble. He has also become infatuated with a female instructor, following her from a distance whenever she comes on campus. Due to his conduct in class, a department head refers him to Student Services for counseling. The female instructor reports his odd behavior to the campus police, who provide her an escort on request. The campus security officer provides the escort service when she requests it; however, upon learning that the male student is no longer attending classes, she stops asking for the service. The reason he is no longer attending classes is because the counseling provided by Student Services was unsuccessful. He preferred to skip class rather than continue the counseling. Because the male student's behavior was not overtly threatening or violent, campus officials took no further action.

In this hypothetical situation, how much information would be disseminated within or outside the ecosystem of the junior college? Because of the confidentiality policies within student services, campus police would not be aware of his mental illness and drug addiction behaviors. The mental health professional providing the confidential counseling would not be aware of his behavior directed toward the female instructor. The city's police department would not be aware of the student's behavior while on campus. Law enforcement officials in another city, where the student lived, would not be aware of his problematic behaviors. Law enforcement officials in the city where the female instructor resided would not be aware of the problem. The community mental health centers would not be aware of the student's problems because he sought treatment on campus. The next college in which he enrolls would not know about his past problems. In short, information about this problem would not leave the various silos within the ecosystem of the college campus. (*Source:* Hypothetical example based on authors' experience)

This same dynamic can and does occur within the ecosystems of other private organizations, such as an industrial plant. In that environment, the added obstacles of personnel confidentiality and nondisclosure agreements initiated by the legal department would also exist. While communication among law enforcement agencies has improved, few or no initiative to improve communication regarding security issues in the private sector has occurred.

While legal experts argue the need for confidentiality in personnel matters, it hinders sharing of relevant security information when a subject moves from organization to organization.

When a threat manager is assessing a situation, he or she should look for evidence of the silo effect and the potential impact of a particular ecosystem on information flow. When the threat manager assists a public or private organization, the threat manager may have to interact with several different segments of the organization to ensure that he or she obtains *all* relevant information. The threat manager, in effect, may have to act as a conduit between the different silos to bring all the different pieces of the puzzle together. He or she will also need to establish the conduit outside the organization, gathering information from other organizational ecosystems. The threat manager will be continuously working to ensure that the information he or she receives is not constricted or filtered by information silos. He or she will be asking the question: With what other organization has the subject interacted and does relevant information exist within those ecosystems?

The threat manager will have to work through information silo problems when considering a protective response. Have all appropriate notifications been made, including to other organizations and all potentially involved law enforcement organizations? Have all potential targets been identified? Have mental health services been informed of their patient's inappropriate conduct?

A very effective way to avoid information silos is to establish threat management teams with representatives from all relevant departments of an organization. Such a team would normally include members from human services, general counsel, operations, the threat manager, internal affairs, the ombudsman, civil rights, and security. Meeting together regularly and openly discussing issues that have come to the individual members' attention since the last meeting will ensure that information flows smoothly among all units of the organization. That flow erodes silos before they can be established.

These meetings are also opportunities to anticipate future threat-related problems within an organization. For example, if the personnel department plans layoffs, the entire team can work together to anticipate resultant problems. The team can share the names of those employees scheduled for the layoff, the members can analyze records from all sections in order to identify employees who may present a safety concern. The team can then work with security or local law enforcement to develop plans to manage the layoffs in a more sophisticated manner.

In a like manner, external meetings could be initiated between counterparts within an industry and representatives from law enforcement to share both information and critical events planned for the future. Regional information sharing meetings made up of law enforcement agencies and security personnel from large employers would also be a deterrent to the creation of silos. The key component to this strategy is to have these mechanisms in place prior to the discovery of problems.

Information silos will not go away for a variety of legal, confidential, and logistical reasons. Protocols can be established to minimize the impact of the silos and create mechanisms both to gather and to disseminate information effectively as part of an overall threat management program. This strategy has proved effective in many large organizations, such as universities and the defense industry. It promises the only antidote to the danger posed by silent silos.

Bunker Mentality (Bogus Bunkers)

The bunker mentality results from focusing so tightly on one aspect of the situation that people become blinded to other risks or threats. Bunker mind-sets fall at each end of the security spectrum. At one end, physical security measures are erected around a target or facility, giving anyone within the perimeter a feeling of safety. As time passes, the security erodes, often by the very actions of the individuals within the security perimeter. Yet, their feeling of complacency prevents anyone from seeing the holes emerging in the physical security measures. The bunker, they assume, is secure when, in reality, insecurity has crept in.

At the other end of the security spectrum, the bunker mentality may emerge when security identifies a subject as a potential risk and then takes whatever measures it can to deflect that subject from the target. The management strategies become so focused on protecting the bunker that threats to other targets are ignored. By protecting its own bunker, it unleashes the at-risk subject on other targets or on the community at large. In not alerting other security organizations, the bunker mentality endangers other targets while protecting its own.

Bogus bunkers, a companion concept to the silo effect, typically affect private organizations and government agencies. Their biggest impact occurs when protective measures or interventions in threat assessment cases are being designed and deployed. The bunker mentality springs from three erroneous beliefs that:

Protective measures alone can be designed that would fortify an organization against all potential threats

An intervention that would expel a threatening subject from an organization's ecosystem will provide adequate safety

It is appropriate to employ any and all interventions and countermeasures to ensure the safety of one target, but leave other targets or the general public at risk

Unless a security unit has unlimited time, money, and resources, such as the United States Secret Service, it is virtually impossible to fortify a location or secure a potential target from all potential harm for an unlimited duration of time. Designing security measures is always the traditional balance of security versus budget, convenience, and practicality. Budget always trumps security. Typically, those who make final security decisions will have to be realistic about how much security for how long. To complicate the situation further, the potential target and those affected by the security measures have to be convinced—and continuously reconvinced— that the inconvenience and indignity of the security is worth what they may discount as the risk of harm. As time passes, the memory of the security risk recedes.

Case Illustration: The Irate Attorney

The chief counsel for a large federal agency in Washington, DC, repeatedly refused to cooperate with the headquarters' building security measures. She claimed that, as one of the top agency executives, she should be allowed unfettered access to and from the building. On numerous occasions, she failed to carry her building pass with her when she left the building and then berated the contract security guards when they refused to let her back into the building without her pass. Although the guards followed security procedures, her hostile and intemperate attitude posed the risk of eroding security by intimidating the guards into accommodating her. (*Source:* Authors' personal knowledge)

Security usually degrades over time. Well-designed security measures are circumvented for convenience or to cater to the desires of the influential. Countless examples illustrate where this occurs:

- Employees prop open a back door, taping over the alarm contact, to accommodate smokers.
- Alarms are turned off after they are frequently tripped by employees.
- Security establishes special access for the influential to avoid security checks.
- Top management or officials do not have to use security badges; security personnel are required to memorize their pictures so that the officials are never inconvenienced by the delay of security procedures.

Many targets and decision makers maintain an in-denial or fatalistic attitude. They respond to security concerns with the belief that nothing has happened in the past; therefore, nothing will happen in the future. They also respond that if somebody really wants to do something, there is nothing we can do to stop them. Both these reasons are used to deny reasonable security recommendations.

Countless times, security is either installed or drastically enhanced immediately *after* some threat becomes public knowledge or a violent act has occurred. Usually, the purpose for doing so is to reassure employees or the public that a location or target is now safe. After a relatively short period of time, the security posture reverts back to the way it was before the violent act. In reality, most security decisions are clouded by nonsecurity considerations, such as fiscal impact, public perception, and a desire not to be too inconvenienced.

When designing protection for an individual, the equation becomes even more complex. Does the target want protection? How much protection will he or she endure and for how long? Will the target allow you to provide meaningful protection or does he or she want just the perception of protection? If the target is a public figure, will the cost of the protection become a political issue? Many public figures, for a variety of reasons, want to maintain the perception that they are "regular guys." Security manifestations, such as motorcades and bodyguards, detract from that perception. Other public figures want the manifestations of security precisely because it gives them an aura of importance.

Many times, protectees are inconsistent in what security they want or will tolerate. While in public, they want a security detail because of the convenience and ease of access to locations. In their private lives, they want security to go away because it intrudes on their privacy. Some public figure targets ignore reasonable security recommendations because they feel that they can take care of themselves or they are adverse to security in general.

Case Illustration: Special License Plates

Traditionally, California state legislators receive special license plates for their personal vehicles. This long-time practice allows them easier access through security checkpoints at the capitol. The plates also let them park illegally and otherwise receive preferential treatment from law enforcement. Over the years, the public has learned to recognize the special plates. Consequently, there have been many incidents of individuals harassing legislators or vandalizing their parked cars. The practice of issuing the special plates continues to this day, despite innumerable objections from security. The trappings of privilege outplay security and common sense. (*Source:* Authors' personal knowledge)

When security is designed and established at a physical location, some type of perimeter security is typically established that includes checkpoints and secure areas. The purpose of the checkpoints is to allow only authorized personnel into the area or to detect and stop harmful objects, such as guns or explosives, from entering the facility. The unintended consequence of this design is that the checkpoint is now the edge of security, which is the location where the threat will be detected. It becomes the point of assault of an attacker and the location of a potential gunfight. Unfortunately, many times the checkpoint is not designed to detect and repel a violent attack safely.

Case Illustration: The Attack on Blair House

Oscar Collazo and Griselio Torresola, two Puerto Rican natives seeking Puerto Rican independence from the United States, decided the best avenue for achieving that goal would be to assassinate President Harry S. Truman. But to get to Truman, the pair first had to get past three Secret Service officers and four White House policemen standing guard on Pennsylvania Avenue outside Blair House. Upstairs, the president napped.

The gunfight began when Collazo walked past the easternmost guard post. Two White House policemen stood outside the guardhouse chatting. Seeing them and another policeman inside the guardhouse, Collazo pulled his pistol and fired at the officer in the guardhouse. That forced Griselio Torresola, at the western end of the property, to begin firing as well. The gunfight lasted under 40 seconds, resulting in Torresola's death, the wounding of Collazo, and a policeman dying with another seriously wounded.

In deciding where to erect security, always ask, "Where do I want the gunfight to begin?" (*Source:* Stephen Hunter and John Bainbridge, Jr., *American Gunfight: The Plot to Kill Harry Truman—and the Shoot-Out That Stopped It*, New York, NY: Simon and Schuster, 2005, pp. 108, 128–132, 204–205, 240–242)

Putting aside the design issue, the personnel assigned to checkpoints are frequently not trained or equipped to be the person at the edge of security. Joe Jackson, the man outraged at the patent lawyer who he thought had stolen his invention for a driver's seat toilet for long-distance truckers, went to the lawyer's office at the Citigroup Center building in Chicago's West Loop. He pulled a pistol on the security guard screening people going up to the office floors. Jackson demanded that the guard escort him to the top floor of the building housing the law firm. As soon as Jackson entered the law offices, the guard fled, taking a train to his home in Indiana. While the guard fled, Jackson killed three people and wounded a fourth. Police SWAT officers killed him. Police were not able to reconstruct how Jackson got to the top floor until the guard contacted them several hours later.[10]

The concept of edges of security also comes into play at courthouses, which in recent years have greatly improved security at the state and local levels. Before, disgruntled spouses did their shooting in the courtroom, but, with the improved security, they have been forced to intercept their spouse or former spouse in the parking lot or at the courthouse entrance—that is, on the public side of security.

Case Illustration: Adding Connecticut to the List

Michael Bochicchio, Jr., and his estranged wife began nasty proceedings over custody of their two children, a boy, 14, and a girl, 12. Bochicchio, a retired Connecticut state trooper, filed for divorce in 2003, but continued living with his family until ordered to leave by a judge in May 2004. The superior court judge found that Bochicchio's "constant requests for affection from his wife ha[ve] created a very tense atmosphere in the home" and that his behavior toward her was "intimidating and harassing."

On June 15, 2005, Bochicchio knew where to find his wife. They were both scheduled for a court hearing on the child custody at around 9:30

that morning. He waited in the parking lot next to the state courthouse. When his wife and her lawyer arrived, Bochicchio approached them and opened fire, killing the wife and wounding the lawyer. He then turned the gun on himself, finally dying later that night.

"Over the past several months, we have seen situations of violence involving the courts in jurisdictions throughout the country," read a statement issued by state Chief Justice William Sullivan and Judge Joseph Pellegrino. "Unfortunately, Connecticut is now on that list." (Source: William Yardley and Avi Salzman, "Divorce Court Shooting Kills Couple and Wounds Lawyer," New York Times, June 16, 2005.

Determined subjects following the path to intended violence will find both the vulnerabilities of security and the locations at the edge of security where an attack can be successful. Like Bochicchio, they need then only lie in wait. Many targets and decision makers are convinced about the need for reasonable security only after there has been an attack or a major security breach.

Case Illustration: The California State Capitol

From the late 1800s until the dawn of the twenty-first century, the California state capitol building has been an open, public building allowing unfettered access for state business and tourists. In the 1970s and 1980s, no less than seven major studies recommended security changes that included restricted access to vehicles in the basement, remote mail delivery, entry screening checkpoints, and architectural improvements to prevent vehicles from driving up next to the building. These recommendations were ignored for philosophical, fiscal, or architectural preservation reasons.

In 1978, a man attempting to contact the governor drove into the capitol basement armed with a rifle. After a short gunfight, police took him into custody. Two years later, in 1980, another man armed with a gun attempted to take a hostage in the legislative bill room. Law enforcement subdued and arrested him. After yet another security study, the legislature in 1983 established security checkpoints at the driveways to prevent unauthorized access to the garage. In 1984, someone threw a Molotov cocktail through a window, causing a fire and over $1 million in damage. Over the years, the capitol and its inhabitants endured countless incidents of mentally ill individuals or disruptive constituents confronting capitol office staff. In 1991, someone mailed an improvised explosive device to the governor. Law enforcement officers disarmed it inside the governor's mailroom.

Despite these incidents, the legislature continued to deny law enforcement recommendations for significant security enhancements.

Not even the 1995 Oklahoma City bombing caused enough concern to convince the decision makers to make the necessary changes. In early 2001, a mentally ill individual crashed an 18-wheel tractor-trailer into the south side of the capitol directly under the senate room where state senators debated the budget. The truck exploded into flames, causing millions of dollars in damage. Legislators finally relented, but only after the 9/11 attacks and several anthrax powder scares. These horrific events provided the political will and funding for entry checkpoints, including magnetometers, x-ray machines, mail screening at a remote site, and physical changes to prohibit unauthorized vehicle access to the building.

The security measures remain in place. However, changes have evolved to ease the impact on legislators and staff, allowing them to circumvent the magnetometers and x-ray machines by flashing their building ID pass. Legislators and other top staff have been given a special driving lane to speed their access into the capitol basement. (*Source:* Authors' personal knowledge)

The major downfall with relying solely on physical security to counter all threats is that security has to be 100% perfect 100% of the time. A determined and resourceful attacker only has to be right or lucky once. A more prudent approach is the combination of reasonable security and a robust threat assessment and management program. That approach lies at the other end of the security spectrum, but it, too, suffers from the risk posed by the bunker mentality.

In an established ecosystem, such as a large business or school, threatening, or trouble-making employees or students come to the attention of those in charge. Typically, due to no-tolerance policies, these ecosystems terminate or expel many of these employees or students. In many of today's corporate cultures, the legal department strongly advocates minimizing liability by terminating employees believed to be potentially threatening or violent. Once the termination takes place, everyone relaxes with the feeling "problem solved." But the problem individual remains a risk, either of coming back to the facility that rejected him or her or of letting loose his or her wrath against another target. The bunker mind-set blinds decision makers to the simple fact that getting rid of a problem individual does not get rid of the problem.

When there is significant on-site security, that security engenders a feeling of safety and insulation from the outside world. In order to keep employees or students safe, problem subjects are removed from the environment. Those managers who were part of the decision feel that the environment is now safe, and everyone can go back to work or class.

Usually, those who know the details of the problem are not allowed to discuss it due to confidentiality policies. Certainly, if officials at another company or school call for references, they are only told the bare details of the subject's employment or attendance with the organization. When a subject's behavior is particularly troubling in these ecosystems, security personnel are advised or instructed to keep watch and prevent the subject from returning to the organization property. If the subject does not immediately attempt to return, the memory fades, and it is back to business as usual inside the organizational bunker because the threat has been expelled. Unfortunately, when organizations employ the intervention of expulsion or termination, it begins the safety process, but does not end the problem. The passing of time or perceived distance does not mitigate a potential threat.

Case Illustration: The Expulsion

Dabrium Jones, who had a history of other disciplinary problems while attending John Jay College of Criminal Justice, began harassing a professor who flunked him on an exam. College authorities expelled him from the school in 2000. Sometime later, police arrested him for trespassing when campus authorities found him in a classroom. He had violated the bunker.

In 2001, school officials promised Jones they would consider readmitting him if he completed a counseling program. On Tuesday, August 28, he again showed up at the campus, but authorities turned him away. They continued to feel that their bunker was safe.

The next morning, Jones again gained entry to the school, this time armed with a knife. He chanced upon Hector Ortiz, the dean of students, and stabbed him repeatedly in the torso and neck. Police arrested Jones, charging him with assault. (*Source:* Associated Press, "Ex-Student Accused of Stabbing Dean," August 29, 2001)

Using the administrative orders threat management strategy may increase the risk, rather than resolve it. This is not to say the strategy should not be used, but in using it no one should assume that the bunker is safe or that other targets are not at risk. While there may be adequate security against an identified threat at the workplace location, the security may not extend to other locations where those responsible for the termination may be found. When employing any intervention, particularly termination or expulsion, methods must be established and maintained to monitor a subject's behaviors, rather than relying on the safety of the bunker or the simple passing of time.

Case Illustration: Laying Off a Paranoiac

An attorney representing Supervisor Steve Ebert of the Cordova, California, Recreation and Park District in a racial discrimination lawsuit, described the plaintiff, Dupree Barber, as paranoid. Barber's neighbors described him as antisocial and a "loner." Yet, none of these concerns seem to have been taken into account when the park district decided to lay off Barber and 17 other employees in a drastic effort to save $800,000.

Two weeks after the dismissals, Barber allegedly lay in wait in the rain for Ebert to arrive for work at 6:00 a.m. As Ebert's Jeep Wrangler turned into the Hagan Community Park in Rancho Cordova, Barber fired at least five rounds into the car. The car drifted several feet before Ebert's dead weight braked the car. Other employees discovered the idling car and its murdered driver when they arrived for work shortly afterward.

Police interviews with park employees almost immediately focused their attention on Barber. By the next day, January 24, 2012, detectives considered Barber a suspect. That afternoon, apparently aware of police interest in him, Barber flagged down a patrolman, explaining that Sacramento County authorities were looking for him. Prosecutors arraigned him on murder charges January 26. (*Sources:* Kim Minugh, "Laid-Off Worker Held in Rancho Cordova Parks Official's Slaying," *Sacramento Bee,* January 25, 2012; Andy Furillo, "Ex-Employee Arraigned in Homicide of Rancho Cordova Parks Superintendent," *Sacramento Bee,* January 27, 2012)

At times, when managing a threatening subject the threat manager is confronted with a dilemma. Should the threat manager apply interventions and strategies in a manner that keeps an identified target safer, but in doing so leaves other potential targets or the public at large at risk? This dilemma can present itself after employee termination or a student expulsion, or when using unconventional methods to divert a subject away from a target. The threat manager has deftly managed the subject away from his or her target, but what should the threat manager do with the information that he or she has indicating that the subject is mentally ill, off medication, and has access to weapons? Should local law enforcement be notified, even if it means the subject will know the source of the report and become angry at the original target? Is there an ethical or moral duty to warn other potential targets when they are discovered in the course of managing a threat case?

Years ago, Park Dietz provided an extreme example of the bunker mentality. During a 1997 interview with Jeffrey Toobin for an article in *The New Yorker,* Dietz, a psychiatrist who ran the Threat Assessment Group, explained his approach to protecting his corporate clients if one of their employees, usually a female, became the victim of a stalker. According to Toobin,

"We'll recommend going to the cops if we see a stalking case where we're confident we can get a felony arrest, pretrial detention, and a probability of incarceration for more than two years—that may happen once a year," Dietz told me. "Or we may see a case where we can get a civil commitment to a mental institution for long enough for the stalker to receive effective treatment. That, too, may happen once a year. Then, there's the case where we feel we can't get the stalker put away for that length of time, and we find that the employee involved doesn't want to be moved to another location. If we can't fix the stalker, can't protect all the employees on our client's premises, and believe there is a continuing danger, then we work out an arrangement with her where she feels fairly treated." Dietz said this meant that the victim is asked to leave her job and the client provides a financial settlement and gives her outplacement.

When Toobin protested that such a solution sounded "outlandish" and asked how often it happened, Dietz replied, "About twice a week."[11] That approach spared the corporate client—the bunker—but put the employee at greater risk. It also put public safety at risk. Rather than hunkering down in the safety of the corporation, would it not be better to continue working with law enforcement, mental health, social services, and any other resource to find ways to manage the stalker?

In the course of business, threat managers develop rapport with threatening subjects and at times even become their confidants. Having that rapport, the threat manager is able to keep track of the subject's behavior and in doing so keeps a target safe. Is the ethical threat manager able to risk that rapport for the greater good on behalf of public safety? These are all difficult problems and the answers to these questions may be different for a threat manager in a public agency, such as the judicial protection unit, than for a private security consultant with a corporate client. We have no easy answers to this conundrum, other than to say that each case has to be assessed on its own merits, always keeping in mind the risks posed by the bunker mentality. Public and private organizations, along with private security consultants, should not rely on the safety of the bunker and the power of termination or expulsion while disregarding the needs of public safety.

Myopic Intervention Strategies

The most challenging aspect of all the facets of threat management comes with the decision of when and how to intervene when a subject exhibits behaviors that potentially pose a threat to an identifiable target. Due to myriad reasons, threat managers can easily fall into the trap of being shortsighted in applying intervention strategies. The concern that the action taken will make the situation worse and potentially cause a violent act hovers over every management decision. Many threat managers hold to the theory that in the vast majority of cases, if the threat manager does nothing, the subject will not commit violence because he or she never would have carried out the act anyway. At the risk of being too blunt, a poorly thought out and executed intervention can be worse than just doing nothing. These concerns, in combination with pressure from potential targets and the complexities of actually implementing interventions, can test the most experienced threat manager.

In a small percentage of cases, the high degree of risk forces the threat manager to take action either to prevent a violent act or to stop behavior so disruptive that it requires a response. At the other end of the spectrum, a much larger percentage of cases assess as so low risk that they allow taking no further action at this time or watching and waiting for the subject's next step. In both these categories of cases, after proper assessment, the threat management team need not struggle to make a decision. The difficulties arise in those cases in the middle of the spectrum, where neither the risk nor the lack of risk can be readily discerned. Unfortunately, most threat managers spend a majority of their time managing these cases.

The choice of interventions depends on the threat manager's training, experience, and approach, and the environment in which the threat manager works. Looking at the same facts under assessment, the threat manager in a law enforcement agency charged with the protection of public officials and government assets will make different intervention decisions compared to a private consultant assisting a medium-size corporation with a problem employee. A threat manager in judicial protection will make different intervention decisions than a mental health professional in a clinical environment or a threat manager in a large multinational corporation.

Some of the differences stem from the types of cases referred to threat managers in the different environments. For example, threat cases referred to law enforcement are usually crimes (or close to crimes). Therefore, the intervention of arrest and prosecution or confrontation and warning interviews will be used most often. Being realistic, a law enforcement threat management unit is oriented, trained, and managed to use law enforcement methods. A mental health unit is oriented, educated, and managed to apply mental health methods because the cases referred to it involve mental health issues.

No doubt, the different cultures in which threat managers work also influence intervention decisions. Typically, a law enforcement agency does not award its officers for deciding not to make an arrest, but instead to use mental health referrals or work with social service agencies to prop up a subject's inhibitors. In a like manner, most mental health organizations likely frown on reporting clients to law enforcement unless required by law. A public figure or private organization wanting to avoid negative publicity may hesitate to apply interventions that could become public knowledge. These types of influences act like blinders on threat managers, forcing their focus into a narrow range.

In some cases, the threat management team resorts to an inappropriate intervention strategy because a powerful individual demands that something be done to make the problem go away. The boss or ultimate decision maker may ignore the team's advice, even the team's best assessment. At other times, the target of an inappropriate contact gets angry or offended and demands punishment for the subject, whether or not the subject actually committed a crime.

Case Illustration: The Chatty Constituent

A state legislator returns to his office around midnight after a night of fundraising receptions. He notices that he has voice mail. He listens to the message and hears an irate constituent berating him about a position he took on a local issue. The constituent's words, though not threatening or obscene, are certainly profane and insulting. Although the constituent left the message at 5:00 p.m. and it is now past midnight, the legislator returns the constituent's call. He engages the constituent in a heated discussion about the issue. The constituent becomes angry, repeats his earlier insulting comments, and profanely yells at the legislator for calling him so late at night.

The next morning, the legislator contacts the chief of the department responsible for legislative security and demands immediate action. He complains that he has been threatened. He wants the constituent immediately arrested and punished. The chief promises the legislator that immediate action will be taken. The chief immediately refers the case to the threat management unit. After interviewing the legislator and listening to the taped message, the unit supervisor advises the chief that they have no cause for arrest and prosecution.

The law does not consider leaving a message on a legislator's voice mail, however insulting and profane, a crime. The constituent did not initiate the legislator's return call, nor did the constituent make any threat during the argument. The constituent, a retired 67-year-old man, had a reputation for taking an active part in local politics. Most considered him a gadfly.

The chief, dismayed by this assessment and feeling trapped by his promise to the legislator to take immediate action, ordered the threat unit supervisor to write up the facts of the case and refer it to the district attorney for prosecution. The prosecutor declined to prosecute. Using the prosecutor's denial as political cover, the chief informed the legislator that the constituent was not going to be arrested. The legislator became angry and demanded that the chief send officers to the constituent's residence to warn him that if he did it again he would be arrested. The chief passed these instructions to the threat management unit supervisor. The supervisor warned the chief that this was a bad idea and could open up the department to civil liability and allegations of harassment.

Frustrated with the response by the unit supervisor, the chief arranged for uniformed patrol officers to go to the residence, contact the constituent, and deliver the message. The constituent became irate at the police officers at his door and attempted to slam the door in their faces. A struggle ensued on the constituent's porch. The officers doused the constituent with pepper spray and placed him under arrest for resisting. All of this took place in full view of the neighbors in the retirement community.

The constituent's version of events in the newspaper the next day painted an embarrassing picture of a drunk legislator calling him in the middle of the night and then sending the police to his door to beat and arrest him for exercising his First Amendment rights. The subsequent lawsuit for false arrest and police brutality was settled out of court. (Source: Authors' personal knowledge)

At times, the bureaucracy of an organization has little understanding of the dynamics of the threat management process and demands actions that are not in the best interests of the case. The bureaucracy wants the problem or the annoyance to go away or at least not to have an impact on its operation.

Case Illustration: Angry Letters

A high-profile government official received tons of correspondence during the year that the mailroom staff handled efficiently. Alerted by that staff, the threat management team closely monitored correspondence from a prolific, angry letter writer. The mailroom supervisor contacted the threat management team to complain about the volume of mail received from this subject. The supervisor took the position that the flow of correspondence from the subject wasted his staff's time processing and forwarding the letters. He insisted that it was the threat management team's job to make the subject stop writing. The threat management supervisor attempted to explain the value of monitoring this subject's thoughts and attitudes toward the public figure as part of an overall intervention strategy. The mailroom supervisor adamantly demanded that the team make the problem go away. However, when the supervisor raised the issue up to the public official's chief of staff, the chief of staff overruled him. (Source: Authors' personal knowledge)

In addition to the external forces we described, the personal characteristics of the threat manager also influence the intervention decision. If the threat manager's training and experience come from law enforcement, he or she will be more comfortable and proficient using the interventions of arrest and prosecution or confrontational interviews. If the threat manager feels uncomfortable talking to mentally ill individuals, he or she will avoid interviewing them. A threat manager who has not developed strong interview skills will frequently hesitate to interview a subject in crisis. The threat manager lacking proficiency in mental health commitments, civil processes, or the legal system will be unable to apply these intervention strategies effectively.

We have described intervention strategies as a range of options. The threat manager must have proficiency in all the options or risk not having the skills necessary to employ the right intervention at the right time in the right way. He or she will resort to choosing an intervention based on his or her preferences or skills, rather than the needs of the particular threat management case. Any gym or fitness center provides an accurate analogy to this problem. Every gym has weightlifters who have developed a huge, well-defined upper body. However, their workouts do not include their lower body. They continue to lift massive amounts of weights and add repetitions to maintain their upper-body beach muscles while neglecting to work their legs. They exercise based on what they are good at, not on what they need, despite the risk of back problems and other injuries.

The practical remedy to this problem requires the professional threat manager to ensure that he or she has all the skills and knowledge necessary to implement the full range of intervention options. If, through self-assessment, he or she recognizes a deficiency in a particular skill, the immediate option may be to partner or act in collaboration with others who possess those skills. We have long been advocates of forming multidisciplinary threat assessment teams or regional task forces to further both the assessment and management of threat cases. This places today's threat manager in a position of being trained or mentored by others, allowing him or her to employ the full range of intervention options effectively.

Despite the challenges of undue influence, bureaucratic obstacles, organizational culture, and threat manager proficiency, the greatest influence on the intervention decision is the attitude and perspective of the threat manager. It is easy to fall into the trap of intervening in threat cases in a myopic manner. All threat managers are confronted with cases that are frustrating, with subjects who are both alarming and annoying. It is easy to concede to undue influence or act out of anger or expediency. The best perspective is asking, "How can I manage this subject at this time in a manner that increases safety toward the target, is consistent and proportionate to the assessed threat, and is sustainable over time?" The best approach that we can offer to counter myopic intervention decisions is the awareness of the factors that can inappropriately affect an intervention decision and always to keep what is called a *high-visual horizon*.

The high-visual horizon concept comes from training in emergency vehicle driving and other types of driver training. The training teaches students to look well ahead while driving on a roadway to anticipate obstacles, dangers, and roadway features before the student gets to them. Doing so allows the driver to observe and react to hazards prior to having to take drastic emergency maneuvers or get into an accident. This concept is also used as a catchphrase to remind others to look far ahead to anticipate future actions and reactions, rather than to focus solely on the here and now and what is immediately to the front. Maintaining a high-visual horizon is an excellent attitude and perspective to maintain when making intervention decisions.

Summary

This chapter raised the alarm about declining resources to support appropriate threat management strategies. Budget shortfalls have forced mental health systems to cut back on the amount of patient services they offer. Law enforcement agencies have been compelled to disband specialized units that once addressed stalking and domestic violence issues. Courts have increased case backlogs and insufficient resources to address problem individuals. All of these constraints mean that threat management strategies previously available to the threat manager are now unavailable.

The chapter also addressed the problem of organizational silos. These silos inhibit, even prevent, sharing information about a problem individual within the organization. Members confined to each silo know something about the subject, but no one within the organization knows everything going on with the subject. Lacking the complete picture, no one within the organization can devise the best strategy for managing the subject. The antidote to the silo effect is to open communication within the organization.

A sister effect to silos is hunkering down in the organization's bunker. This mentality infects both ends of the security spectrum. At one end, the bunker mentality assumes that once physical security measures are in place, the organization need do nothing more. Physical security, the bunker mentality assumes, will keep everyone safe, even though physical security tends to degrade over time. At the other end of the security spectrum, the bunker mentality treats expelling or getting rid of a problem subject as a solution to the organization's problem. In fact, it may unleash the risk within the community at large. Again, the antidote to the bunker mentality is to open communication with counterparts and colleagues in other organizations and local governments.

Finally, we discussed the risk of adopting myopic threat management strategies. Threat managers tend to invoke those strategies with which they are comfortable or about which they feel most knowledgeable, even if other strategies may, in fact, be more appropriate or successful. The cure for this nearsightedness is training and teamwork with other specialists. Threat management teams offer the best way to ensure that all threat management strategies are considered and the most appropriate is selected.

Notes

1. Yep, M. (2011, October 12). Topeka, Kansas, actually decriminalized domestic violence. http://feministing.com/2011/10/12/yep-topeka-kansas-actually-decriminalized-domestic-violence; Lamb, J. (2011, October 12). Domestic violence law repealed in Topeka, Ks., to save money. *Kansas City Star.*
2. Bassett, L. http://www.huffingtonpost.com/2011/10/12/domestic-violence-topeka-kansas_n_1007357.html
3. Heasley, S. (2011, March 9). Mental health cuts are "national crisis," report finds. www.disabilityscoop.com
4. *Brown, Governor of California, et al. v. Plata et al.,* Case 09–1233, 2011 WL 1936074 (2011, May 23).
5. Bay State Mental Health: A funding crisis, March 20, 2011, New England Center for Investigative Reporting, http://necirbu.org/investigations/bay-state-mental-health-a-funding-crisis/bay-state-mental-health-a-funding-crisis/
6. Weiss, D. C. (2011). Civil justice in San Francisco is collapsing due to budget cuts. *ABA Journal,* July 19, 2011 (http://www.abajournal.com/news/article/civil_justice_system_in_san_francisco_is_collapsing_due_to_budget_cuts_judg/).
7. Egelko, B. (2011, July 19). S.F. courts warn of budget disaster, huge delays. www.sfgate.com
8. For a detailed discussion of this decision, see Calhoun, F. S., & Weston, S. W. (2009). *Threat assessment and management strategies: Identifying the howlers and hunters* (pp. 121–126) Boca Raton, FL: CRC Press.
9. For a detailed discussion of the range of threat management strategies, see Calhoun, F. S., & Weston, S. W. (2003). *Contemporary threat management: A guide for identifying, assessing, and managing individuals of violent intent* (pp. 183–262). San Diego, CA: Specialized Training Services, and Calhoun, F. S., & Weston, S. W. (2009). *Threat assessment and management strategies: Identifying the howlers and hunters* (pp. 10–13) Boca Raton, FL: CRC Press.
10. Coen, J., & Janega, J. (2006, December 9). Gunman believed to be former client of slain attorney. *Chicago Tribune;* Johnson, C. K. (2006, December 9). Shooter thought he was cheated over invention. *Chicago Tribune.*
11. Toobin, J. (1997, February 24 and March 3). Stalking in L.A.: Is there any way to stop a stalker? *New Yorker,* 80–81.

Case Studies on Cutbacks, Silos, Bunkers, and Myopia

12

In this chapter, we focus on two shooting incidents, both of which were closely related to colleges. Each college seemed incapable of raising the alarm in sufficient time to prevent the tragedies that followed. At Virginia Tech in 2007, silos prevented campus officials from seeing the situation in its entirety. At Pima Community College in Tucson in 2011, a bunker mentality spared the campus from violence, but not the community at large. In both incidents, budget shortfalls prevented the mental health system from adequately treating the two shooters, even though both clearly had mental health issues. And in both incidents, myopic threat management strategies fueled the failure to identify, assess, and manage the subjects. We again want to emphasize that we are in no way criticizing the men and women in law enforcement or the respective college administrations who dealt with these situations. We present these cases to illustrate the concepts that we have been discussing and to prompt continued thought and positive changes.

Events Leading Up to April 16, 2007, at Virginia Tech

Prior to Seung Hui Cho's 18th birthday, the partnership between Virginia's public schools and the mental health system served him well. Cho's elementary school teachers noticed his withdrawn behavior and reached out to his parents to get him help. Diagnosed with "selective mutism," Cho received counseling during the summer prior to entering seventh grade. His eighth grade teachers identified suicidal and homicidal ideations in his writing assignments. The Columbine shootings inspired Cho's writings that year. At the school's request, Cho's parents sent Cho for a psychiatric evaluation at the Multicultural Center for Human Services. That agency prescribed antidepressant medications. Cho responded well to the medicine, enough so that his doctors took him off the medicines a year later.[1]

During his high school years, the staff at Westfield High School enrolled him in an individual educational program (IEP) to help him with his shyness and inability to respond well to classroom settings. During his junior year, Cho continued with the therapy at the Multicultural Center. He graduated high school in 2003 with a 3.5 grade point average, making the honors program. Both his guidance counselor and his therapist viewed him as a success.

Overruling the advice of his parents and counselors, Cho decided to attend Virginia Tech in Blacksburg, Virginia, some 4½ hours from his home in Centreville. The Virginia Tech campus sprawls out alongside the small town of Blacksburg. The college has almost 30,000 students. Concerned that Cho would not receive adequate individual attention at so large a university, counselors at his high school alma mater gave him a contact at the high school should he need help in college. Cho never reached out for that support.

Privacy laws prevented his Westfield High School counselors from notifying their counterparts at Virginia Tech about his mental health history. Conversely, having reached his majority age, privacy laws prevented officials at Virginia Tech from contacting Cho's parents after he began engaging in disturbing behaviors. Those same privacy considerations also contributed to the erection of a number of silos within the Virginia Tech community. Various officials on and off the campus grew concerned with Cho's mental health, but they did not share their individual concerns with each other.[2]

Cho's freshman year seemed uneventful, although he did have neatness issues with his first roommate and changed rooms. During his sophomore year, he developed a passion for writing, thinking of himself as a brilliant novelist. In the fall of 2004, he submitted a book proposal to a New York publisher. The following spring, Cho switched majors from business information systems to English. The publisher rejected his proposal, which his family later reported seemed to depress him and put a chill on his enthusiasm for writing.[2]

During his junior year (the 2005–2006 school year), problems began. Cho moved back into a college dorm with suitemates. They observed odd behavior on his part, including stabbing the carpet with a knife in a girl's room. One of his English professors, the poet Nikki Giovanni, expressed concern over the violence described in his writing. She also asked him to cease taking pictures of classmates with a camera he held under his desk. Giovanni took the trouble of writing to the chair of the English Department to make a record of Cho's disturbing writings and behavior in preparation for having him removed from her class.[2]

The chairwoman, Dr. Lucinda Roy, removed Cho from Giovanni's class and tutored him one on one. When he refused her advice to seek counseling, Roy alerted the Division of Student Affairs, the Cook Counseling Center, the Schiffert Health Center, the Virginia Tech campus police, and the College of Liberal Arts and Human Sciences about her concerns over Cho. This alert brought Cho's situation to the attention of the university's care team, which had responsibility for addressing students with problems.[2]

In the fall of 2005, Cho's problem behaviors worsened. In late November, a female student complained to campus police that Cho had made "annoying" contacts with her, using the Internet and telephone and in person, using a disguise. Campus police officers interviewed Cho and referred him to the

Office of Judicial Affairs, part of the university's disciplinary system. The female, however, refused to press charges.[3]

After the police interviewed Cho, he voluntarily telephoned the Cook Counseling Center. Counselors there screened him over the telephone. Cho made an appointment to go to the center, but did not keep it.[4]

In early December, resident advisors (RAs) at one of the dormitories exchanged e-mails about Cho and his inappropriate contacts with the female student. He had sent her various instant messages using a variety of strange aliases. The e-mail traffic referred to his November contacts with the first complainant, showing that the RAs knew about that approach.[4] No action appears to have been taken place beyond the exchange of e-mails.[4]

A week later, on December 6, a second female student filed a complaint with campus police concerning "disturbing" instant messages that she had received from Cho. She asked the police to ensure that Cho stayed away from her and would have no further contact. Police confronted Cho and warned him to leave the student alone. After the police left, Cho sent one of his suite-mates an instant message saying, "I might as well kill myself." The suitemate reported the threat to Virginia Tech campus police. Campus police officers hauled Cho into the station house, where a prescreener from the New River Valley Community Services Board evaluated him. The prescreener assessed Cho as "an imminent danger to self or others." A magistrate ordered Cho committed to the Carilion St. Albans Psychiatric Hospital for an overnight evaluation. A psychologist there determined that Cho did not present an imminent danger to himself or others.

The next day, a staff psychiatrist at the hospital concurred. The psychiatrist recommended outpatient counseling, but made no effort to collect any other information concerning Cho's behavior. A special justice conducted a commitment hearing, ruling in accordance with the psychiatrist's evaluation. The justice ordered follow-up treatment on an outpatient basis. Cho kept an appointment with the campus Cook Counseling Center. The hospital sent the center a psychiatric summary of Cho's evaluation, but neither the center nor the care team followed up on Cho in the new year.[4]

In April, Cho engaged in an angry confrontation with one of his writing professors, who found Cho's writing so inappropriate that he asked Cho to drop his class. The professor did not report the incident. Around that time, Cho wrote a paper for his creative writing class that described a student who hated his fellow students and planned to kill them and then himself. In the fall of 2006, another writing professor warned the associate dean of liberal arts and human sciences about Cho's writings and class demeanor. The dean, however, found "no mention of mental health issues or police reports on Cho," even though such records did, in fact, exist. Cho again dropped off the school radar.[5]

In February 2007, Cho bought a handgun online, picking it up at a pawn-broker across the street from the university. He waited the requisite 30 days prescribed by Virginia law and bought another pistol. The store put in the background check required by law, but they found no record of mental health issues. They did not see any record of Cho's involuntary commitment the previous year. During March and early April, Cho purchased magazines and ammunition for the two pistols. He also practiced firing the weapons for an hour at a local indoor firing range. He made several videotapes of himself ranting against the world and the wealthy. He also wrote out a journal detailing his complaints against those who had more than he did. He mailed the tapes and journal to NBC on April 16, after he had killed Emily Hilscher and Ryan Christopher at the West Ambler Johnston dorm, but before he killed 25 students and five faculty members—then himself—at the Norris Hall classroom building.[6]

According to the report of the Virginia Tech Review Panel, "numerous incidents occurred" during Cho's junior year at the university that showed "clear warnings of mental instability." The report noted that "various individuals and departments within the university knew about each of these incidents." Nonetheless, "the university did not intervene effectively. No one knew all the information and no one connected all the dots." The silos within the university prevented effective communication among the various academic departments, campus police, and the mental health community. University officials blamed federal laws regarding the privacy of health and education records for their failure to communicate with each other. The review panel, however, pointed out that those laws provided "ample leeway to share information in potentially dangerous situations." The report also cited a "lack of resources" within the mental health system as contributing to the failure to follow up with Cho after his involuntary commitment.[7]

Consequently, Virginia Tech's institutional silo mentality, combined with budget shortfalls in the county mental health system and the failure of the court and the police to record Cho's involuntary commitment, all united to allow Cho to drift along untreated and ignored by everyone except his teachers and fellow students, who observed his behavior firsthand. They recognized him as a potential danger and even reported their concerns to their superiors, but those concerns remained within the English Department.

The campus police department knew about Cho's harassment and stalking of two female students, but did not share that information with the care team. Indeed, the police did not have a representative on the team. The police also knew about Cho's suicide threat and subsequent involuntary commitment, but they did not pursue the matter after Cho's discharge. The lack of follow-up indicated the myopic approach taken toward Cho. Having brought him before the magistrate and gotten an order for the commitment, the police acted as though that was all that was needed. The hospital staff, too, acted as though one overnight stay and unscheduled outpatient treatments would solve Cho's issues. The tragedy on April 16, 2007, resulted directly from these budget shortfalls, university silos, and myopic threat management strategies.

More than anything, Cho's attack on Virginia Tech illustrates just how dangerous silos can be.

Events Leading Up to January 8, 2011, at Congresswoman Giffords's "Congress on Your Corner" Event in Tucson, Arizona

Unlike the silos that so hamstrung officials at Virginia Tech in their attempts to manage Seung Hui Cho, officials, faculty, and police at Pima Community College, a much smaller organization, shared their information about the problematic behaviors engaged in by their student, Jared Loughner. Instead, a clear bunker mentality plagued the college. Although college officials strongly suspected him of being a danger to himself or others, their myopic management strategy entailed an administrative action to suspend him. In solving their problem with Loughner, college officials unleashed him on the Tucson community at large.

Unlike the muted Cho, Loughner engaged in loud, erratic behavior that brought him to the attention of other students, teachers, and campus police. He enrolled in the Tucson community college in the fall of 2005. Throughout his time at the school, students and faculty observed wildly inappropriate behavior on his part. "The first time I was really struck by him was because he used inappropriate reactions to people's emotional content," a classmate in an advanced poetry class remembered. "He would laugh at things that were sad. He just didn't seem to be aware of what was going on." A campus police report described Loughner's comments in the class as "a huge leap from the context of the poem and said things about abortion, wars, killing people, and 'why don't we just strap bombs to babies?'" Another student confessed to being scared of Loughner: "I wasn't scared of him physically, but I was scared of him bringing a weapon to class."[8]

Loughner took an algebra class in the summer of 2010. His behavior ultimately prompted the professor to kick him out of the class. One woman taking the class became so frightened of him that she intentionally sat by the door, keeping her purse ready, should she need to flee the classroom. "We have a mentally unstable person in the class that scares the living crap out of me," she wrote in one e-mail. "He is one of those whose picture you see on the news, after he has come into class with an automatic weapon." After 3 or 4 weeks of repeated disruptions, the professor removed Loughner from the class.[9]

On five separate occasions, campus police responded to reports of a disturbance involving Loughner. Finally, school officials ran out of patience. Working with the campus legal staff, administrative officials drafted a letter for the campus police to deliver to Loughner at home. The letter suspended him immediately and warned him not to come on campus except for a meeting to go over the Code of Conduct process and suspension status. On October 4, Loughner and his parents met with administrators. During the meeting, Loughner expressed his intent to withdraw from the school.

Again working together with their legal staff, campus administrators mailed Loughner a follow-up letter on October 7. The letter advised him that if he intended to return to the community college, he would first have to resolve his Code of Conduct violations. The letter also required him "to obtain a mental health clearance indicating, in the opinion of a mental health professional, his presence at the College does not present a danger to himself or others." That letter was the last contact between Loughner and Pima Community College.[10]

No silos prevented school officials from sharing information and coordinating their response to the problem student. After Loughner's suspension, campus police monitored his Internet postings and distributed his photograph in case he returned to the campus. They put school officials on alert to report immediately to the police any sightings of Loughner on or near the campus. Sergeant Dan Simmons sent an e-mail to other college officials on December 23 reporting that one of his officers "happened to find" videos that Loughner had posted on YouTube. Simmons described the postings as "more drivel from Jared Loughner." He added, "Doubt there is anything to do about it." The college police commander wrote in an e-mail dated December 28 that he would "have a photo of Jared copied and given to the swing shift crew and have them conduct more frequent checks of the Northwest Campus."

The school's bunker mentality resulted in the school taking care of itself, but not sharing its concerns with Tucson police or the mental health community. Although campus officials clearly assessed Loughner as dangerous (the October 7 letter requiring him to get a mental health evaluation prior to returning to school showed that assessment), no one appears to have shared those concerns with any off-campus agency. By cutting Loughner loose from the school, they set him adrift in the city, alone with his delusions and fixations. The continued police monitoring of his Internet postings and the warning to be alert to his potential return to campus showed the ongoing concern about Loughner, but the concerns focused on the safety of the campus and its inhabitants. Such a myopic focus blinded campus officials and police to the potential risk he posed to others in the Tucson community.

On January 8, 2011, Loughner went to the shopping center where Congresswoman Gabriel Giffords was hosting one of her "Congress on Your Corner" sessions, allowing her constituents to meet her and express their views on the issues of the day. As he approached the gathering, he pulled his pistol. He aimed his first shot into the congresswoman's head and then fired indiscriminately and randomly into the crowd. Bystanders subdued him when he tried to reload the pistol. In all, he killed six people and wounded more than a dozen more. Amazingly, Giffords survived the head shot.[11]

Lessons Learned

1. Although stymied by different mentalities, the shootings at the two schools underscore the vital importance of information sharing and avoiding any degree of hunkering down in a bunker. At Virginia Tech, information silos hampered the school's ability to deal adequately with the seriously ill Cho. At Pima Community College, the school's bunker mentality resulted in a failure to see the potential risk to the Tucson community, not just the community college.

2. Budget cuts to the mental health system were cited as the reason no one tried to follow up with Cho after his involuntary commitment. Undoubtedly, similar budget woes probably affected any treatment that Loughner sought.

3. Similarly, the myopic management strategies applied at both schools served as blinders cutting off a larger perspective of each problem. In both situations, a law enforcement response of confrontational warnings did not result in a long-term change in behaviors.

4. At Virginia Tech, the subsequent mental health commitment was an appropriate response by law enforcement; however, the lack of follow-up and information sharing stymied an adequate long-term mental health intervention.

5. Privacy laws and concerns were cited as obstacles in both these cases. Most if not all privacy laws allow exceptions for those subjects who make threats or pose a danger. Although privacy laws are seen by some as insurmountable obstacles, they would not have prevented campus law enforcement from sharing all the information at their disposal with their mental health counterparts.

6. In both these incidents, no evidence indicates that the campus police shared their contact records on the subjects with local law enforcement. Undoubtedly, Cho and Loughner left the campus and mingled with the community at large. Cho left long enough to buy two weapons off campus. Many examples exist of efficient information sharing between law enforcement agencies when it concerns crimes such as auto burglary or sex crimes. Similar protocols can be established concerning subjects who pose a risk to public safety.

7. We have posed in this chapter—indeed, throughout the book—a number of concepts that have an impact on how threat managers respond to potentially threatening situations. Keeping aware of the negative concepts, such as cutbacks, silos, bunkers, and myopic management strategies, offers the best strategy for minimizing their effects. Conversely, exploiting the positive concepts, such as the need-to-knows and the differences in the various venues for violence, can powerfully improve the threat management process.

Notes

1. Mass Shootings at Virginia Tech, April 16, 2007. Report of the Virginia Tech Review Panel presented to Governor Kaine, Commonwealth of Virginia, August 2007, p. 21.
2. Mass Shootings at Virginia Tech, April 16, 2007. Report of the Virginia Tech Review Panel presented to Governor Kaine, Commonwealth of Virginia, August 2007, p. 22.
3. Mass Shootings at Virginia Tech, April 16, 2007. Report of the Virginia Tech Review Panel presented to Governor Kaine, Commonwealth of Virginia, August 2007, pp. 22–23.
4. Mass Shootings at Virginia Tech, April 16, 2007. Report of the Virginia Tech Review Panel presented to Governor Kaine, Commonwealth of Virginia, August 2007, p. 23.
5. Mass Shootings at Virginia Tech, April 16, 2007. Report of the Virginia Tech Review Panel presented to Governor Kaine, Commonwealth of Virginia, August 2007, pp. 23–24.
6. Mass Shootings at Virginia Tech, April 16, 2007. Report of the Virginia Tech Review Panel presented to Governor Kaine, Commonwealth of Virginia, August 2007, pp. 23–29.
7. Mass Shootings at Virginia Tech, April 16, 2007. Report of the Virginia Tech Review Panel presented to Governor Kaine, Commonwealth of Virginia, August 2007, p. 2.
8. Simon, M. (2011, January 13). Jared Loughner's background reveals series of warning signs. *CNN: This Just In.*
9. Fahrenthoid, D. A. (2011, January 9). Jared Loughner's behavior recorded by college classmate in e-mails. *Washington Post.*
10. Smith, D. (2011, January 8). Pima College statement on alleged Giffords shooter. Tucson Sentinel.com
11. Fahrenthold, D. A., & Williams, C. (2011, January 9). Tucson shooting suspect Jared Loughner appears to have posted bizarre messages. *Washington Post.*

Appendix A: Glossary of Threat Management Terminology

This document represents the joint work efforts to date of a work group from the Association of Threat Assessment Professionals in partnership with the University of Nebraska Public Policy Center. (© Association of Threat Assessment Professionals; CRC Press, Taylor & Francis Group; and University of Nebraska Public Policy Center.) The definition of those terms without a specific source reference is based on the common usage in the field of threat management.

Administrative Action: A threat management intervention involving the use of disciplinary action within an organization or structure to manage problem individuals (e.g., firing, withholding services, suspension, barring from a particular location or activity; Calhoun & Weston, 2009).

Affective Violence: Affective violence, sometimes called impulsive, emotional, or reactive violence, is an unplanned act of violence that occurs in response to a perceived threat in the immediate environment (Meloy, 2006).

Americans With Disabilities Act (ADA): The Americans With Disabilities Act of 1990 established comprehensive legislation covering civil rights for people with disabilities. It is published in the United States Code and is often referred to by the titles and chapters of the code that contain the law. More information about the ADA is available at http://www.ada.gov

Anchors: Anchors are factors that provide stability; in threat assessment, anchors could be used to provide support or stability to a subject who is struggling or represent reasons that an individual would not engage in targeted violence (de Becker, 1997).

Approach Behavior: This refers to the type, frequency, and intensity of the subject's attempts to be physically proximal (close) to the target. Approach behavior includes successful and unsuccessful attempts to approach the target (Scalora et al., 2002).

Arrest: An arrest can be a threat management intervention. It is the act of detaining someone in legal custody, usually be a law enforcement officer. The actual deprivation of a person's liberty can be physical detention for a short or prolonged period of time in response to a criminal charge (Bureau of Justice Statistics, 2011).

Attack: Carrying out (or attempting to carry out) the intended violence against the target (Calhoun & Weston, 2003).

Attack-Related Behaviors: Specific behaviors that are needed in order to launch a physical assault on a target. These behaviors are displayed as steps on the pathway to violence (Calhoun & Weston, 2009).

Behavioral Indicator: An observable action that provides evidence of an underlying element that may be relevant to a threat assessment and management case; for example, a subject's actions (e.g., talking to himself or herself) might lead the threat assessor to believe that the person has a mental health disorder that influences the level of threat posed by that individual (Bulling, Scalora, Borum, Panuzio, & Donica, 2008).

Behavioral Threat Assessment: Threat assessment orientation based on the idea that the subject will exhibit identifiable behaviors indicating the intent to commit an act of targeted violence (Calhoun & Weston, 2003).

Behaviors of Concern: Behaviors of concern are the observable, identifiable behaviors that an individual exhibits while he or she is progressing on the pathway of violence (Calhoun & Weston, 2003).

Black Swan Event: An event that is rare, predictable only in retrospect, with extreme impacts (Meloy, 2011; Talib, 2007).

Breach: The word breach is commonly used when referring to a gap or break. In threat assessment contexts, this commonly refers to a situation where usual security measures have been circumvented (Calhoun & Weston, 2003).

Bunkers: The use of the term bunker is linked to the common use of the phrase "bunker mentality," in which an individual or group becomes defensive and surrounded by fortifications (real and virtual) to keep information in or detractors out. Adopting a bunker mentality in threat assessment can lead to under- or overestimation of risk (Calhoun & Weston, this volume).

Case Dynamics: The continuous interaction between what is known and unknown in a particular case, and the evolving assessments used to determine the appropriate protective response at any given point in time (Calhoun & Weston, this volume).

Chain of Custody: This is a process used to document the chronological history of evidence to maintain the security, integrity, and accountability of its handling.

CirCon Factors: "CirCon" is an acronym for "circumstances, content and contextual factors" related to a subject's inappropriate communication or contact (Calhoun & Weston, 2003).

Civil Action: Civil actions are orders issued by a court to convince the subject to stop threatening behaviors or stay away from the target and are periodically employed as a threat management intervention (e.g., restraining, stay-away, protective orders) (Calhoun & Weston, 2009).

Code of Ethics: Refers to the ethical code developed by the Association of Threat Assessment Professionals outlining appropriate behavior and decision making in threat assessment and management (Association of Threat Assessment Professionals, 2010).

Cognition: The simplest definition of cognition is thinking; in more complex terms, it is the processes in the human mind involved in acquisition, storage, retrieval, and processing of information. Individuals with poor cognition may have difficulty visualizing alternatives to violence and receiving assistance for grievances.

Cognitive Complexity: This is a psychological construct that refers to a person's ability to perceive nuances or subtle differences. A person who has high cognitive complexity is sensitive to small changes in a task, activity, behavior, or the environment; someone with low cognitive complexity is less likely to detect these differences. Sometimes this is referred to as intuition or street smarts. A person may have high cognitive complexity but little formal education (Scott, 1962).

Communication Channels: The media used to transmit messages are referred to as "communication channels." Threat assessment uses this phrase when referring to the ways that information about threatening individuals can be gained by threat assessment teams (Calhoun & Weston, this volume).

Confidentiality: Confidentiality refers to the process of safeguarding sensitive information, usually involving case intelligence or personal information. Confidentiality is sometimes framed as an individual's right to have his or her personal information kept private.

Content Factors: The information contained and conveyed in the words, style, and method of a threat (Calhoun & Weston, 2003).

Contextual Factors: Sometimes referred to as situational factors. In threat assessment, the context refers to the situation and environment surrounding the subject or the target. These can be personal, organizational, or on a larger scale (e.g., economic climate, world news, etc.) (Scalora & Bulling, 2007).

Credible Threat: A threat, direct or veiled, that is thought to be real, not just hypothetical. One test of whether a threat is credible is the ability and intent of the entity posing the threat (de Becker, 1997).

Criminal Intelligence: This phrase refers to any information that is collected, analyzed, or distributed for use in inhibiting or monitoring criminal activity (International Association of Chiefs of Police National Law Enforcement Policy Center, 1998).

Cultural Competence: Organizationally, this is a set of behaviors, attitudes, and policies that make it possible for people to work effectively across cultures. In threat assessment, it is having knowledge of culture differences and the ability to foresee how those differences may impact the investigation, analysis, or management of a case (U.S. Department of Health & Human Services, 2005).

Directly Communicated Threat: This is an unambiguous statement of threat to either the target or law enforcement detailing intention to commit an act of targeted violence (Meloy, 2011).

Domino Effect: This phrase is used generally when referring to the cumulative effect an event can have when it initiates a succession of similar events. In threat assessment and management, it is often used to describe the tendency for the loss of one inhibitor to affect other aspects of a subject's life and create a downward spiral where other inhibitors are compromised as well (Calhoun & Weston, this volume).

Duty to Warn/Protect: Legal directive to mental health professionals in most states: If they have knowledge of a possible act of harm by someone in their care directed at a third party, they are required to act reasonably to protect the potential victim from the threat. This stems from a U.S. Supreme Court decision in the 1970s (*Tarasoff v. Regents of the University of California*) that established the professional's duty to provide warning as a way to protect the third party from danger.

Empathy: In mental health, empathy typically means being able to recognize and feel what another is feeling, usually in a therapeutic context. In threat assessment, empathy is often used as a way to build rapport with the target or subject.

Energy Burst: A subject may have what is termed an energy burst as part of the pathway to violence. This is a preattack increase in intensity (frequency and/or duration) or variety of warning behaviors, usually indicating that an attack is imminent (Meloy, 2011).

Environmental Influences: The sum of background factors (peer group, security, access to weapons, etc.) affecting the situation of both the subject and the target. This includes organizational or cultural factors that impact tolerance or reporting of behaviors on the pathway to violence (Kiilakoski & Oksanen, 2011).

Evidence Collection: The process of gathering, maintaining, and preserving evidence for use in investigation and prosecution.

Evidence Preservation: Ensuring that evidence is collected and maintained in a proper manner that will preserve the forensic value of the evidence.

Extremist Violence: Violent action for which the impetus of the attack is born out of an ideological system, usually intended to enact some change or disrupt activities deemed unacceptable by followers of that ideology (Gerwehr & Hubbard, 2007).

Fact Finding: Process of acquiring information and evidence (about the target, the subject, contacts, communication, past and present behavior, context) to support accurate and complete assessment of risks and the best way to defuse them (Calhoun & Weston, 2009).

FERPA: Acronym for Family Education Rights and Privacy Act. This federal law (20 U.S.C. § 1232g; 34 CFR Part 99) governs the gathering, maintenance, and accessibility of educational records. Schools need written permission from the student to release educational records to anyone other than the student. Schools may disclose records, without consent, to certain parties under specific conditions, including complying with a judicial order or lawfully issued subpoena, to appropriate officials in cases of health and safety emergencies, and to state and local authorities, within a juvenile justice system, pursuant to specific state law.

Final-Act Behavior: Prebreach preparations made by the person(s) posing a threat right before the threat is carried out. This can include acts like disseminating reasons for the attack or executing a last will and testament (Calhoun & Weston, 2009).

Fixation: A fixation is generally an extreme preoccupation with something, be it another person, an activity, or an idea. It can be adaptive in the form of romantic love, parental love, or loyalty, but can also cross into pathology when it involves a grievance, personal cause, or public figure (Meloy, 2011).

Grievance: A grievance is generally defined as the cause of someone's distress or reason for complaint/resentment; in threat assessment contexts, it takes on additional meaning to include a highly personal meaning for the subject, often fueling a feeling of being wronged and translating into behaviors related to a sense of mission, destiny, loss, or desire for revenge (Calhoun & Weston, 2003).

HIPAA: Acronym for Health Insurance Portability and Accountability Act. The HIPAA Privacy Rule requires covered entities to protect individuals' health records and other identifiable health information. Of primary importance to threat assessment professionals are the security, accountability, and confidentiality of medical records covered by this act. The Privacy Rule permits use and disclosure of protected health information, without an individual's authorization or permission, for national priority purposes to law enforcement officials under specific circumstances (See 45 C.F.R. § 164.512). Disclosure must also be made to someone believed to be able to prevent or lessen a threat or to law enforcement if the information is needed to identify or apprehend an escapee or violent criminal.

Howlers (AKA Barkers): Howlers are individuals who, though they have inappropriate, bizarre, or threatening contact with the target, never intend on following a path to violence (Calhoun, 1998; Calhoun & Weston, 2003, 2009).

Howler Types (Calhoun & Weston, 2009):

Binder howlers: Individuals who threaten to facilitate a personal relationship with the target.

Celebrity-seeking howlers: Individuals who are motivated to threaten individuals because of their high public profile.

Controller howlers: Individuals who threaten as means of control over the target, usually a partner or family member.

Copycat howlers: Individuals who threaten as a reaction to other threats or reports of violence.

Crusader howlers: Individuals who threaten as a means to further a personal cause.

Deluded howlers: Individuals who threaten as a result of a delusional relationship (or potential relationship) with the target.

Delusional howlers: Individuals for whom delusional content plays a direct role in their threats.

Dirty-trickster howlers: Individuals who threaten in order to implicate a third party as the perpetrator of the threats.

Habitual howlers: Individuals who make threats on a continual basis, much like a hobby.

Impersonal howlers: Individuals who threaten someone they do not know.

Intimidator howlers: Individuals who threaten as a way of intimidating the target, who is typically a member of one of their social circles (e.g., supervisor, coworker, teacher, classmate).

Maintainer howlers: Individuals who threaten as an attempt to continue a relationship that the target wishes to end.

Personal howlers: Individuals who threaten someone they know.

Seeker howlers: Individuals who threaten as a means to establish an intimate relationship with the target, even when the target has repeatedly rebuffed them.

Self-defender howlers: Individuals who threaten as a defensive reaction to a perceived threat or attack from the target.

Sinister howlers: Individuals who threaten in order to scare the target.

Human-on-Human Violence: Deliberate actions taken by a human against another human with the intention of causing harm.

Hunters (AKA Biters): Hunters are individuals who intend to follow a path toward violence and behave in ways to further that goal (Calhoun, 1998; Calhoun & Weston, 2003, 2009).

Ideation: The *Merriam-Webster Dictionary* defines ideation as "the capacity for or the act of forming or entertaining ideas." In threat assessment contexts, this term takes on the added meaning of entertaining ideas specific to the utility and acceptability of violence as a means to address the subject's particular grievance (Calhoun & Weston, 2003).

Identification: Thoughts of the necessity and utility of violence by a subject that are made evident through behaviors such as researching previous attackers and collecting, practicing, and fantasizing about weapons (Meloy, 2011).

Impromptu Violence: This is an act of spontaneous violence often sparked by situational or contextual triggers (Calhoun & Weston, 2003, 2009).

Inappropriate Communication or Contact: Contact or communication with the target that is unwanted and intended by the subject to further the motives behind the threatening behavior. Contact can be written, verbal, or behavioral in nature and delivered in a variety of ways. These may be perceived by the target as intimidation, harassment, threatening, or out of context (abbreviated as IC&C) (Calhoun & Weston, 2009).

Information Analysis: Careful consideration of converging evidence in a case to ascertain the level of threat posed and progress toward violence.

Information Gathering: Process of obtaining information from all available sources to inform the analysis and decision making in a threat assessment (Fein & Vossekuil, 1998).

Information Sharing: Facilitation of the flow of information among entities responsible for a case so that all parties have access to current, relevant information on which to base decision making (Department of Defense, 2007).

Information Silos: Information that is not shared across disciplines or agencies is sometimes referred to as being in a silo. The word silo originates from the towers or pits used to store grain. The term is also used to refer to information or knowledge that is kept separate, is tightly controlled, and is not shared. When information about a threat or potentially threatening situation is not shared appropriately, it can inhibit attempts to assess or manage it (Calhoun & Weston, this volume).

Inhibitors: In threat assessment, this is anything that serves to decrease the likelihood that a subject's behavior will escalate to an act of targeted violence (e.g., familial bonds, strong friendships, or employment); sometimes referred to as buffers (Calhoun & Weston, 2003).

Insider Threat: An individual with access to a facility or organization who uses that access to disrupt or cause harm to the organization or others involved with that organization (Cappelli, 2005).

Intended Violence: Violent acts that meet the following criteria: intent to commit the act; selecting an attack mode that ensures injury, death, or property damage; and a motive that does not profit the attacker (Calhoun & Weston, 2003).

Interrogation: Purposeful questioning of a subject to obtain accurate, useful, and timely information relevant to an investigation (Boetig & Bellmer, 2008).

Intervention: An action or process that has the effect of modifying behavior, thinking, or emotions. In threat assessment, an intervention is the action taken in implementation of a threat management strategy (e.g., interviewing, monitoring, etc.) (Calhoun & Weston, 2003).

Intervention/Inhibitor Dichotomy: Disciplinary actions toward a subject are often required in threat management to ensure a target's safety; however, confrontational interventions can also negatively affect a subject's well-being. The relationship between the target's safety and the subject's well-being can be described as a dichotomy in some situations because each impacts the other and often suggests different threat management decisions. Both should be considered and continuously assessed after intervention (Calhoun & Weston, this volume).

Intervention Synergy: The case dynamic intensified by the stimulus of what the threat manager or target does or does not do in response to the threat situations (Calhoun & Weston, this volume).

Intervention Vectors: Similar in concept to intervention strategies, this is the range of levels of confrontation with the subject of a threat management case (Calhoun & Weston, 2003).

Interview Approaches: Strategies to engage a subject in the interview in order to elicit information (Calhoun & Weston, 2003).

Interview Strategy: Plan for the goals and approaches to an interview (e.g., deciding what information will be sought, how the subject will be redirected, where the interview will take place, etc.) (Calhoun & Weston, 2003).

Intimacy: Real or perceived close personal relationship, sometimes accompanied by physical or sexual contact (Jenkins, 2009).

Intimacy Effect: The closer the interpersonal relationship (degree of intimacy) between the threatener (subject) and the threatened (target), the greater is the likelihood of threats being carried out. This intimacy is based upon the subject's perception of the relationship, which may be delusional and completely unknown to the target (Calhoun & Weston, 2003).

Investigation: This is an active process of seeking out and finding information relevant to a threat assessment case.

Investigative Interview: Any verbal interaction between a law enforcement officer and a civilian for which the purpose is gathering information (Boetig & Bellmer, 2008).

JACA: JACA is an acronym for justification–alternatives–consequences–ability. This acronym suggests four questions that can help determine level of threat posed by a subject: J: Does the person feel justified in using violent means? A: Does the subject perceive that he or she has alternatives to rectify the grievance? C: How salient are the consequences of this activity to the subject? A: Does the subject believe that he or she has the ability to carry out the intended violence (de Becker, 1997)?

Last Resort: The subject's decision to end his or her life can lead to an act of targeted violence as a means of attaining fame or martyrdom in addition to the suicide attempt (Meloy, 2011).

Leakage: Leakage is an accidental or gradual escape. In threat assessment it is used to describe when a subject shares information with a third party that reveals clues related to his or her thinking, planning, or execution of an act of targeted violence (O'Toole, 2000).

Liability: Legal responsibility or obligation related to professional actions or inactions.

Mental Health Commitment: Sometimes referred to as civil commitment, this is a legal action that forces an individual into mental health care. Jurisdictions differ in the legal definitions and criteria for commitment, but generally two criteria must be met: (1) the person must have a mental disorder and (2) the mental disorder contributes to dangerousness that the subject exhibits by actions or threats to himself or herself (suicide or inability to care for self) or others (homicidal or actively threatening harm to another person).

Mental Illnesses:

Mood Disorders: Disorders that include prolonged excessive emotion. Threat assessors should be aware that symptoms can include clouded judgment along with other symptoms:

Depression: Depression can be a major mental disorder or a short-term, reactive state. A major depressive episode includes symptoms that occur over 2 weeks or more. Symptoms of depression include sadness, loss of interest/pleasure, sleep disturbance, weight change, psychomotor disturbance, fatigue, feelings of worthlessness, cognitive disturbance, and recurring thoughts of death. Suicide is associated with major depression and is of great concern to threat assessors.

Mania: Clinically, mania is a period in which an individual experiences elevated, expanded, or irritable mood and grandiosity; decreased sleep; increase in verbal communication; distractibility; increase in activity or psychomotor agitation; and excessive involvement in pleasurable activities.

Personality Disorders: Mental disorders characterized by unhealthy patterns of thinking and behavior. There are several types of personality disorder, but three symptoms are of most concern to threat assessors:

Borderline: Often characterized by desperate attempts to avoid abandonment (real or perceived), a pattern of frequent, unstable relationships, unstable self-image, impulsive behavior across multiple domains (including sexual activity, spending money, substance abuse, driving recklessly, eating dysfunction) (American Psychiatric Association [APA], 2000; Meloy, 2001).

Narcissistic: Clinically characterized as having a grandiose sense of importance; a belief in being special or unique; fantasies of excessive intelligence, power, beauty, wealth, etc.; sense of entitlement; exploitative of those around them; need for admiration; arrogance; envious of others or believes that they are envious; lacking in empathy; and arrogance or superior attitude/behavior (APA, 2000).

Paranoid: Unwarranted suspicion that others are harming them in some way, questioning of loyalty of those around them, bearing of grudges, reluctance to trust or confide in others for fear of exploitation, and perceiving of threats or slights when none are present (APA, 2000; Meloy, 2001).

Thought Disorders: Mental disorders that include a variety of symptoms related to a disruption in the ability to communicate or think clearly. Two key symptoms of thought disorders are of concern to threat assessors:

Delusion: A delusion is an incorrect belief that is caused by a thought disturbance; it can be of a number of different types including grandiose, jealous, persecutory, somatic, and erotomanic (APA, 2000).

Hallucination: In clinical terms, a hallucination is any sensory experience that is perceived by someone to be occurring externally for which there is no stimulus present. These can take the form of any perceptual experience from any of the five senses (APA, 2000).

Monitoring: Monitoring falls into one of two types, active or passive, delineated as follows:

> **Active:** Threat management interventions that are dynamic and involve real-time observation of a subject's behavior and/or movements through means such as surveillance or wiretapping.

> **Passive:** Threat management interventions that involve the use of nonintensive methods of tracking a subject's behavior, such as having a third party report on conduct (Calhoun & Weston, 2003).

Multidisciplinary Team: A group of professionals from different disciplines assembled to provide their perspectives and expertise in the fulfillment of a function such as threat assessment and management (BusinessDictionary.com, 2011).

Myopic Management: Myopia is a difficulty in viewing distant things due to nearsightedness. Myopic management refers to the style of management that focuses on short-term goals with immediate payoffs at the expense of strategies with superior but distant payoffs (Mizik, 2010; Calhoun & Weston, this volume).

Novel Aggression: In threat assessment, this refers to new acts of violence committed by the subject that are unrelated to his or her planned act of targeted violence (Meloy, 2011).

Opportunistic Violence: These are acts of intended violence involving general or nonspecific selection of a victim (Calhoun & Weston, 2003).

Overt Threat: Threat of a direct nature, describing a possible future act against the target (e.g., I will kill you) (O'Toole, 2000).

Pathway to Violence: A series of sequential steps—from its beginning with a felt grievance to violent ideation, research and planning, specific preparations for violence, critical breaches of security or other boundaries, to a concluding attack—indicating that an individual is progressing toward an act of targeted violence (Calhoun & Weston, 2003; Fein et al., 2002).

Physical Security: Physical security is the sum of the physical protective measures (e.g., key locks, security guards, security cameras, etc.) designed to detect, mitigate, or eliminate a threat (Reddy et al., 2001).

Predatory Violence: Predatory violence is an act that is planned by the attacker and does not involve reactive emotional components or an imminent threat to the attacker. It is sometimes referred to as instrumental, premeditated, proactive, or cold-blooded violence (Meloy, 2006).

Preparation: After deciding on a course of action and conducting the necessary background work, the subject must prepare for the actual attack. Behaviors associated with this include acquiring weapons, assembling equipment, arranging transportation, observing significant dates, rehearsing, conducting final-act behaviors, or costuming (Calhoun & Weston, 2003).

Proportionate Responses: The principle of "proportionality" refers to the balance that is struck between achievement of a goal and the cost to achieve it. Legal use of proportionality usually refers to a legal punishment being equivalent to the severity of the crime. Military use of the phrase is often related to use of force in response to aggression. Proportionate responses in threat assessment and management refer to strategies that employ measures comparable to the level of risk presented by the subject (Calhoun & Weston, this volume; Gardam, 1993).

Protective Fact Finding: Process of gathering detailed information surrounding an inappropriate communication or contact, including background on the subject, current behaviors, links to the target, and triggers for the communication. This information is used to create safety plans for the target (Calhoun & Weston, 2006).

Protective Response: Actions taken in response to a criminal act or imminent threat to secure the target and ensure the target's safety (Calhoun & Weston, 2003).

Psychopathy: In its clinical interpretation, psychopathy is generally conceptualized as a condition in which a specific combination of personality and behavioral factors exist. These factors include a superficiality and charming aspect, unreliability, lack of remorse, insight or affective reaction, dysfunction in interpersonal relationships, antisocial and dangerous/risky behavior, and lack of life planning (Meloy, 2001).

Radicalization: Conversion of a follower of a legitimate belief system to an extremist ideology based on that system, often with the intent of using the individual to commit or support a future act of violence (Silber & Bhatt, 2007).

Rapport Building: Establishing a sense of connection between the interviewer and the interviewee to facilitate communication and information sharing (Keats, 1993).

Redirection: Technique of refocusing the subject's attention away from the target and toward another person, organization, or activity (e.g., toward the threat assessment professional or law enforcement agency) (Calhoun & Weston, 2003).

Referral: Process of sending an individual to another professional with the proper expertise to address the particular situation.

Research and Planning: Seeking information about a target to facilitate an attack. This can include any number of dimensions, including surveillance of the target, Internet searches, testing security around the target, and researching methods of attack (Calhoun & Weston, 2003).

Risk Assessment: Risk assessment began in systems engineering. In threat assessment, it is used as a phrase that encompasses a process through which options for decreasing risk are considered along with the potential outcomes associated with their implementation, both positive and negative (Haimes, 2004).

Scope of Practice: Recognizing the limits of knowledge, experience, and capabilities that one possesses and performing only functions within the boundaries of professional training and duties (American Psychological Association, Inc., 2002).

Stalking: A cluster of behaviors, including unwanted communication, approach, or other contact, usually intended to threaten, harass, coerce, or intimidate the target into meeting the demands of the perpetrator (Kropp, Hart, & Lyon, 2002). (It is important to review stalking laws in your jurisdiction to ensure that you know the legal definition and specific behaviors listed in the law.)

Subject Interview: A threat management intervention that involves direct contact with the subject. The subject interview can have many different purposes, including information gathering, refocusing or redirecting the subject, and warning or confronting the subject (Calhoun & Weston, 2009).

Substance Abuse: A maladaptive pattern of substance use leading to clinically significant impairment or distress as manifested in one (or more) of the following: failure to fulfill obligations (family, work, school, etc.), use of substances in hazardous situations, recurrent substance-related legal troubles, or continued use despite frequent interpersonal difficulties related to this use. In threat contexts, substance abuse often has an impact on the subject's impulse control and may contribute to an erosion of inhibitors.

Surveillance: Actively but unobtrusively observing a subject to gather information about their activities and whereabouts (*Webster's New World Law Dictionary*, 2010).

Tail Risk: Probabilities of risk at the extreme ends (tails) of a normal distribution. In threat assessment, this pertains because targeted violence has a very low rate of occurrence; however, the risk should not be underestimated based on statistical probability that it will or will not happen (Meloy, 2011).

Take No Further Action at This Time: A deliberate, justified decision to assign a case inactive status (Calhoun & Weston, 2009).

Target: The general definition of a target is a person, object, or place that is the aim of an attack. In threat assessment and management, it is the point of fixation for intended violence. This can include people, buildings, or more general concepts (Calhoun & Weston, this volume).

Targeted Violence: Violent incidents involving an identifiable subject (perpetrator) who possesses the intent and potential to cause harm to an identifiable target (Borum, Fein, Vossekuil, & Berglund, 1999; Fein & Vossekuil, 1998; Fein, Vossekuil, & Holden, 1995; Reddy et al., 2001).

Terrorism: Act of violence or threats of violence used to further the agenda of the perpetrator while causing fear and psychological distress (Schmid, 2006).

Third-Party Control or Monitoring: Using a reliable third party to exercise control over the subject or unobtrusively monitor his or her behavior (Calhoun & Weston, 2009).

Threat Assessment: A fact-based method of assessment/investigation that focuses on an individual's patterns of thinking and behavior to determine whether, and to what extent, he or she is moving toward an attack on an identifiable target (Borum et al., 1999).

Threat/Control Override: A condition in which the individual believes he or she is not in control of his or her actions, but instead is being commanded by an outside, usually malevolent force (Link & Stueve, 1994).

Threat Management: Managing a subject's behavior through interventions and strategies designed to disrupt or prevent an act of targeted violence.

Threat Management Process: The threat management process is the entirety of the steps taken to identify, assess, and manage a threat assessment case. This includes developing, implementing, and monitoring a thorough plan unique to each subject and situation that includes protective measures for the intended target (Fein et al., 1995, 2002).

Threat Management Strategy: A coordinated plan of direct or indirect interventions with the subject that, based on current information regarding level of threat posed, is designed to defuse the risk in a given situation at a particular point in time.

Threat Management Team: A cross functional, multidisciplinary team approach to assist in assessing threatening situations and developing threat management plans. The team meets regularly and as needed in crisis situations to review potential and active threat cases (Deisinger, Randazzo, O'Neill, & Savage, 2008).

Threat Manager: The person who has primary responsibility for initiating, investigating, assessing, and managing threat cases. This person should have experience and training in threat assessment/management before assuming the role of manager (Calhoun & Weston, 2003, 2009).

Triggers: A trigger is an event or action that initiates a response of some
type. In threat assessment, a trigger initiates action on the part of the
subject, moving him or her along the path to violence. Identifying
potential triggers is part of the threat assessment process (Drysdale,
Modzeleski, & Simons, 2010).

Types of Targeted Violence:

> **Domestic Violence:** Domestic violence is a pattern of behavior
> in which one intimate partner uses physical violence, coer-
> cion, threats, intimidation, isolation, and emotional, sexual,
> or economic abuse to control the other partner in a relation-
> ship (American Bar Association Commission on Domestic
> Violence, 1999).

> **Workplace Violence:** Targeted violence, threats, bullying, harass-
> ment, intimidation, etc. that occurs in the workplace—by
> someone within the organization (e.g., disgruntled employee)
> or outside the organization (may or may not be associated with
> an employee of the organization) (Rugala, 2004).

> **Public Figure:** A target with a high public profile, such as a govern-
> ment official, politician, or entertainer.

> **Organizational:** An act of violence in which the target is an orga-
> nization or group, rather than an individual person. Though
> individuals may be harmed during the act, they are not the pri-
> mary objective of the attacker.

Veiled Threat: Threat of an indirect nature, vaguely describing the possibility of negative consequences for the target (e.g., "Someday you will
get what is coming to you") (O'Toole, 2000).

Venues for Violence: Locations in which violence occurs or could potentially occur, including (but not limited to) workplaces, residences,
and schools (Calhoun & Weston, this volume).

Victim Interview: Interview involving the target of the threatener (subject).

Victim Management: Working with the target to determine what a potential victim knows and needs to know, and how he or she finds out
about the subject's behaviors. Providing too much information can
unnecessarily cause distress for the victim, while not presenting
enough can lead to unsafe situations (OSHA, 2004).

Victim Selection: The process by which a subject focuses on a target for
his or her intended violence. This can include specific selection or
opportunistic victims that happen to be at the location of an attack
or included in some broad group toward which the subject has a
grievance (Calhoun & Weston, this volume).

Violence: An intentional act of harm.

Violence Content: The nature and intensity of violent rhetoric included in
inappropriate contacts and communications (Meloy, 2011).

Violence Risk Assessment: A continuous investigative and analytical process of evaluating an individual's probability of committing an act of violence based on personal and situational variables by an individual qualified (through training, experience, or education) to make risk determinations and recommendations for response, management, and mitigation of that risk (Hart, 1998; Rogers, 2000; ASIS International [ASIS] & Society for Human Resources Management [SHRM], 2011).

Violence Risk Factors: Reliable factors that have an established correlation with violent crime (Meloy, 2001).

Violence Risk Screening: A broad determination by a threat management team as to whether an individual's behavior shows cause for concern and thus threat management procedures should be initiated (ASIS & SHRM, 2011).

Violent Ideation: The process of forming and entertaining thoughts about violence as an acceptable means to address a grievance (Bruns, Disorbio, & Hanks, 2007).

Vulnerability: Vulnerability has many meanings depending on context. According to Homeland Security definitions, it refers to degree to which a target is at risk for attack or disruption; in mental health circles, vulnerability is an innate propensity for a disorder or symptom cluster, which may only manifest given certain triggers. In threat assessment, vulnerability typically is closer to the Homeland Security definition, referring to the target's vulnerability to the subject's violent intent or threats (Department of Homeland Security [United States], 2006).

Watch and Wait: Unobtrusive monitoring of the subject while waiting to see if he or she will take additional actions in relation to the target (Calhoun & Weston, 2009).

Witness Interview: Interview involving a third party, usually to inquire about information concerning threatening behaviors or contacts by the subject, or background information on the subject's past or current behavior or mental status.

References

American Bar Association Commission on Domestic Violence. (1999). *A guide for employees: Domestic violence in the workplace.* Washington, DC.

American Psychiatric Association. (2000). *Diagnostic and statistical manual of mental disorders* (4th ed., text rev.). Washington, DC.

American Psychological Association, Inc. (2002). Ethical principles of psychologists and code of conduct. *American Psychologists, 57*(12), 1060–1073. doi: 10.1037//0003-066X.57.12.1060

ASIS International & Society for Human Resources Management. (2011). Workplace violence: Prevention and intervention. Alexandria, VA: ASIS International.

Association of Threat Assessment Professionals. (2010). ATAP code of ethical conduct. Retrieved from http://atapworldwide.org/associations/8976/files/documents/ATAP-code-of-ethics.pdf

Boetig, B. P., & Bellmer, A. R. (2008). Understanding interrogation. *FBI Law Enforcement Bulletin, 77*(10), 17–21.

Borum, R., Fein, R., Vossekuil, B., & Berglund, J. (1999). Threat assessment: Defining an approach for evaluating risk of targeted violence. *Behavioral Sciences and the Law, 17,* 327–337.

Borum, R., & Reddy, M. (2001). Assessing violence risk in Tarasoff situations: A fact-based model inquiry. *Behavioral Sciences and the Law, 19,* 375–385.

Bruns, D., Disorbio, J. M., & Hanks, R. (2007). Chronic pain and violent ideation: Testing a model of patient violence. *Pain Medicine, 8,* 207–215. doi:10.1111/j.1526-4637.2006.00248.x

Bulling, D., Scalora, M., Borum, R., Panuzio, J., & Donica, A. (2008). Behavioral science guidelines for assessing insider threats. Retrieved from http://digitalcommons.unl.edu/publicpolicypublications/37

Bureau of Justice Statistics. (2011, December 16). Terms and definitions: Law enforcement. Retrieved 2.20.2012, from http://www.bjs.gov/index.cfm?ty=tdtp&tid=7

BusinessDictionary.com. (2011). Multidisciplinary team. Retrieved from http://www.businessdictionary.com/definition/multidisciplinary-team.html

Calhoun, F. S. (1998). *Hunters and howlers: Threats and violence against federal judicial officials in the United States, 1789–1993.* Ann Arbor, MI: University of Michigan.

Calhoun, F. S., & Weston, S. W. (2001). *Defusing the risk to judicial officials: The contemporary threat management process.* Alexandria, VA: National Sheriffs' Association.

Calhoun, F. S., & Weston, S. W. (2003). *Contemporary threat management: A guide for identifying, assessing, and managing individuals of violent intent.* San Diego, CA: Specialized Training Services.

Calhoun, F. S., & Weston, S. W. (2006). Protecting judicial officials: Implementing an effective threat management process. *Bureau of Justice Assistance Bulletin,* June.

Calhoun, F. S., & Weston, S. W. (2009). *Threat assessment and management strategies: Identifying the hunters and howlers.* Boca Raton, FL: CRC Press.

Cappelli, D. (2005). Preventing insider sabotage: Lessons learned from actual attacks [PowerPoint slides]. Retrieved from www.cert.org/archive/pdf/InsiderThreatCSI.pdf

de Becker, G. (1997). *The gift of fear: Survival signals that protect us from violence.* New York, NY: Little Brown.

Deisinger, G., Randazzo, M., O'Neill, D., & Savage, J. (2008). *The handbook for campus threat assessment & management teams.* Stoneham, MA: Applied Risk Management.

Department of Defense. (2007). Memorandum for secretaries of the military departments. Retrieved from http://cio-nii.defense.gov/docs/InfoSharingStrategy.pdf

Department of Homeland Security (United States). (2006). National infrastructure protection plan. Washington, DC: DHS.

Drysdale, D. A., Modzeleski, W., & Simons, A. B. (2010). Campus attacks: Targeted violence affecting institutions of higher education. U.S. Secret Service, U.S. Department of Homeland Security, Office of Safe and Drug-Free Schools, U.S. Department of Education, and Federal Bureau of Investigation, U.S. Department of Justice. Washington, DC, 2010.

Fein, R., & Vossekuil, B. (1998). *Protective intelligence and threat assessment investigations: A guide for state and local law enforcement officials.* Washington, DC: U.S. Department of Justice, Office of Justice Programs, National Institute of Justice.

Fein, R. A., Vossekuil, B., & Holden, G. A. (1995). Threat assessment: An approach to prevent targeted violence (pp. 1–7). National Institute of Justice Research in Action.

Fein, R. A., Vossekuil, B., Pollack, W. S., Borum, R., Modzeleski, W., & Reddy, M. (2002). *Threat assessment in schools: A guide to managing threatening situations and to creating safe school climates.* Washington, DC: U.S. Secret Service & U.S. Department of Education.

Gardam, J. G. (1993). Proportionality and force in international law. *American Journal of International Law, 87*(3), 391–413.

Gerwehr, S., & Hubbard, K. (2007). What is terrorism? Key elements and history. In B. Bongar, L. M. Brown, L. E. Beutler, J. N., Breckenridge, & P. G. Zimbardo (Eds.), *Psychology of terrorism.* New York, NY: Oxford University Press.

Haimes, Y. Y. (2004). *Risk modeling assessment and management* (2nd ed.). Hoboken, NJ: Wiley-Interscience.

Hart, S. D. (1998). The role of psychopathy in assessing risk for violence: Conceptual and methodological issues. *Legal and Criminological Psychology, 3,* 121–137.

International Association of Chiefs of Police National Law Enforcement Policy Center. (1998). Criminal intelligence. Retrieved from http://www.ojp.usdoj.gov/BJA/topics/CI_Paper_0703.pdf

Keats, D. M. (1993). *Skilled interviewing.* Melbourne, Australia: Australian Council for Educational Research.

Kiilakoski, T., & Oksanen, A. (2011). Soundtrack of the school shootings: Cultural script, music, and male rage. Young, 19(3), 247–269. doi: 10.1177/110330881101900301

Kropp, P. R., Hart, S. D., & Lyon, D. R. (2002). Risk assessment of stalkers: Some problems and possible solutions. *Criminal Justice and Behavior, 29*(5), 590–616.

Link, B., & Stueve, A. (1994). Psychotic symptoms and the violent/illegal behavior of mental patients compared to the community. In J. Monahan & H. Steadman (Eds.), *Violence and mental disorder: Development in risk assessment.* Chicago, IL: University of Chicago Press.

Meloy, J. R. (2001). *Violence risk and threat assessment: A practical guide for mental health and criminal justice professionals.* San Diego, CA: Specialized Training Services.

Meloy, J. R. (2006). Empirical basis and forensic application of affective and predatory violence. *Australian and New Zealand Journal of Psychiatry, 40,* 539–547. doi: 10.1111/j.1440-1614.2006.01837.x

Meloy, J. R. (2011). Approaching and attacking public figures: A contemporary analysis of communications and behavior. In C. Chauvin (Ed.), *Threatening communications and behavior: Perspectives on the pursuit of public figures.* Washington, DC: The National Academies Press.

Mizik, N. (2010). The theory and practice of myopic management. *Journal of Marketing Research (JMR)*, 47(4), 594–611. doi:10.1509/jmkr.47.4.594

Occupational Safety and Health Administration. (2004). *Guidelines for preventing workplace violence for health care & social services workers.* Retrieved from http://www.osha.gov/Publications/osha3148.pdf

O'Toole, M. E. (2000). The school shooter: A threat assessment perspective. Critical Incident Response Group, National Center for the Analysis of Violent Crime, FBI Academy.

Reddy, M., Borum, R., Berglund, J., Vossekuil, B., Fein, R., & Modzeleski, W. (2001). Evaluating risk for targeted violence in schools: Comparing risk assessment, threat assessment, and other approaches. *Psychology in the Schools, 38*, 157–172. doi:10.1002/pits.1007

Rogers, R. (2000). The uncritical acceptance of risk assessment in forensic practice. *Law and Human Behavior, 24*(5), 595–605.

Rugala, E. A. (2004). Workplace violence: Issues in response. Department of Justice, Federal Bureau of Investigation.

Scalora, M. S., & Bulling, D. J. (2007). *Developing threat assessment best practice standards: Leveraging behavioral science strategies to enhance decision-making.* Lincoln, NE: University of Nebraska.

Schmid, A. P. (2006). Frameworks for conceptualizing terrorism. *Terrorism and Political Violence, 16*(2), 197–221.

Scott, W. A. (1962). Cognitive complexity and cognitive flexibility. *Sociometry, 25*(4), 405–414.

Silber, M. D., & Bhatt, A. (2007). Radicalization in the West: The homegrown threat. Retrieved from http://www.nypdshield.org/public/SiteFiles/documents/NYPD_Report-Radicalization_in_the_West.pdf

Talib, N. N. (2007). *The black swan: The impact of the highly improbable.* New York, NY: Random House.

U.S. Department of Health & Human Services (2005, October 19). What is cultural competency? *Office of Minority Health.* Retrieved February 20, 2012, from http://minorityhealth.hhs.gov/templates/browse.aspx?lvl = 2&lvlID = 11

Webster's New World Law Dictionary. (2010). Surveillance. Hoboken, NJ: Wiley Publishing, Inc.

Appendix B: Association of Threat Assessment Professionals' Code of Ethical Conduct

Introduction and Applicability

The Association of Threat Assessment Professional's Code of Ethical Conduct (hereinafter referred to as the Ethics Code) consists of an Introduction and specific professional conduct standards for ethical practice. The Introduction discusses the intent, organization, procedural considerations, and scope of application of the Ethics Code. This Ethics Code sets both aspirational goals, to guide Association Members (hereinafter referred to as Members) toward the highest ideals of violence risk assessment, also referred to as threat assessment; and violence risk management, also referred to as threat management; as well as providing enforceable expectations of appropriate conduct in certain areas of practice. Most of the Ethics Code is written broadly, in order to apply to members in varied roles, although the application of an Ethics Code may vary depending on the context. The Ethics Code is not exhaustive. Conduct not directly addressed by the Ethics Code has not been determined as ethical or unethical.

This Ethics Code applies only to Members' activities that are part of their scientific, educational, or professional roles as violence risk assessment/threat assessment and management professionals. Areas covered include but are not limited to research; teaching; public service; policy development; development of assessment instruments; conducting assessments; developing or delivering intervention or case management plans; organizational consulting; forensic activities; program design and evaluation; and administration. This Ethics Code applies to these activities across a variety of contexts, such as in person, postal, telephone, Internet, and other electronic transmissions. These activities shall be distinguished from the purely private conduct of Members, which is not within the purview of the Ethics Code.

Membership in the ATAP requires a commitment from Members and student affiliates to comply with the standards of the ATAP Ethics Code and to the rules and procedures used to enforce them. Lack of awareness or misunderstanding of the Ethics Code is not itself a reasonable defense to a charge of unethical conduct.

The procedures for filing, investigating, and resolving complaints of unethical conduct are described in the current Rules and Procedures of the ATAP Ethics Committee. ATAP may impose sanctions on Members who violate the standards of the Ethics Code, including termination of ATAP membership, and may notify other bodies and individuals of its actions. In addition, ATAP may take action against a Member for other misconduct, as outlined in the Association Bylaws.

The Ethics Code is intended to provide guidance for Members and standards of professional conduct that can be applied by the ATAP. The Ethics Code is not intended to be a basis of civil liability. Whether a Member has violated the Ethics Code standards does not, by itself, determine whether the Member may have any legal liability, whether in a court action, the enforceability of a contract, or other legal or regulatory actions.

The modifiers used in some of the standards of this Ethics Code (e.g., *reasonably, appropriate, potentially*) are included in the standards when they would (1) allow professional judgment on the part of Member, (2) eliminate injustice or inequality that would occur without the modifier, (3) ensure applicability across the broad range of activities conducted by Member, or (4) guard against a set of rigid rules that might be quickly outdated. As used in this Ethics Code, the term *"reasonable"* means the prevailing professional judgment of violence risk assessment (threat assessment) and management professionals engaged in similar activities in similar circumstances, given the knowledge the Member had or should have had at the time.

It is recognized that Members represent, and also integrate, a range of professional backgrounds (e.g., law, medicine, law enforcement, behavioral science, security, human resources, etc.). In the process of making decisions regarding their professional behavior, Members must also consider this Ethics Code in addition to applicable laws during the performance of their professional duties. In applying the Ethics Code to their professional work, Members may consider other materials and guidelines that have been adopted or endorsed by scientific and professional organizations and the dictates of their own conscience, as well as consult with others within the field.* If this Ethics Code establishes a higher standard of conduct than is

---

* It is understood that each profession represented within the ATAP membership enumerate core competencies and standards in explicit and implicit ways. Such competencies and standards may be enumerated in a variety of manners, including but not limited to profession-based ethical standards, professional or specialty guidelines, statutory and regulatory sources as well as informally defined standards of practice. Therefore, it is also understood that each Member will need to consider these other elements in any decision regarding his or her conduct as well.

required by law, Members must attempt to meet the higher ethical standard. If Members' ethical responsibilities conflict with law, regulations, or other governing legal authority, Members make known their commitment to this Ethics Code and take steps to resolve the conflict in a responsible manner. If the conflict is irresolvable via such means, Members may adhere to the requirements of the law, regulations, or other governing authority.

Ethics Code

1. Resolving Ethical Issues

1.01 Misuse of Members' Work
If Members learn of misuse or misrepresentation of their work, they take reasonable steps to correct or minimize the misuse or misrepresentation.

1.02 Conflicts Between Ethics and Law, Regulations,
or Other Governing Legal Authority
If Members' ethical responsibilities conflict with law, regulations, or other governing legal authority, Members make known their commitment to the Ethics Code and take steps to resolve the conflict. If the conflict is irresolvable via such means, Members may adhere to the requirements of the law, regulations, or other governing legal authority.

1.03 Conflicts Between Ethics and Organizational Demands
If the demands of an organization with which Members are affiliated or for whom they are working conflict with this Ethics Code, Members must clarify the nature of the conflict and make known their commitment to the Ethics Code, and to the extent feasible, resolve the conflict in a way that permits adherence to the Ethics Code.

1.04 Informal Resolution of Ethical Violations
When Members believe that there may have been an ethical violation by another Member, they attempt to resolve the issue by bringing it to the attention of that individual, if an informal resolution appears appropriate and the intervention does not violate any confidentiality rights that may be involved. (See also Standards 1.02, Conflicts Between Ethics and Law, Regulations, or Other Governing Legal Authority, and 1.03, Conflicts Between Ethics and Organizational Demands.)

1.05 Reporting Ethical Violations
If an apparent ethical violation has substantially harmed or is likely to substantially harm a person or organization and is not appropriate for informal

resolution under Standard 1.04, Informal Resolution of Ethical Violations, or is not resolved properly in that fashion, Members take further action appropriate to the situation. Such action might include referral to state or national committees on professional ethics, to state licensing boards, or to the appropriate institutional authorities. This standard does not apply when an intervention would violate confidentiality rights or when Members have been retained to review the work of another Member whose professional conduct is in question. (See also 1.02, Conflicts Between Ethics and Law, Regulations, or Other Governing Legal Authority, and 9.01, Reporting Ethical Concerns.)

1.06 Cooperating With Ethics Investigations and Committees
Members will cooperate in ethics investigations, proceedings, and resulting requirements of ATAP. In doing so, they will address any confidentiality issues. Failure to cooperate is itself an ethics violation. However, making a request for deferment of adjudication of an ethics complaint pending the outcome of litigation or related disciplinary process does not alone constitute noncooperation.

1.07 Improper Complaints
Members do not file or encourage the filing of ethics complaints that are made with reckless disregard for or willful ignorance of facts that would disprove the allegation.

1.08 Unfair Discrimination Against Complainants and Respondents
Members do not deny persons employment, advancement, admissions to academic or other programs, tenure, or promotion based solely upon their having made or their being the subject of an ethics complaint. This does not preclude taking action based upon the outcome of such proceedings or considering other appropriate information.

2. Competence

2.01 Boundaries of Competence
(a) Members provide services, teach, and conduct research in areas only within the boundaries of their competence or expertise, based on their education, training, supervised experience, consultation, study, or professional experience.

(b) Where scientific or professional knowledge in the discipline of violence risk assessment and threat assessment establishes that an understanding of factors associated with age, gender, gender identity, race, ethnicity, culture, national origin, religion, sexual orientation, disability, language, or socioeconomic status is essential for effective implementation of their services or research, Members have or obtain the training, experience, consultation, or supervision necessary to ensure the competence of their services, or they make appropriate referrals.

(c) Members planning to provide services, teach, or conduct research involving populations, areas, techniques, or technologies new to them undertake relevant education, training, supervised experience, consultation, or study.

(d) In those emerging areas in which generally recognized standards for preparatory training do not yet exist, Members nevertheless take reasonable steps to ensure the competence of their work and to protect clients, research participants, and others from harm.

(e) When assuming forensic roles, Members are or become reasonably familiar with the judicial or administrative rules governing their roles.

2.02 Maintaining Competence

Members undertake ongoing efforts to develop and maintain their competence.

2.03 Bases for Scientific and Professional Judgments

Members' work is based upon established scientific and professional knowledge of the discipline. (See also 2.01, Boundaries of Competence.)

2.04 Delegation of Work to Others

Members who delegate work to employees, supervisees; or research or teaching assistants; or who use the services of others, such as interpreters, take reasonable steps to (1) avoid delegating such work to persons who have a multiple relationship with those being served that would likely lead to exploitation or loss of objectivity; (2) authorize only those responsibilities that such persons can be expected to perform competently on the basis of their education, training, or experience, either independently or with the level of supervision being provided; and (3) see that such persons perform these services competently. (See also 3.05, Multiple Relationships; 4.01, Maintaining Confidentiality; 8.01, Bases for Assessments; 8.02, Use of Assessments; 8.03, Assessment by Unqualified Persons.)

2.05 Personal Problems, Considerations, or Conflicts

(a) Members refrain from initiating an activity when they know or should know that there is a substantial likelihood that personal problems, considerations, or conflicts will prevent them from performing their work-related activities in a competent manner.

(b) When Members become aware of personal problems, considerations, or conflicts that may interfere with their ability to perform work-related duties adequately, they take appropriate measures, such as obtaining professional consultation or assistance, and determine whether they should limit, suspend, or terminate their work-related duties.

3. Human Relations

3.01 Unfair Discrimination

In their work-related activities, Members do not engage in unfair discrimination based on age, gender, gender identity, race, ethnicity, culture, national origin, religion, sexual orientation, disability, socioeconomic status, or any basis proscribed by law.

3.02 Sexual Harassment

Members do not engage in sexual harassment. Sexual harassment is sexual solicitation, physical advances, or verbal or nonverbal conduct that is sexual in nature, that occurs in connection with the Member's activities or roles as a Member, and that either (1) is unwelcome, is offensive, or creates a hostile workplace or educational environment, and the Member knows or is told this or (2) is sufficiently severe or intense to be abusive to a reasonable person in the context. Sexual harassment can consist of a single intense or severe act or of multiple persistent or pervasive acts. (See also 1.08, Unfair Discrimination Against Complainants and Respondents.)

3.03 Other Inappropriate Conduct

Members do not knowingly engage in behavior that is harassing or demeaning to persons with whom they interact in their work, or in conjunction with their affiliation with the Association, based on factors which include, but are limited to, a person's age, gender, gender identity, race, ethnicity, culture, national origin, religion, sexual orientation, disability, language, or socioeconomic status.

3.04 Avoiding Harm

Members take reasonable steps to avoid harming their clients, students, supervisees, research participants, organizational clients, and others with whom they work, and to minimize harm where it is foreseeable and unavoidable.

3.05 Multiple Relationships

(a) A multiple relationship occurs when a Member is in a professional role with a person and (1) at the same time is in another role with the same person, (2) at the same time is in a relationship with a person closely associated with or related to the person with whom the

Member has the professional relationship, or (3) promises to enter into another relationship in the future with the person or a person closely associated with or related to that person.

A Member refrains from entering into a multiple relationship if the multiple relationship could reasonably be expected to impair the Member's objectivity, competence, or effectiveness in performing his or her functions as a practitioner, or otherwise risks exploitation or harm to the person with whom the professional relationship exists.

Multiple relationships that would not reasonably be expected to cause impairment or risk exploitation or harm are not unethical.

(b) If a Member finds that, due to unforeseen factors, a potentially harmful multiple relationship has arisen, the Member takes reasonable steps to resolve it with due regard for the best interests of the affected person and maximal compliance with the Ethics Code.

(c) When Members are required by law, institutional policy, or extraordinary circumstances to serve in more than one role in judicial or administrative proceedings, at the outset they clarify role expectations and the extent of confidentiality and thereafter as changes occur. (See also 3.04, Avoiding Harm, and 3.07, Third-Party Requests for Services.)

3.06 Conflict of Interest

Members refrain from taking on a professional role when personal, scientific, professional, legal, financial, or other interests or relationships could reasonably be expected to (1) impair their objectivity, competence, or effectiveness in performing their functions as practitioners or (2) expose the person or organization with whom the professional relationship exists to harm or exploitation.

3.07 Third-Party Requests for Services

When Members agree to provide services to a person or entity at the request of a third party, Members attempt to clarify at the outset of the service the nature of the relationship with all individuals or organizations involved. This clarification includes the role of the Member (e.g., consultant, assessor, case manager, or expert witness), an identification of who is the client, the probable uses of the services provided or the information obtained, and the fact that there may be limits to confidentiality. (See also 3.05, Multiple Relationships, and 4.02, Discussing the Limits of Confidentiality.)

3.08 Exploitative Relationships

Members do not exploit persons over whom they have supervisory, evaluative, or other authority such as clients, students, supervisees, research participants, and employees. (See also 3.05, Multiple Relationships.)

3.09 Cooperation With Other Professionals

When indicated and professionally appropriate, Members cooperate with other professionals in order to serve their clients/patients effectively and appropriately. (See also 4.05, Disclosures.)

4. Privacy and Confidentiality

4.01 Maintaining Confidentiality

Members have a primary obligation and take reasonable precautions to protect confidential information obtained through or stored in any medium, recognizing that the extent and limits of confidentiality may be regulated by law or established by institutional rules or professional or scientific relationship. (See also 2.04, Delegation of Work to Others.)

4.02 Discussing the Limits of Confidentiality

(a) Members discuss with persons and organizations with whom they establish a scientific or professional relationship the relevant limits of confidentiality.

(b) Unless it is not feasible or is contraindicated, the discussion of confidentiality occurs at the outset of the relationship and thereafter as new circumstances may warrant.

(c) Members who offer services, products, or information via electronic transmission inform clients of the risks to privacy and limits of confidentiality.

4.03 Recording

Before recording the voices or images of individuals to whom they provide services, Members obtain permission from all such persons or their legal representatives if required by law and regulation in the jurisdiction in which they are conducting their work.

4.04 Minimizing Intrusions on Privacy

(a) Members include in written and oral reports and consultations only information germane to the purpose for which the communication is made.

(b) Members discuss confidential information obtained in their work only for appropriate scientific or professional purposes and only with persons clearly concerned with such matters.

4.05 Disclosures

(a) Members may disclose confidential information with the appropriate consent of the client or another legally authorized person on behalf of the client unless prohibited by law.

(b) Members disclose confidential information without the consent of the individual only as mandated by law, or where permitted by law for a valid purpose such as to (1) provide needed professional services; (2) obtain appropriate professional consultations; (3) protect the client, Member, or others from harm; or (4) obtain payment for services from a client, in which instance disclosure is limited to the minimum that is necessary to achieve the purpose.

4.06 Consultations

When consulting with colleagues, Members do not disclose confidential information that reasonably could lead to the identification of a client, research participant, or other person or organization with whom they have a confidential relationship unless they have obtained the prior consent of the person or organization or the disclosure cannot be avoided, and/or they disclose information only to the extent necessary to achieve the purposes of the consultation. (See also 4.01, Maintaining Confidentiality.)

4.07 Use of Confidential Information for Didactic or Other Purposes

Members do not disclose in their writings, lectures, or other public media, confidential, personally identifiable information concerning their clients, students, research participants, organizational clients, or other recipients of their services that they obtained during the course of their work, unless (1) they take reasonable steps to disguise the person or organization, (2) the person or organization has consented in writing, or (3) there is legal authorization for doing so.

5. Advertising and Other Public Statements

5.01 Avoidance of False or Fraudulent Statements

(a) Public statements include but are not limited to paid or unpaid advertising, product endorsements, grant applications, licensing applications, other credentialing applications, brochures, printed material, directory listings, personal resumes or curricula vitae, or comments for use in media such as print or electronic transmission, statements in legal proceedings, lectures and public oral presentations, and published materials. Members do not knowingly make public statements that are false or fraudulent concerning their research, practice, or other work activities or those of persons or organizations with which they are affiliated.

(b) Members do not make false or fraudulent statements concerning (1) their training, experience, or competence; (2) their academic degrees; (3) their credentials; (4) their institutional or association affiliations; (5) their services; (6) the scientific or clinical basis for, or results or degree of success of, their services; (7) their fees; or (8) their publications or research findings.

(c) Members claim degrees as credentials only if those degrees (1) were earned from a regionally or nationally accredited educational institution or (2) were the basis for licensure by the state in which they practice.

5.02 Statements by Others

(a) Members who engage others to create or place public statements that promote their professional practice, products, or activities retain professional responsibility for such statements.

(b) Members do not compensate employees of press, radio, television, or other communication media in return for publicity in a news item. (See also 1.01, Misuse of Members' Work.)

(c) A paid advertisement relating to Members' activities must be identified or clearly recognizable as such.

5.03 Media Presentations

When Members provide public advice or comment via print, Internet, or other electronic transmission, they take precautions to ensure that statements (1) are based on their professional knowledge, training, or experience in accord with appropriate literature and practice; (2) are otherwise consistent with this Ethics Code; and (3) do not indicate that a professional relationship has been established with the recipient. (See also 2.03, Bases for Scientific and Professional Judgments.)

6. Education and Training

6.01 Design of Education and Training Programs

Members responsible for education and training programs take reasonable steps to ensure that the programs are designed to provide the appropriate knowledge and proper experiences, and to meet the requirements for licensure, certification, or other goals for which claims are made by the program.

7. Research and Publication

7.01 Plagiarism

Members do not present portions of another's work or data as their own, even if the other work or data source is cited occasionally.

7.02 Publication Credit

(a) Members take responsibility and credit, including authorship credit, only for work they have actually performed or to which they have substantially contributed. (See also 7.02b, Publication Credit.)

(b) Principal authorship and other publication credits accurately reflect the relative scientific or professional contributions of the individuals involved, regardless of their relative status. Mere possession of an institutional position, such as department chair, does not justify authorship credit. Minor contributions to the research or to the writing for publications are acknowledged appropriately, such as in footnotes or in an introductory statement.

7.03 Duplicate Publication of Data

Members do not publish, as original data, data that have been previously published. This does not preclude republishing data when they are accompanied by proper acknowledgment.

8. Assessment

8.01 Bases for Assessments

(a) Members base the opinions contained in their recommendations, reports, and diagnostic or evaluative statements, including forensic testimony, on information and techniques sufficient to substantiate their findings. (See also 2.03, Bases for Scientific and Professional Judgments.)

(b) When Members conduct a record review or provide consultation or supervision and an individual examination is not warranted or necessary for the opinion, Members explain this and the sources of information on which they based their conclusions and recommendations.

8.02 Use of Assessments

Members administer, adapt, score, interpret, or use assessment techniques, interviews, tests, or instruments in a manner and for purposes that are appropriate in light of the research on or evidence of the usefulness and proper application of the techniques.

8.03 Assessment by Unqualified Persons

Members do not promote the use of assessment techniques by unqualified persons, except when such use is conducted for training purposes with appropriate supervision. (See also 2.04, Delegation of Work to Others.)

9. Procedure for Addressing Ethical Concerns

9.01 Informal Resolution

Members who have concerns about possible ethics violations on the part of another ATAP member are encouraged to first attempt to bring such concerns to the attention of that member in order that it might be resolved at the lowest level of intervention. It is the goal of the Association that the members would work together to resolve the raised concerns. (See also 1.04, Informal Resolution of Ethical Violations.)

9.02 Reporting Ethical Concerns

In any situation where the possible violation is unable to be resolved informally, is egregious in nature, poses a potential risk to the safety or well-being of another person and/or poses risk to the reputation of the Association, the member who has identified the ethical concern must report the possible violation to ABOD Sergeant at Arms, or as an alternative the Association President, in a timely manner. Members making a report of ethics violation may request anonymity. While every attempt will be made to honor this request, it may become necessary to name a complainant in the course of due process. (See also 1.05, Reporting Ethical Violations.)

9.03 Report Screening

(a) Upon receipt of a report of possible ethics violation, the ABOD Sergeant at Arms will evaluate the merits of the concerns contained in the report. If after review, and in consultation with the Association President, the nature of the allegation(s) requires additional investigation, the Sergeant at Arms will notify the Association Ethics Committee of the referral and facilitate any such investigation/action that may be necessary to adequately evaluate the concerns.

(b) The Sergeant at Arms will attempt to work with involved parties to address the concerns in a manner which is satisfactory to those members as well as consistent with the Association Code of Ethics. In those cases where resolution is not reached, the Sergeant at Arms will refer the case, investigative notes, and recommendations to the Association Ethics Committee.

(c) In all cases reported to the Association, the Sergeant at Arms will maintain documentation related to the concerns raised, involved parties, investigation outcome, and case disposition. Further, the Sergeant at Arms will provide semiannual reports to the Association Ethics Committee. This documentation will be made available to ABOD upon request.

History and Effective Date Footnote

This document was created in this form and submitted to the ATAP Board of Directors for approval on March 1st, 2010. Portions of this content have been adapted with permission from the American Psychological Association's (APA's) Ethical Principles of Psychologists and Code of Conduct 2002, adopted by the APA's Council of Representatives on August 21, 2002. Copyright © 2002 by the American Psychological Association. APA has in no way provided endorsement for this use, or advised, assisted, or encouraged the Association of Threat Assessment Professionals (ATAP) to utilize the APA Code of Ethics. APA is in no way responsible for the decision of the ATAP to utilize the APA Code of Ethics, or for any actions or other consequences resulting from such use by the ATAP.

ATAP wishes to thank the APA for the support of our effort and for their work in promoting ethical professional conduct in professional practices.

Index

A

Abdo case, 35–36
ability
    accessibility of target, 73
    venue selected, 69–70
abuse of substances, *see* Substance abuse
accessibility
    of target, 71–73
    weapons, 79–80
Acme Corporation, 13–14
active monitoring, 203
administrative action, 193
administrative order, 17
advertising, 221–222
affective violence, 193
alcohol, *see* Substance abuse
Allen case, 106
always known variables, 65
American Judges Foundation, 136
Americans With Disabilities Act (ADA), 193
Amy C. example, 43–44
analysis, *see* Information analysis
anchors, 193
anger
    employees, 41–42, 49–51
    letters, 181
    spitter, 8–9
antiabortion activities, 21–29
anti-Semitism, 145
Appalachian State University, 39
applicability, 213–215
approach behavior, 63–65, 193
Aronwald case, 105–106
arrest, 17, 194
Aryan Nations, 127–128
Ashbrook, Larry, 140
assessment
    "at this time" freeze, 13–14
    current *vs.* prior, 42
    domestic partners, threats to, 138
    Ethics Code, 223–224
    gathering information, 87–88
    gathering places, threats to, 141
    known facts at this time, 18–19
    lack of standard model, 55
    minimization of, 21–29
    public figures, threats to, 134
    Randall case, 91–92, 95
    representatives, potential attacks, 146–147
    short shelf life, 41
    situations, 53–54
    workplace violence potential, 144–145
assistant DA case, 72
Association of Threat Assessment
    Professionals (ATAP), 55–56, *see also* Ethics Code
ATAP, *see* Association of Threat Assessment
    Professionals (ATAP)
attack, 194
attack-related behaviors, 194
attention seeker stalkers/assassins, 130
"at this time"
    elements, threat management, 13–14
    format of threat assessments, 18–19
Austin C. example, 41–42
avenging behavior
    inhibitors, 101–102
    venue selection, 141–142
avoiding harm, 218

B

Barber case, 177
Barton, Mark, 109, 140
Baty, Jessica, 104
behavior
    avenging, inhibitors, 101–102
    of concern, 194
    violent employee, 49–51
behavioral indicators, 194
behavioral threat assessment, 194
behavior history, *see also* History
    subject's own, 74–75
    toward target, 82